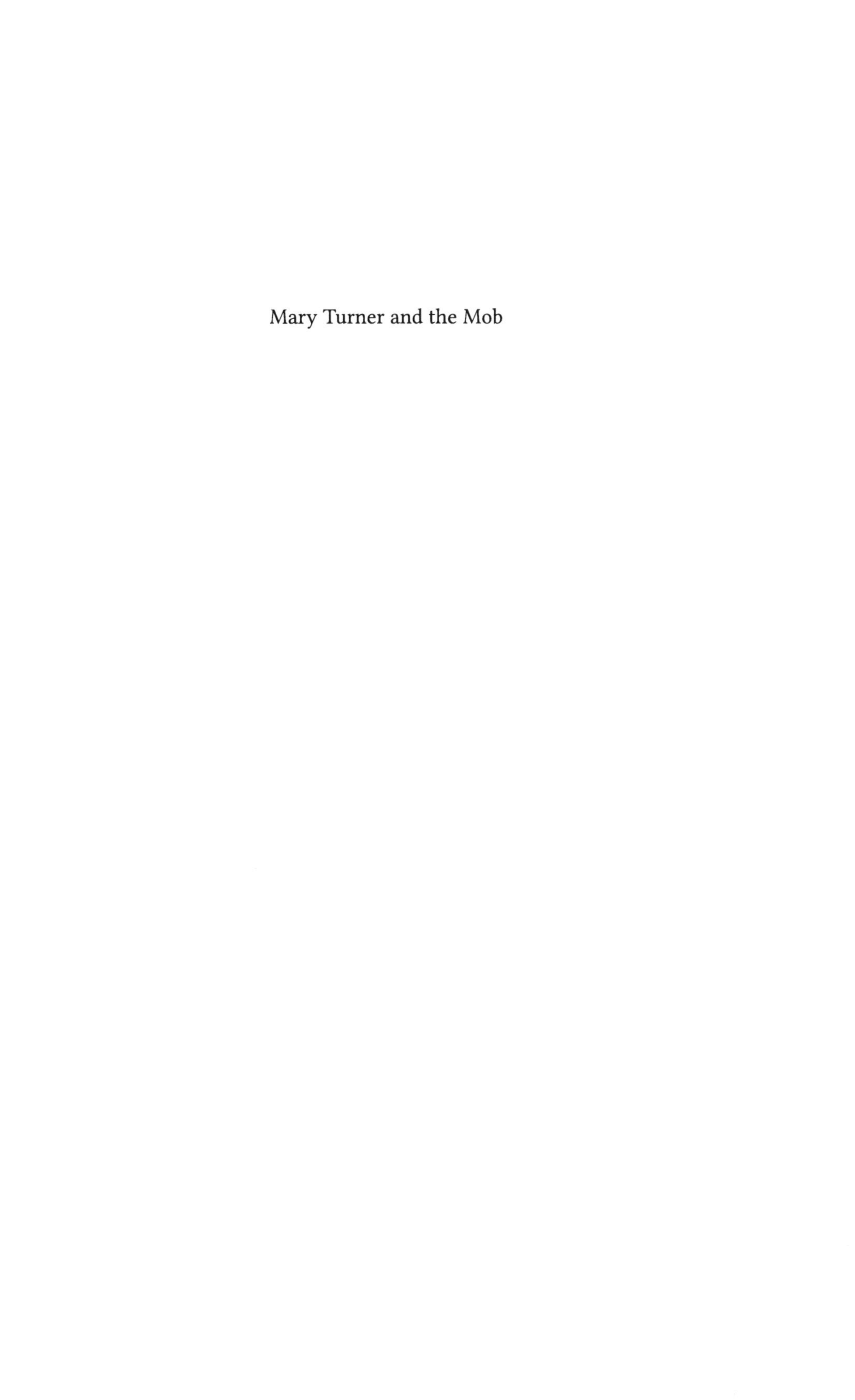

Mary Turner and the Mob

MARY TURNER AND THE MOB

The Brooks-Lowndes Race Riot of 1918 in History and Memory

THOMAS AIELLO

THE UNIVERSITY OF
SOUTH CAROLINA PRESS

Published by the University of South Carolina Press
Columbia, South Carolina 29208

uscpress.com

Printed in the United States of America

Library of Congress Cataloging-in-Publication Data
can be found at https://lccn.loc.gov/2024038704

ISBN: 978-1-64336-504-6 (hardcover)
ISBN: 978-1-64336-505-3 (ebook)

CONTENTS

LIST OF TABLES

Introduction

Race, Gender, and Violence

Mary Turner was a vulnerable Black woman, eight months pregnant, in the deepest Jim Crow South. When her husband was lynched and she protested the injustice, a mob gathered her up, took her down to the river, and hung her by her feet from a nearby tree. There they set her on fire. They sliced open her abdomen and pulled out her fully formed baby, watching it fall to the ground before taking turns stomping it into nothingness. As the horrified woman's screams resounded through the riverbed, the crowd finally put her out of her misery, riddling her broken body with bullets.

Or so the story went.

First told by Walter White after his investigation into the attack for the NAACP in June 1918, a month after the infamous lynching, the story of Mary Turner was retold with relish and to great effect by proponents of a federal anti-lynching law, by civil rights activists making a case for the brutality of the white South, and by historians who have used her story for similar historical ends. As Julie Buckner Armstrong has demonstrated, it has appeared in artistic and literary sources, as well, including works by sculptor Meta Warrick Fuller and writers such as Angelina Weld Grimké and Jean Toomer. The closing section of Toomer's *Cane* involves a poet, Ralph Kabnis, being driven to distraction by the story of Mame Lamkins, a pregnant Georgia woman lynched after defending her husband.[1]

The Turner narrative is one that has helped those who study it theorize the gendered assumptions of white southerners, to provide a counternarrative to the "defense of white womanhood" trope that informs so many of the lynch law justification excuses. It demonstrates the real vulnerability of the

Black population in the post-emancipation age. As Jennifer D. Williams has explained, the "traumatic effects of lynching tend to transpire through acts of secondary witnessing like oral culture, photographs, literature, and journalistic accounts."[2] The collective trauma isn't simply in the act itself but also in its retelling. And as with all retellings, the trauma that is the subject of lynching narratives grows in its continued sharing.

In each of these settings—artistic, theoretical, metaphorical—the Walter White story of Mary Turner is semiotically true. But it isn't historically accurate. While the metaphors matter and do important work on their own, so too does the historical narrative. By telling the story of the brutalized pregnant victim and her baby, the narrative of the violence in south Georgia's Brooks and Lowndes Counties became one of a particular lynching. In reality the Turner lynching was part of a larger mass casualty event that killed several Black residents before her death and several more after it. Even when the lynchings that preceded the murder of Turner were included in the narrative, it remained a lynching story, one that served the NAACP's ends to help enact a federal antilynching law. When White's account is believed and the events of the story take place solely in May 1918, that makes total sense, and historians are right to make that interpretation. The story was retreaded in the form White intended, for example, by leading historians like Leon Litwack, Lerone Bennett Jr., and Philip Dray.[3]

But the final death in what had become a lynching rampage in Brooks and Lowndes Counties occurred on June 3, 1921, Jefferson Davis's birthday, in Savannah, when a claimed coconspirator in the murder that started the rampage was legally hanged after being convicted of rape in superior court. Not only was June 3 of symbolic importance to white south Georgia because it was a state holiday, the birthday of the Confederate president, reifying all the white supremacist tropes upon which that conviction was based, but it also was two days after the Black Wall Street section of Tulsa, Oklahoma was burned to the ground. The lynching of Mary Turner was one of many in a regional rampage that began ten months after the 1917 race riot in East St. Louis, Illinois, and ended two days after the Tulsa Race Riot of 1921. It was decidedly part of a powerful wave of race riots that witnessed its loudest impact in the Red Summer of 1919 but spread from 1917 to 1921 in the years surrounding World War I.

The definitional line between riots and lynchings has never been static, but the names themselves have been vitally important. "The history of lynching is inseparable from the history of its rhetoric and representation," explain Amy Louise Wood and Susan Donaldson.

> The ways in which various groups or constituencies defined, discussed, and imagined it had everything to do with whether they deemed it socially legitimate or illegitimate, or treated it as a local inevitability or a national crime. Today, we can never know what exactly happened at a lynching or understand the full depth and range of experience, as our only access to this past is through its representation in news accounts, descriptive narratives, or photographs, all of which provide only limited and ideologically-charged perspectives.[4]

Christopher Waldrep had described the contemporary debate over what constituted a lynching and the role that naming played in the process of validating collective murders. Early twentieth-century reformers like Ida B. Wells and Jessie Daniel Ames emphasized that lynchings were community-sanctioned events, making reporting of them in the local press essential to how they were defined.[5] Though NAACP investigations were crucial to understanding racialized murders and are similarly crucial to this account, Wells, William Work of Tuskegee, and the NAACP all developed their statistical counts of lynchings through newspaper accounts. So journalistic representations, however defensive or racist local white editors might be, were a fundamental part of what lynching was, and because of the inconsistent nature of that coverage, the definition of lynching itself was regularly contested.[6]

It was particularly contested in times of white riots that included multiple victims. Waldrep uses the 1919 Elaine, Arkansas, massacre as an example. William Work, whose statistical counts of lynchings became the early standard, included in his lynching count for 1919 the murders of four brothers, Elihu, Louis, Gibson, and Leroy Johnson, based on his interpretation of local news coverage of the deaths. The NAACP originally did not include them, seeing their deaths as tragic, to be sure, but not lynchings by their particular definition. NAACP officials eventually capitulated and added the Johnson murders to their count, but they did not budge on including the burning of a white man's body in Deer, Arkansas. The man had committed suicide prior to the burning, and thus, the organization argued, his death should not be considered a lynching. Work, however, "held fast to the importance of neighborhood discourse" and kept the man in his count.[7]

The NAACP wanted a federal anti-lynching law, and the lobbying effort, described in greater detail in chapter 4, required more specific justification than community sentiment to convince legislators of the need. The most prominent of the bills that emerged from Congress defined a lynch mob as three or more persons and threatened the towns and counties where lynchings occurred with fines, hewing to the community sentiment paradigm while providing something more specific. After the failure of those early efforts, however, the NAACP loosened its standards and by the mid-1920s was reporting more annual lynchings than were Work and Tuskegee.[8]

Others wanted an even broader definition. The Associated Negro Press in 1932 defined lynching as "any death to an individual or individuals inflicted by two or more privately organized citizens, who impose such violence with correctional intent." The communists included labor violence in their definition.[9] The NAACP was sympathetic to such broadening. The association was itself founded in the wake of the 1908 Springfield race riot and knew that publicizing lynching was one of the most effective tools to dramatize racial bigotry in the South. If a limited social scientific definition of lynching like that used by Ames and Work held sway, then "lynchings" could be eliminated without a constituent elimination of "the prejudice, brutality, and violence that lynching represented."[10]

Walter White, also a principal player in the narrative that follows, was part of that rebellion against the more positivist approaches of Tuskegee, Ames's Association of Southern Women for the Prevention of Lynching, and others. He indicted white southern culture, backwardness, and Christianity as elements that contributed to racial violence, which themselves were symptoms of the larger white southern disease.[11] The debates continued for decades after the Brooks County violence, as did the disease, and though the conflicts were not over the differences between race riots and lynchings, they demonstrated the importance of naming in classification efforts. Unjust deaths were always tragic, but how racialized violence was publicly conceptualized was more than a description of deaths. It was a stakes game that framed southern racism.

The debate demonstrates the historical contingency of such definitions and the need for historians to take a broad view of what constituted racial violence, whatever it might be called and whatever positivist category in which a given murder might be placed.[12] That said, interpreting acts of racial violence as race riots in a wave of riot behavior does provide contextual benefit to the historical project. Whether an individual murder was a lynching by any technical accounting does not diminish the horror of an event that continued in one form or another with general regularity from the 1880s to the 1930s. Race riots, however, appeared in waves, killed multiple people, and served to control communities not through fear but through mass attack. They were defined not by multiple perpetrators but by multiple victims. When one of the victims became the story, the mass attack was subsumed into the story of an individual lynching. For contemporaries the definition of those mass attacks was less important, because groups like the NAACP could still marshal their resources and use the incident to portray the "southern disease." For historians, however, classifying the violence as part of a wartime wave of mass casualty racist events better contextualizes both the deaths in south Georgia and the full scope of the riot wave.

Ashraf Rushdy has produced one of the most sustained analyses of lynching definitions and argues for dual capacious and specific definitions of the practice to better contextualize the continuity of the violence beyond the bounds of the traditionally understood lynching period between the 1880s and 1930s. His capacious definition, that "a lynching is an act of extralegal collective violence by a group alleging pursuit of summary justice," can easily include the violence in south Georgia in 1918. He notes an important continuum between individual lynching acts and "other forms of extralegal policing of social groups," which include race riots. Riots, he argues, "differ from lynchings only in that they have multiple victims and occur in more widespread terrain. They often start with lynchings and develop into riots. These kinds of riots would be counted as lynchings." The notion that "some riots can be lynchings or can contain lynchings as part of the actions of the riot" is instructive.[13] If definitional deficiencies are remedied in aid of contextualizing the development of the eras in which lynchings occur, then Rushdy's notion of lynchings occurring within riots or riots comprising groups of lynchings makes the case that categorizations best serve temporal understanding. While the lynching of multiple victims in south Georgia in 1918 was symbolized by one lynching in particular, the problem with the particular categorization of the events comes not in contesting the "act of extralegal collective violence by a group alleging pursuit of summary justice." Though innocents not involved in the murder of Hampton Smith, whose death was the catalyst for the racial rampage, were killed and the trauma of the acts was felt by Black residents throughout the area, Rushdy's capacious lynching definition very much describes the mob's action in Brooks and Lowndes Counties. Lynchings within riots, however, do not validate the presence of a race riot, and in triangulating the reasons for and the temporal context of such events, the location of the acts in the timeline of the wartime riot wave places the violence as a constituent part of a decidedly specific wave of mass killings that took place in rural and urban areas between 1917 and 1921. The distinction is all the more important in this particular instance, because one incident of lynching and horrific violence effectively eliminated the riot's other victims from contemporary and popular historical attention. Reframing the 1918 acts as a race riot, then, does not deny the individual lynching acts but instead restores them within a capacious riot definition to both acknowledge the entirety of the victims and to place the event within the Red Summer wave.

When the south Georgia attack is contextualized as a race riot, the racial animus in the region can be seen as emanating from a broader conflagration sparked at least in part by the hypocrisies of claims of war-era egalitarianism in the United States. The World War I period gave lie to American claims of democratic supremacy abroad because of overt acts of racial terrorism at home. Happening alongside an explosion of anti-immigrant sentiment throughout the country, the white racial violence of the war era was not a new phenomenon but a concentrated manifestation of the diffuse acts of white supremacist aggression that had been present since the seventeenth century. The long history of slavery, Jim Crow, and racism in south Georgia created the specific conditions for the attack, but the region witnessed many lynchings from the 1880s to the 1930s. This was one of its only large-scale mass murders—five people were retributively murdered in Brooks County in 1894—and it happened as such murders were occurring across the country, North and South, in urban and rural areas, as that concentrated racial violence and the ubiquitous lack of consequences for those perpetrating it created a contagious permissibility for those seeking to carry out attacks.

Historians have not drawn such connections in this particular case because of the power of the Turner narrative. Walter White's report, however, was wrong. Mary Turner, I argue, was not pregnant when she was lynched. One of the lynching victims White claimed to have verified actually had just moved to Brunswick. White's document is riddled with factual inaccuracies. He was twenty-four years old in June 1918, and his trip to south Georgia was only his second investigating effort. There is no real surprise that the tenuous nature of these stories would lead him to some early mistakes, but they were compounded for two principal reasons. First was the power of the story he told. When his account of the Turner lynching appeared in the *Crisis*, it shook the nation in a way previous lynching stories had not and led to the artistic, theoretical, and historical emphasis that dominated after the fact. Second, there is evidence to suggest that White later knew he had gotten the story wrong and intentionally covered up the new information to salvage his original account.

It is significant that no major historical analysis of lynching appeared in the thirty years following World War II and that lynching studies did not begin in earnest until the 1980s. Miscommunications of factual accuracy and divergent interpretations are understandable in a discipline that is relatively new.[14] As Amy Louise Wood and Susan Donaldson explain, "Lynching haunts our social memories, but we are reluctant to grasp it or hold it carefully up for view. In this sense, lynching perhaps acts less like a lens and more like a prism, since our perception through it is multiple and refracted, and it can obfuscate as much as it clarifies."[15]

Such is not to say that Mary Turner was not actually lynched or that lynching is not its own horror existing beyond the realm of its physical details. Her death, however it occurred, was a brutal outgrowth of white supremacy, as were the deaths of the men who suffered at the hands of the mob. Her family still suffers from its effects today. The trauma of racial murder in all its forms exists in both the past and present—or perhaps in the various presents in which it is experienced, by those who were killed and those who have been left to experience it in collective memory and literary and artistic representation. In their foundational text on trauma theory, Shoshana Felman and Dori Laub describe "the practical hazards of listening—of coming to know"—which "lead to a rethinking of the crucial role the (always threatened) preservation of the truth, of knowledge and reality, plays in the enablement of psychological survival—in the very ability to sustain and continue life after catastrophes." In describing the trauma of World War II in Europe, they make a case applicable to racial violence in the United States. It is "a trauma we consider as the watershed of our times"; it is not "an event encapsulated in the past" but a "history which is essentially *not over*, a history whose repercussions are not simply omnipresent (whether consciously or not) in all our cultural activities, but whose traumatic consequences are still actively *evolving*."[16]

That active evolution is particularly acute in the racial trauma of south Georgia. White supremacy was lived in the region as a colonial relationship, and as Aimé Césaire has argued, colonization "dehumanizes even the most civilized man; that colonial activity, colonial enterprise, colonial conquest, which is based on contempt for the native and justified by that contempt, inevitably tends to change him who undertakes it."[17] Individual outgrowths of racialized violence, the symptoms of the colonial disease, have a virology that spreads to everyone involved. Dozens of white people participated in the race riot in Brooks and Lowndes Counties, and thousands participated tangentially in the act by approvingly visiting the sites of the deaths. That participation, and even the tacit approval given by the broader white populace that was not physically present but saw no need for legal remedy, served as its own form of trauma, the creation of Césaire's colonial monsters. Local white people were, as Michael Rothberg has described, “implicated subjects.” A white citizen of the region who did not participate in the violence was not a direct victim or perpetrator “but rather a participant in histories and social formations that generate the positions of victim and perpetrator.” Implicated subjects, as defined by Rothberg, “help propagate the legacies of historical violence and prop up the structures of inequality that mar the present.”[18] The Black population in the region experienced a more immediate, crippling trauma as a result of the acts. Mary and Hayes Turner had an eight-year-old son who survived the ordeal but was forced to watch as his mother was taken. Several Black employees of white rioters were forced to attend some of the lynchings; the Black residents of Valdosta, Georgia, frequently worked in the rural agricultural areas of the surrounding counties, which meant that there was no meaningful division between urban and rural in Black south Georgia. Everyone knew everyone. The trauma spread across the bounds of place to all who feared for their own safety.

It also spread through time. Though the names and circumstances of the other victims of the violence have largely been forgotten by locals, Black and white, the murder of Mary Turner still resonates, intentionally suppressed by white people as a detriment to civic growth. That suppression, its own response to trauma, manifests in silence surrounding the attack but also more viscerally in continued desecration of the historical marker standing near the site of Turner’s killing, a marker erected only after years of negotiation with a recalcitrant white leadership. (A new marker at a new site in nearby Hahira, Georgia, was erected in 2021.) The trauma for the Black population still resonates acutely, the scars of the rampage showing most clearly after acts of new racial violence, in particular the 2013 murder of Kendrick Johnson, for whom legal justice has never come. Though official reports declared Johnson’s murder at a local high school an accident, no one among Valdosta’s Black population was convinced. Protests continued for more than a decade. They still continue. “Just like Mary Turner” was a common phrase in the years following Johnson’s death, but new acts of racial violence were not necessary to manifest the trauma of older aggressions. They carried through the century following the race riot. One local man, Rufus Morrison, giving an interview in 2002, claimed to have been at the Turner lynching. When her baby was cut out, he recounted, birth matter spilled out onto him, causing lesions that never healed. Though the historical facts of the account were untrue, the broader ontological facts were.[19] The man was describing the scars of trauma, a trauma that had redounded through the generations to all Black residents in the area. Those scars, whether physical or psychic, still remain, evincing what Cathy Caruth has called the "belatedness" of trauma, an effect that comes through the process of knowing. "The complex ways that knowing and not knowing are entangled in the language of trauma" define the modes in which people experience past trauma in the present, particularly when the underlying basis of that trauma—in this case white supremacy—has remained a constant in the region.[20] This account is an attempt at knowing, while acknowledging that not knowing will always be a constituent part of a traumatic tale.

The racial scars of the trauma associated with Turner's death specifically and violent white supremacy more broadly were overt, but so too were the scars of gender. It was, after all, Turner's birth matter that created the unhealed lesions on the remembering witness. Thus such racial violence must also be viewed through a gendered lens. Georgians lynched eighteen women between 1886 and 1957, the most of any state save Mississippi, which lynched twenty-nine, but the story of Mary Turner took precedence, largely because of White's particularly gruesome account.[21] As Julie Buckner Armstrong has argued, "When lynching is perceived as a national event or recalled in historical memory, the bodies in question are male." Thus "what made Turner's story stand out for [James Weldon] Johnson is also what made it become a hidden memory for others years later."[22] Armstrong's account is the most complete evaluation of the Turner lynching and its legacy, and this book is not an attempt to undo the important work she and other scholars have undertaken. The legacy of the Turner lynching in cultural production, with which Armstrong is principally interested, remains the same whether or not the facts of the attack actually contradict that influential narrative.

"Although black women and men had struggled equally for liberation during slavery and much of the Reconstruction era, black male political leaders upheld patriarchal values," bell hooks explains. "As black men advanced in all spheres of American life, they encouraged black women to assume a more subservient role. Gradually the radical revolutionary spirit that had characterized the intellectual and political contribution of black women in the 19th century was quelled."[23]

It is a reality all the more relevant in the modern moment, as violence against Black female bodies appears in the news with regularity. The uprisings against racialized police brutality that occurred in the summer of 2020 emphasized a variety of murders by those tasked with protecting the population, but among them was Breonna Taylor, who was killed in her home after being awakened by members of the Louisville Police Department. She was among forty-eight Black women killed by police between 2015 and 2020, most of whom never received the national profile that Taylor did.[24] In that sense Taylor's death, like Turner's before her, served as a representation of violence against Black women whose deaths did not garner the same headlines. The trauma associated with both murders, then, though a century apart, fed both political concerns and actual pain about violence against Black women more broadly. They were public signposts of a reality lived for so many in the shadows of larger public concern.

As Maria De Longoria has explained, "The black woman's body represented the ultimate identification of white manhood. The use, abuse, and display of this body was so grossly entangled with honor and violence that honor often was demonstrated through violence directed at that body."[25] De Longoria argues that the violence associated with such representations only increased after slavery, after Black women were no longer the legal property of white men. "In a society that created true womanhood, there had to be a balance of power, so to speak. There had to be an image or a scripted behavior for those who were not entitled to pedestal status."[26] In direct contradistinction to that true woman, an image of the Black Jezebel arose, a woman who had nefarious motives and was not to be trusted. She did not have the maternal or caring instinct that came with the caricature of the mammy. This framing of Black womanhood as a threat to white southern values and the order of civil society left it outside the bounds of protected womanhood as conceived in the simplistic conceptions of chivalry carried by many white southern men.[27]

Patricia Morton has argued that American historiography and other forms of academic scholarship have included Black women with a surprising regularity, but the images that scholarship presents disfigure the roles and lives of Black women, resulting in a broader set of stereotypes that have worked in conjunction with popular culture to create an image that comes to the forefront only in caricature.[28] Though "black women may be embraced as symbols of female strength and pathos, they are still not embraced as equals." It is that "still-immense perceptual barrier dividing 'good' and 'bad'" that disallows American women of different racial backgrounds from their ability "to make common cause."[29]

W. Fitzhugh Brundage wrote the foundational account of lynching in Georgia and demonstrated the contingency that results from a secondary source base built on such disfiguring stereotypes. Brundage's *Lynching in the New South* helped to incorporate sociological theory into the social history of southern racial violence and to validate the study of organized racial violence as a field. For all of its strong work, however, the book's brief account of the mob violence in Brooks and Lowndes Counties not only gets the bulk of its information wrong but also never mentions the Black woman involved. His analysis argues that "women lynching victims, with few exceptions, were accused of murder or complicity in other violent crimes." He maintains that "even during the tense atmosphere before and after lynchings, black women perhaps could voice their opinions and anger without suffering extralegal violence themselves." This analysis is, in aggregate, helpful in understanding the role of Black women in the broader lynching scenario, but it leaves women like Turner as one of those few exceptions who was unable to voice her opinion or anger without suffering a violent reprisal.[30]

Brundage categorizes lynchers into four different categories: small terrorist mobs "that made no pretense of upholding the law"; small private mobs "that exacted vengeance for a wide variety of alleged offenses"; posses, which could range in size and "often overstepped their quasi-legal function and were themselves responsible for mob violence"; and mass mobs, "numbering from more than fifty to hundreds and even thousands of members," which "punished alleged criminals with extraordinary ferocity."[31] The south Georgia race riot managed to traverse the lines of all four of Brundage's categories, largely because rioters who kill multiple people act differently in different settings. When the violence in south Georgia is understood as a race riot, the instability of such common categories is more apparent.

Mass racial violence is described by many names. *Massacre*, *atrocity*, *pogrom*, and *riot* are often used interchangeably in historical accounts of events prior to World War II. David F. Krugler has described such attacks as "antiblack collective violence."[32] Brent M. S. Campney marshals the term *racist violence* to broadly construe violent outgrowths of white supremacy, from the heavily reported riots and lynchings to the less sensationalized acts of property damage, forced removal, and even rape.[33] My account attempts to broaden the scope of racist violence; I include, for example, a state execution in Savannah in 1921 as part of the events in Brooks and Lowndes Counties in 1918. But I focus attention on the more sensationalized, publicized events represented by the former terms. While *pogrom* is the only descriptive name that has racial coding built into its definition, and while the racial murders in south Georgia fall easily within the bounds of its dictates, I use *riot* more broadly because of the common usage surrounding mass casualty events associated with the Red Summer. In 1959 sociologist Allen Day Grimshaw distinguished between "Southern style" race riots and "Northern style" race riots. Incidents in Atlanta in 1906, Springfield, Illinois, in 1908, Washington, DC, in 1919, and Tulsa in 1921 fell into the former category, along with those in smaller communities like Elaine, Arkansas, and Longview, Texas. "In every such riot," he argues, "violence is largely one-sided and consists of attacks, of varying degrees of organization, by whites on Negroes and on the Negro community." He identifies the cause of all such riots, Elaine and Longview notwithstanding, as a perceived assault on white womanhood. Northern-style race riots, he argues, had longer causal build-up, tensions growing over time for a multitude of reasons, and featured a Black population willing to fight back in some measure. He includes lynching as a separate category of incidents involving only one or two victims. If one were to adjust Grimshaw's formula to replace assaults on white womanhood with an immediate causal stimulus, his formula certainly puts Brooks and Lowndes Counties under the organizational banner of a southern-style race riot and better situates them—particularly when compared with Brundage's limited lynching categories—in the context of the Red Summer wave that surrounded it between 1917 and 1921.[34]

Such an analysis is vital to understanding lynchings like that of Turner and those who met their death in the same rampage. The emphasis on Turner, however, has also pulled historical focus from the rampage itself. There had been significant race riots earlier in the century—Atlanta in 1906, Springfield in 1908—but the war brought record levels of mass violence, pushed by Black expectations following World War I military service and white anger and fear as more and more Black migrants were moving into urban areas. This was supposed to be a war to make the world safe for democracy, but African Americans simply did not see it. On top of that, campaigns by the NAACP, French support of Black troops, and other civil rights efforts sparked a massive backlash by the white population, leading to retributive racial violence around the country.

The bulk of that violence centered on what James Weldon Johnson dubbed the Red Summer of 1919. But the first surge in race-related attacks, which had always maintained a baseline level of constancy, came at the war's beginning rather than its end. A broader view of the Red Summer that places its onset in 1917 with the race riots in East St. Louis and Philadelphia and recognizes its conclusion as the Tulsa race riot in 1921 better encapsulates the breadth of racial violence in the era, including the period of US involvement in the war and the full run of its economic aftermath.

East St. Louis, for example, was approximately 10 percent Black, and virtually everything within its bounds was segregated. In February 1917, 470 Black workers were hired as scabs for an American Federation of Labor strike in the city, fueling racial tensions between the Black and white working class on both the Missouri and Illinois sides of the Mississippi River. On July 1, several white men drove through a Black neighborhood firing guns. Soon after, two white plainclothes policemen walked through the same neighborhood and were shot and killed, probably by residents who believed that the officers were there to do them harm. Angry white mobs sought revenge, killing and mutilating Black residents and burning Black homes and businesses. At the riot's end, thirty-five Black residents and eight white assailants were killed, and hundreds were left homeless.[35]

Five years later, in Tulsa, Oklahoma, violence erupted on May 31, 1921, caused by both esoteric and pragmatic factors. The Black population of Tulsa had thrived in the wake of World War I. Their business district, known as Black Wall Street, was an affront to a white population that had not experienced a commensurate financial boon. More immediately, a Black man, Dick Rowland, was falsely accused of raping a white woman, and fearing a lynch mob, a group of Black men assembled at the jailhouse to protect him. A white mob inevitably arrived, and the two groups exchanged gunfire, killing several white and Black men. The violence continued, fueled by the white assumption that any Black self-defense was an affront to white citizens of Tulsa, and the next day a mob of five hundred white men confronted about one thousand Black men. Attackers burned a church full of people, and as the congregants ran out, whites began picking them off one by one. More than four square blocks in the Black neighborhood were burned to the ground. As many as three hundred Black residents and twenty white were killed in the catastrophic violence.[36]

In between these two poles was Johnson's Red Summer. Chicago in 1919, for example, had doubled its Black population since 1916, a result of the first major wave of the Great Migration, leading to mass resentment among many white residents, which soon gave way to anger. It was an attitude "nurtured on the killing floors in the stockyards, on all-white blocks threatened with Black occupancy, and in parks and on beaches that were racially contested," as historian William Tuttle has explained.[37] On July 27, 1919, Eugene Williams was swimming in Lake Michigan and inadvertently drifted over into the "white" section of the lake. He was stoned by white people and drowned. The police did not arrest anyone. Instead they arrested a Black man who complained that they were not doing their jobs. That incident set off a week of violence that resulted in twenty-three Black deaths and fifteen white deaths. More than five hundred were injured and almost one thousand left homeless.[38]

There were similar conflicts in cities like Houston, Omaha, Knoxville, Charleston, Philadelphia, and Washington, DC. But such incidents were not limited to urban centers. There were also race riots in Waco and Longview, Texas, and in even smaller communities like Elaine, Arkansas.[39] In the fall of 1919, Black sharecroppers in and around Elaine attempted to organize a union and withhold their cotton crop from market until they received a higher price. When deputy sheriffs tried to break up an organization meeting, one of them was killed. In retaliation whites in the region went on a rampage, killing dozens of Black farmers. After the massacre no whites were arrested, but twelve Black men were convicted of the deputy's murder. They were sentenced to death, and sixty-seven other Black men were given prison sentences of up to twenty years in retributive show trials. The NAACP worked diligently on the sharecroppers' behalf, and in 1923 the Supreme Court overturned their convictions, but the association was powerless to compensate for the lives lost.[40]

Much of the violence in those urban areas was caused by tensions resulting from the Great Migration. Between 1910 and 1940, 1.75 million Black people left the South, doubling the Black population outside of the region. People escaped because of agricultural problems, Jim Crow, racial violence, and other reasons. Most went to urban hubs in the North: Washington, Philadelphia, New York, Pittsburgh, Cleveland, Detroit. Others moved to urban hubs in the South. Some, a much smaller number, went west.

The violence in south Georgia, then, acted as both a prompt for the Black southern out-migration, helping to feed what Johnson would call the Red Summer the following year, and an exemplar of the racially-motivated mob violence that such demographic shifts caused. It was, like the race riots that accompanied it, an act of social violence, an assault, in the words of Grimshaw, "upon individuals, or their property, solely or primarily because of their membership in social categories."[41] Race riots did not supplant lynchings in any way. There were also seventy-eight lynchings in 1919, the Red Summer year. But the riots were considered different because they were a mass casualty mob event not contained by a single act or cause. With the exception of incidents in places like Elaine and Longview, they took place in decidedly urban areas, and rioters usually killed by means other than rope and tree. Another of those riots, one that did not happen in an urban area and that did kill by hanging, happened in two counties in south Georgia in the summer of 1918, a year after the violence in East St. Louis and a year before that in Washington and Chicago. The last victim of that south Georgia violence was hanged on June 3, 1921, two days after the violence in Tulsa began to subside. It was multifaceted mob violence that killed at least eight, and possibly many more, in the period of the broadly defined Red Summer of race mob violence.

Christopher Waldrep, in describing the Elaine race massacre, notes that "Americans had grown accustomed to reports of urban racial violence," but coming as it did "a year after the Georgia lynchings, in October 1919," newspaper readers discovering the horrors happening in rural Arkansas had context for anticipating that kind of mass casualty event.[42] In other words, for events defined historically largely by their newspaper coverage, the south Georgia rampage was part of the connective tissue helping readers comprehend the rural outgrowths of the Red Summer the following year. It was a race riot related to the other race riots in the wave.

The reason it has not been included in such historical interpretations is because of the emphasis placed by the NAACP on one of those murders, that of Mary Turner, who, the association claimed, was only protesting her husband's lynching, was more than eight months pregnant, and had her unborn child cut from her body and stomped to death before she was burned alive and shot repeatedly. Walter White's gruesome account of Turner's lynching took the focus off the broader racial violence in the area and limited it to that against one woman. His was not an intentional omission. It was a way of focusing the trauma of the event on one example that would drive home the situation's severity to readers across the country. In the process he created a narrative that has had an inordinate impact on the historiography. Turner's lynching has been depicted in poetry, fiction, and sculpture. It has been the subject of one monograph and been included in numerous others. Turner has her own display panel at the Smithsonian's National Museum of African American History and Culture. She has become the quintessential example of white southern brutality against Black female bodies in the period from 1880 to 1930.

This influence is important, her narrative a powerful reminder of the power of racism and the vulnerability of the Black population in general and of Black women in particular during the Jim Crow era. Her story has played an important role both locally and nationally. There are multiple stakeholders with a vested interest in the account of her death. Her relatives still live in the area. Her story has done powerful feminist and antiracist work that has played a role in the ideology of millions. She has, in her influence, earned her display panel at the Smithsonian. This narrative does not seek to diminish any of that influence. As Brundage noted in his own study of Georgia race violence, "To observe that some lynchings were literally banal is not to deny the obvious significance of the symbolism and ritual evident in other lynchings."[43]

I do, however, argue that the violence in Georgia's Brooks and Lowndes Counties in May 1918 belongs less in the context of lynching history, as it is usually portrayed, and instead in the context of the history of race riots in a broadly conceived interpretation of the Red Summer as running from 1917 to 1921. It was, whatever the terminology, an organized mass killing, a large-scale embodiment of Campney's racist violence. The reason it has not been so contextualized is because of the emphasis on Turner's death. Her death was no less horrifying for the misstatement of its particulars, but the historiographical emphasis it receives is specifically because of those misstatements. And while this narrative does not ascribe any treacherous motives to White, who presented those particulars to the nation, I do argue that by the end of the summer of 1919, his misrepresentation of that account was in some measure intentional.

Of course, intentional misrepresentations are also a hallmark of white southern journalism related to lynchings. "White southern newspapers helped to shape the racist discourse of their time," argues historian Susan Jean. They "wielded tremendous power in creating ostensibly factual representations in order to convey particular messages," and those messages were directed to both Black and white citizens in a given community.[44] Claims that justified lynchings and other violent behavior gave white people license to engage in them and Black residents a gauge of how fearful they should be of further reprisals. That being the case, historians of lynching have to ask, "How much that is quantifiable, indeed, how much that is plausible can be derived from these reports?" Comparing accounts from various newspapers can help triangulate various factual elements embedded in such accounts, but it is a process that "adds the assumptions of the historian to a chain of uncertainties."[45]

This is an account concerning a chain of uncertainties in which the historian makes a series of assumptions based on interpreted evidence. But so too are all historical accounts. My assumptions and interpretations are the most reasonable conclusions to be drawn from the available material, though I acknowledge that much of that material was skewed by racism in intent and presentation. Mine is different from previous accounts of the events because I use far more material and have found new sources unused previously by historians, and new evidence of necessity creates new interpretations.

Many of those new sources are decidedly white and southern in origin. While this book questions the motives of white voices in the media and on the ground in late-1910s south Georgia, I ultimately draw qualified conclusions from those voices that directly contradict some of the Black voices in the region at the same time. Despite some of the evidentiary failings of the 1619 Project, the effective totality of its work, along with books like Isabel Wilkerson's *Caste*, demonstrates the importance of those voices in reimagining the historical narrative.[46] Taking Black voices seriously, however, only works when they are held up to the same critical lens as others. No one is silent in this story, and my conclusions come from interpretations of the likelihood of various versions of events, contextualized by the veracity and potential motives of their sources.

Throughout the chapters that follow, accounts of various assaults and lynchings demonstrate the contested space that was information sharing in the South, both on the opinion page of local newspapers and on the front page. It demonstrates the contingency of such accounts, the ability of such stories to change easily through time and space, and thus the difficulty for historians of parsing those decidedly different data sets to determine some measure of factual accuracy.[47]

The first chapter describes the precipitating attack and the resulting race riot, placing them within the context of the region's shifting demographics and the longstanding phenomenon of debt peonage that formed the bedrock of the agricultural economy in south Georgia and north Florida. Chapter 2 continues the story by describing the one murder that took place in Lowndes County before moving on to a broader analysis of racial violence in the region and the nation in the period of World War I. Race riots engulfed many areas of the country, and lynchings were at least a semiregular phenomenon in the counties of south Georgia and north Florida. While much of that violence was the result of demographic upheaval, it was also in the South a causal factor of the changes, helping spur the first major wave of the Great Migration.

Chapter 3 begins by describing the regional journalistic response to the mayhem, analyzing both the motivations behind white local coverage and the trajectory of its arguments. It then broadens its analysis to the national media response, demonstrating how the riot was subsumed for many into the image of one lynching in particular. So much racial violence was experienced through media characterization, and historical memories of lynchings and riots are determined through those experiences. In this case historical memory was also shaped by an influential investigation by White and the NAACP. Chapter 4 tells the story of that investigation, its successes and its missteps. A legislative effort for an anti-lynching law escalated after the attack, built largely on White's report, but the NAACP temporarily surrendered in that brief battle in the long fight for federal legislation after receiving information that contradicted White's claims. To that end, the chapter closes by analyzing pregnancy claims in other lynchings and the power of myth in recounting events for which journalists and investigators had only secondhand knowledge.

But the events had yet to end. Chapter 5 recounts the continued racial violence in the region following the principal murders of the riot, emphasizing in particular the manhunt for a supposed accomplice in the original precipitating assault. Shorty Ford was rumored to have been present at the original debt peons' revolt, and someone authorities claimed to be him was captured in Jacksonville. Though the man captured was clearly not the one white authorities were seeking, he was convicted nonetheless and was executed in Savannah in June 1921, just days after the Tulsa race massacre. That continuation of the violence into the next decade also occurred in the press, and chapter 6 evaluates a telling debate in the *Portland Morning Oregonian* about the facts of the violence in south Georgia and White's continued changing accounts of the story over the course of his long career.

It was a traumatic story, whatever its changes, and I undertake the effort with an acute awareness of the collective trauma still experienced by those in south Georgia. "Victims of severely traumatizing events may never fully escape possession by, or recover from, a shattering past," explains Dominick LaCapra in another evocation of trauma theory. "How," he asks, "may one eschew rewriting or apologetically glossing history yet 'brush [it] against the grain' (in Walter Benjamin's phrase) to recover different possibilities for the present and future?"[48] This book offers no remedy for the future. That work is being done by activists both locally and across the country and by local stakeholders, who worked so diligently with the Georgia Historical Society to erect a new marker for Mary Turner and the riot's other victims after the desecration of its predecessor. I instead attempt to more fully contextualize the events of 1918, arguing that, first, the full number of victims is better served and the totality and scope of that trauma is better explained by reading the violence as one of several rural outgrowths of the Red Summer wave between 1917 and 1921, and second, that the reason it usually is not framed as such is because the investigation of Walter White was factually incorrect.

Similarly, this book also makes much of the fact that Turner was not pregnant at the time of her gruesome killing, as it is at the core of the mythmaking surrounding the race riot, but such is not to say that pregnant women and actual children were not affected by the events. As Amol Shah and Bradford Kilcline have explained, "Trauma complicates at least 6% to 7% of all pregnancies, and it is the most common cause of nonobstetric morbidity and mortality in pregnancy."[49] Public health studies have demonstrated that such traumas increase at the intersection of race and socioeconomic status, leading to preterm births, which are the leading cause of infant mortality.[50] Pregnancies, then, were in fact decidedly affected by the race riot. And they were affected by white supremacy, Jim Crow, and the artificially enforced poverty that made it possible, beginning long before this particular act of racial violence in south Georgia and extending well beyond it.

Thus the account of the south Georgia race riot presented here is intended in no way to diminish that trauma nor the historical work of pathbreaking researchers like Julie Buckner Armstrong and Christopher Meyers. This account is built off source material that they did not have access to, principally the immediate local reporting of the Valdosta newspaper and the NAACP correspondence of executive secretary John R. Shillady, along with a variety of other newly discovered primary sources. That new information and sourcing, however, does not counteract the contingency present in such data sets, a contingency that dominates so much of lynching source material. "Because lynching was so often perpetrated through spectacle and sensationalism," explain Amy Louise Wood and Susan Donaldson, "any attempt to represent it risks re-engaging in that spectacle or exploiting the sensationalism once again."[51] Because of that contingency, historical presentations of racist violence in the Jim Crow South are inevitably the researcher's best hypothesis based on substantively incomplete data, no matter how much new data a researcher is able to find.

What follows is my best hypothesis.

CHAPTER ONE

The Revolt and the Rampage

Claude Hampton Smith was born January 4, 1893, the sixth and final child of Dixon and Mary Smith. The couple was not native to the area—Dixon was from South Carolina and Mary from Alabama—but they made their home in Brooks County, purchasing a 180-acre farm in the 1870s before expanding it to 200 acres the following decade. Hamp, as he was known to the family, had a sister, Emma, and four brothers, Willie, Tommy, Walter, and Bob, all of whom were significantly older than their late-arriving kid brother. But the men in the family remained close to him, because they continued to live at home into their adulthood, working the family farm. Hamp's older sister was married and out of the house early in his life, so the youngster grew up in a household surrounded by his mother and men. It could be a rugged place, but it was a stable one, Hamp absorbing both the science and racial codes of farming in south Georgia from his father and brothers. It was there he learned the nature of Georgia's debt peonage system and its advantageous use for white farm owners.[1]

THE REVOLT

Peonage in the South developed from the slave labor settlement following emancipation, wherein impoverished freedpeople were forced into signing year-long contracts that took away their ability to bargain for their labor.[2] In March 1867 Congress made peonage illegal, arguing that "the holding of any person to service or labor under the system known as peonage is hereby declared to be unlawful." The statute was originally dealing with a version of the practice taking place in the Territory of New Mexico but was applied more broadly as the nineteenth century progressed. That application was solidified in a series of peonage cases in the Gulf South states in the early twentieth century. In *United States v. Clyatt*, a 1902 peonage case in Pensacola, prosecutors claimed that in south Georgia and north Florida, particularly in the turpentine business, the practice of using debt peonage as a source of involuntary labor was widespread. Meanwhile, a series of twelve indictments for violations of the 1867 law appeared in the federal courts of the Southern District of Georgia. Judge Emory Speer, a native of Monroe County who proved an ardent opponent of both the morality and legality of peonage, clearly explained in June 1903 that such cases were violations of laws against involuntary servitude. "No other crime is so subtle in its operation, more destructive in its results than that which degrades the public conscience, until it can tamely and without protest witness the unlawful slavery of the citizen." Thus it was that Georgia passed its relatively vague "contract labor law" on August 15, 1903, to reframe the white South's defense of the practice and act as a check against such indictments.[3]

The plan worked. One investigation in 1907 estimated that one third of plantations "operating from five to one-hundred plows" were holding their Black workers in a state of peonage. In the early twentieth century, two Black men, one a doctor, took a young Black girl to Valdosta on the pretense of a "pleasure trip." They then "manufactured a claim against her for medical services" and sold her to the McRee family, who ran a notorious convict labor camp at Kinderlou Plantation just outside of the city. The two men were caught, appearing in Speer's court. "I am afraid if you had remained in Africa that you both would have become leaders of bands of slave catchers," the judge told the two Black men before fining them for the offense, "who swoop down on the unprotected kraals of the Hottentots or Congo and seize the defenseless people and bear them off and sell them into slavery."[4]

The state's peonage system was facilitated by its agricultural demography. Almost half of all farms in the South as of 1920 were operated by tenants, but tenant farms made up 66.6 percent of the total in 1920 Georgia, 200,954 farms. This was an increase of 8.4 percent from 1910 and 17 percent above the national average. Meanwhile, owners like Smith operated 102,123 farms in the state, but that did not mean they were going to do all the work of the farm. The lopsided use of farm tenancy in Georgia meant that those owners operating their own farms had a smaller labor supply to choose from, and since the conditions under which they worked were daunting for potential laborers, the pay was minimal or nonexistent, and workers had no stake, ephemeral or otherwise, in the outcome of the farm as did tenants, peonage became the vehicle by which farmers like Smith could keep an operation profitable. And in the racially coded labor system of the rural South, the vast majority of peons were Black.[5]

The vulnerabilities faced by Black farm laborers increased exponentially when that work was done in a state of peonage. Part of that vulnerability was an increased susceptibility to lynching: Black men who owned property were statistically less likely to be lynched, as Amy Kate Bailey and Stewart E. Tolnay have demonstrated.[6] But the peonage system inherently exploited vulnerability. An August 1919 letter from south Georgia's Coffee, a small hamlet in Bacon County, to the NAACP's national headquarters in New York, attested to the avarice that attended debt peonage. "I am in slavery," the letter writer explained. "All I want to do is leave this place. I am here at this place and my husband are working turpentine and the poor men here are only getting something to eat, and not very much of that, and when a man gets ready to leave he are not allowed to go. We got to show what these wicked men and women do, but the boss man will not allow no officer to come in here."[7]

Table 1. Georgia Farm Workers, 1920

Workers, Type of work	N	*Black workers* (n)	%
Male, turpentine	4,889	4,332	88.6
Male, farm	73,709	50,267	68.2
Female, farm	31,896	29,003	90.9

SOURCE: *Fourteenth Census of the United States, vol. 3, Population, 1920, Occupations* (Washington, DC: USGPO, 1923), 903, 905.

Another came from Darien, Georgia. "I a poor widow woman will tell you my trouble and if the Good Lord be willing I am asking you to help me if you can. My name is Nona Harris. Now in January my son was here with me in Darien, and this white man sent the sheriff for him and they carry my son back to Forest Glen and make him work for this same man til a debt of $329.50 is paid and he say he will send back and get the whole family of us and put us all on the chain gang or back on his farm if I don't pay the money to him by the first of April."[8]

Pete Daniel, who published the seminal study on southern debt peonage, has argued that "most complaints from the rural South charged that coercion, not laws, kept the victims [of peonage] at their jobs." Some were arrested for petty crimes, with white men paying their fines. At other times, as Len Cooper explains, white landowners "swindled the sharecropper into debt so permanent he could never work himself out of it." Using fines was probably the most common organized effort. Others took the indigent and traded a room for work, then billed for food and other amenities that kept employees in an overwhelming cycle of debt. "This peonage system was the dying gasp of that reign of terror called slavery," explains historian Elizabeth Clark-Lewis, "and the people didn't want to let go of it."[9]

To the north of Valdosta in Jasper County, federal agents launched a 1921 investigation into the peonage farm of John S. Williams. They told Williams it was illegal to "work a negger against his will," and he was shocked to learn it. "I and most all of the farmers in this county must be guilty of peonage," he told agents. The following year, he was tried for running what was called in the press a "murder farm." Clyde Manning, Williams's Black overseer, admitted at the trial to killing eleven of the workers after those original federal agents left Jasper County. Some he beat to death, others he drowned, others he chopped with an axe. He did so under orders from Williams, who worried about their possible testimony in a federal trial. And while the plantation owner was convicted and sentenced to a long prison term, the trial demonstrated both the brutality of the system and its ubiquity in places like Jasper County.[10]

Before that, however, the war was playing havoc with the region's debt peonage system, so much so that in early May 1918, Florida governor Sidney Johnston Catts instructed county sheriffs in the state to arrest all labor recruiters operating without a license. "Labor agents have been active in sending men from this to other states for government work," one report explained, "in many instances taking them from government work in this state and industries in some cases have been badly crippled."[11] The turpentine industries of north Florida, in other words, were losing impoverished workers to recruiters offering better wartime opportunities away from the deadly business.

The same was true for the farms of south Georgia, so Hamp Smith was careful to work with officials in Brooks and Lowndes Counties to ensure there was plenty of potential labor arrested so that he could pay their fines and bind them to his farm. It was an effort with which officials were familiar. To help farming and industry develop in the region, for example, Brooks and Lowndes Counties would also become the convict leasing capital of the area, with Kinderlou plantation just outside Valdosta's city limits near the Brooks County border run as a particularly brutal prison labor and peonage camp. Even though convict lease had been abolished in Georgia in 1908, a version of the system continued in a chain gang program that still included private elements that leased misdemeanor convicts to counties to work on public roads, and it ensured that peons on farms would be treated as brutally as the convicts. Smith's exploitation of that system was, to be sure, a successful venture. In 1916 Hamp was able to move away from his father's property and purchase a 450-acre farm of his own just outside of Barney. Using debt labor to maintain cheap overhead, he expanded his operation, acquiring an additional 300 acres and making himself one of the most prominent residents of the county.[12]

Just before his first land acquisition, Smith met and married Leila Bertha Simmons. Bertha, as she was known, was born on October 7, 1892, the daughter of William G. and Mary L. Simmons. Bertha moved to the new farm just outside of Barney and in late 1917 became pregnant with the couple's first child.[13]

It seemed to be an idyllic rise by a local boy made good in the de facto slave system of the New South, but all was not well. Any business built on debt peonage carried with it the potential fault lines that attended such cruelty. "Trouble with farm labor," reported the *Butler Herald*, "was not new to Smith."[14] This was an approving, racially coded admission that Hamp Smith ran his farm with overt brutality. The area was in the heart of the turpentine belt of south Georgia and north Florida, regularly coming under federal scrutiny for violence and duplicity toward Black workers. Nearby Kinderlou faced several federal charges for illegally trading in human beings. Smith's cruelty toward bound labor and the likelihood that at least a portion of that labor was acquired illegally—that some of those workers were being held against their will in a state of modern slavery—were characteristic of the violent form of white supremacy endemic to the region, and to be known for "trouble with farm labor" in a region where such behavior was so normalized was illustrative of a particularly notorious brutality.

Thus it was that on Thursday, May 16, 1918, as Congress, mired in the xenophobia of war, enacted the infamous Espionage Act, Smith and his pregnant wife had a quiet dinner before retiring to their bedroom, where he noticed that his Winchester rifle was missing. As he began to tell his wife about the absence, a shot fired through the window hit him in the chest, killing him. Bertha, "wild with terror," ran out onto the porch, then circled around the house, where she was attacked. "Evidences of a terrible struggle," such as "bits of Mrs. Smith's torn clothing" on the ground, testified to the brutality she suffered. Most accounts had her being shot through the right breast while on the ground, the bullet exiting from her upper shoulder. After shooting Bertha, the attackers ransacked the house, taking clothes and bullets along with the rifle. They tried to escape in Smith's car but could not operate it. Despite Bertha's claim of two attackers, there were three sets of footprints around the house, leading authorities to assume that three attackers were involved. Bertha Smith was "terribly mistreated and wounded," according to local reports, before crawling to a brook near the house. She washed her wounds in the stream, remaining in hiding there for several hours before traveling a half mile to the home of a Black family around 1:00 AM. There she named Sidney Johnson and a man named Julius as her attackers.[15]

The violence enacted against the Smiths was a rebellion against the approximation of slavery that the white South had erected in the post-Reconstruction decades through convict lease and debt peonage. Immediately the family of the victims sprang into action. Smith's brother Walter was made executor of his estate. William and Mary Simmons of Garden Valley, near Butler in Taylor County, traveled to Brooks County with other family members to be with their daughter for her convalescence. Their presence showed immediate results. "Mrs. Smith's condition is better today," the *Tifton Gazette* reported on May 18.[16]

Smith's body was taken to McGowan Undertaking Company, owned by Samuel Edward McGowan, to be prepared for burial. McGowan was not native to the area—he was born in 1879 in North Carolina—but the undertaker made his way to south Georgia, married his wife, Florence, a local woman, and had four children. The last of them, Samuel Jr., was born on August 8, 1917, nine months before the Brooks County rampage. McGowan was successful, adjusting to his new community and establishing an influential Quitman mortuary.[17]

McGowan continued to play a role as events unfolded, as did his assistant, a Black man named George U. Spratling. Spratling was born on October 22, 1881, the child of a local Quitman minister, George M. Spratling, and his wife, Ida Ellis. A resident of Quitman his entire life, Spratling married his first wife, Addie, in 1902, and over the next eight years, the two had four children. The century's second decade was difficult for Spratling, however. Addie died, and in 1918, the year of the lynching rampage, he married again, this time to the much younger Clara. He was thirty-six, she was twenty-one, but the two created a new home and had twins, a son and daughter, the following year.[18]

Both McGowan and Spratling played pivotal roles in the lynchings that followed, but before the mortuary owner led the lynch mob, he prepared Smith's body for the funeral. The ceremony took place on Saturday, May 18, at the Pauline Church north of Quitman, with the service conducted by Rev. W. T. Gaulden, a friend of the family. It was "tense with emotion, the feeling of the people over the foul murder of the young farmer being apparent," reported the *Valdosta Times*.[19]

Bertha's mother stayed with her, while her father, along with Mrs. G. H. Boles, Mrs. R. L. Green, and Miss Carmerine Huitt, all returned home to Reynolds after Smith's funeral. One of those who traveled to south Georgia with Simmons wrote an account of the trip for the local *Butler Herald*, describing the story of the attack on the Smith family based on Bertha's account. By this report, Smith was shot while his wife stood beside him. "The brute then rushed in the room and fired into the prostrate form, the deadly missile passing through the body and into the floor of the room." Bertha "in frantic fear stepped over the dead body of her husband and attempted to make her escape through the dining room . . . where she was caught and dragged into the yard, maltreated." Despite the fact that Bertha had passed out during the attack, "to cover up their fiendish, hellish acts," one of the perpetrators "fired a shot, going through her body, while she lay a helpless victim on the ground, the leaden missile passing through her right chest, puncturing the lung." Assuming she was dead, the attackers then went back into the house to rob it, "thinking that a large amount of money, the proceeds of the sale of timber a few days previous, was still in the house."[20]

That this version of the events differed in significant ways from the initial local reports demonstrates the instability of such accounts. Accounts were presented in nearby local newspapers from Thomasville, Tifton, Cordele, Homerville, and Waycross. They tended to match because they were all building from the reporting of the Thomasville paper. Though its counterparts were not syndicating the coverage, they were clearly pulling from the same source. The account from Taylor County was different because it was the only one coming from a substantially different point of reference. It is another reminder of the contingency of these accounts. White newspaper stories often played a role in justifying white violence, to be sure, and none of the accounts described the actions of Smith's workers as the functional slave revolt that it was. But the Black violence they were responding to was the routinized outgrowth of virulent white supremacy. White violence, the aberrant outgrowth of virulent white supremacy, had yet to happen. These early differences demonstrated that even before factoring in the ulterior motives of white southern reporters, unanimity of factual accuracy across time and space was always a fraught endeavor.[21]

Whatever its relationship to accounts emanating from local newspapers, however, the *Butler Herald*'s first-person narrative insisted that the timber money that the would-be robbers were looking for was not in the house and that her bullet wound actually brought Bertha back to consciousness. "She in some manner walked and dragged herself to a branch about three hundred yards from the house." She stayed there, "hidden behind some logs in the water and mud for three hours. She then made her way to a friendly negro house about a half mile distant," where help was called. Bertha was taken to "the home of Mrs. Joyce, a widow," and stayed there until the arrival of her father.

Emma E. Joyce had been married to a farmer named James J. Joyce, but he died in his thirties, leaving his widow and her four children alone at the farm in Barney. There was plenty of room and plenty of help at the Joyce farm for Bertha Smith to recuperate until the arrival of the Simmons family.[22]

Now, however, her father was back in Taylor County. The funeral was over, Bertha was recovering, still preparing to have her baby, and things seemed to have settled for the Smith and Simmons families. But for others, things were not settled at all. "I want you to know that I have not rested," one of Smith's brothers addressed him over the open casket at his funeral. "I have been through swamps, through mud and water to my waist to get the brute."[23]

THE RAMPAGE

When Hamp Smith was murdered, white farmers in the region were already on edge, largely agitated by resentment at government regulatory policy. The region's economy had suffered following the Civil War, well into the 1880s, saved at least in part by the introduction of long-staple Sea Island cotton and the arrival of another railroad in 1889, the Georgia Southern and Florida, which gave the area its first north-south transportation connection. With an economic recovery in full swing, Valdosta built a new courthouse for Lowndes County in 1904, and in 1906 the state legislature chartered South Georgia Normal College for the city. Three more railroads arrived by the time the school opened for classes in 1913.[24]

But there were problems. Georgia segregated its railroads in 1891 and everything else soon after. The state implemented disenfranchisement laws in 1908. And despite the seeming flourishing of Valdosta, further economic problems were on the horizon. In 1915 the boll weevil arrived, damaging the farm economy all over again and ensuring that white landowners would hedge their bets by further relying on indigent Black workers held in bondage through debt peonage. At the same time, the region sought to attract tourism and nonagricultural industries as a broader hedge. The Dixie Highway began construction in 1915, moving through south Georgia and providing motorcar access to the area, giving urban white residents in Quitman and Valdosta a stake in cultivating a reputation that would not offend venture capital or paying customers.[25]

Segregation and disfranchisement hindered that reputation, but so too did the behavior of the locals. Beginning in 1916, the farmers of Brooks and Colquitt Counties began protesting against the federal requirement of cattle dipping in aid of reducing the tick population. On May 25, 1916, seven dipping vats were dynamited in Brooks County. Two men, Jeff and Arden Keel, were arrested after drawing guns on the federal inspector who had come to inspect their cattle. In neighboring Colquitt County two days later, a mass meeting of more than a thousand people demanded that the tick eradication program end; several of the speakers told the crowd "that they would die before submitting to any such trampling of their rights," to great applause. There had been dynamiting in Colquitt, as well, to the approval of the massive crowd.[26]

Throughout the following year, several farmers in Lowndes, Brooks, and Colquitt Counties who refused to dip their cattle were prosecuted. On August 16, 1917, sixteen Lowndes County dipping vats were dynamited. Authorities originally assumed that only nine vats had been destroyed, but the vandals had also cut the rural telephone lines, making reporting more difficult. It took county commissioners months to rebuild the vats, finally restoring operational status in early January, at which point they were dynamited yet again. County commissioners offered a $600 reward for any information about the perpetrators, and Georgia governor Hugh Dorsey offered another $250, but no one was caught for the crimes. The following month, in February 1918, the Keels were finally convicted in federal district court on charges of resisting a federal officer in the discharge of his duty for the gun incident more than a year prior.[27]

Neither reward nor conviction, however, would stanch local anger over the federal scourge of cattle dipping. On April 11, 1918, just a month prior to the revolt at Smith's farm, eight more dipping vats were dynamited in Lowndes County. "Without knowledge as to the personnel of the outlaw band, it is patent that every member of it—whether composed of three men or a dozen—is not only an unworthy citizen, but a desperado and a menace to the community," decried the *Atlanta Constitution* in language that it later used to decry the region's lynchings. "Those dynamiters should be taught that Georgia is a state of law and order, and of progress, and it behooves the authorities of every county in which this form of outlawry still lives—and such counties are few—to concentrate their attention upon the business of stamping it out."[28]

Compounding the dynamiting terror that hung over the region in the spring of 1918, Valdosta's Southern Bank and Trust, one of the region's largest financial institutions, closed its doors on March 22 and planned to turn over the bank's books to state authorities for liquidation. Worried that the bank's collapse could cause the region to plunge into depression, other banks in the area offered to contribute to its rival's coffers to keep it afloat. Without time to fully investigate the institution's finances, however, state banking authorities were deemed to be a better option. The bank's president issued a statement affirming its solvency, trying to reassure customers that "every depositor will be paid in full." Depositors were not convinced, and as the state audit commenced, the tenuous stability of the region's economy hung in the balance.[29]

Further demonstrating that tenuous stability, local farmers in Lowndes County who did fear cattle ticks and wanted to protect their herds pooled their resources and attempted to rebuild the vats themselves. Their hold on economic solvency in a region where the largest bank had just collapsed was too tenuous to risk losing the cows to disease. Still, they were just as resentful of federal intervention as their anti-dipping counterparts. They realized that to rebuild the vats properly, they needed federal guidance, but they demanded that the finished product would be their private property. The farmers assured officials that the property transfer would guarantee that no new dynamiting would occur.[30]

A month prior to the Hampton Smith killing, the *Moultrie Observer* also worried over violence against those opposed to US participation in World War I. The paper did not support the war protestors, but "the work of the mob in dealing with these offenders will run to dangerous extremes if the government does not also deal firmly with it." If officials were not careful, "this work of the mob would ultimately go to the extreme of taking life without process of law." Such behavior turned well-meaning people into those they hated. "We do not want to adopt German tactics in this country, in the army or in civil life." It was an odd complaint from a white south Georgia newspaper, one seemingly unaware that the same argument could be made about those engaging in mob violence against suspected Black criminals or in reaction to them.[31]

At the same time, Claude Reviere, a Black man from Moultrie, was sentenced by the Colquitt County superior court to life in prison for the murder of John Williams. Williams was also Black, meaning that the crime would likely be redressed in the courtroom. Lynchings remained substantively rare relative to the number of murder trials that occurred during the era, but the potential impetus for extralegal action often disappeared when both the victim and alleged perpetrator were Black.[32] While hegemonic control of Black lives and bodies was in aid of sustaining an antebellum power relationship, it was also about protecting against perceived threats to those who met the standard of white legitimacy, and Reviere's crime was no threat to that dynamic.

While Reviere was beginning his life sentence, Robert Presley, a Black Brooks County farmer, went to the Bank of Pavo, a few miles from Barney, and purchased a one-thousand-dollar liberty bond on the first day of the campaign.

It was an act, the *Moultrie Observer* explained, that "bespeaked the loyalty of the colored farmers in this section."[33]

But to most white people in the area, such acts of generosity were beside the point. On April 14, 1918, days after the latest dynamiting, J. F. Husbands, a white farmer two miles outside of Valdosta, shot and killed Will James, "noted negro chicken thief," who he claimed was trying to enter his chicken coop. Husbands was not punished; the guilt of James was assumed by all, as was the merit of the extrajudicial death sentence.[34]

Ten days prior to the Smith murder, another prominent local who took advantage of debt peonage was killed in nearby Sirmans, Florida, just to the south of Quitman. W. C. Lamb was a turpentine operator, a member of the industry so notorious for debt peonage, and after his murder one of his workers, John Wesley, was suspected of the offense. Wesley disappeared after the crime, leaving all white people in the area on edge, fearing further race trouble.[35]

Much of the violence in the region was a function of demographic changes. Both Brooks and Lowndes Counties had Black majorities, apartheid areas ruled by white minorities largely unconcerned about the welfare of their counterpart population. Between 1900 and 1910, Brooks County's population increased more than 25 percent, and its rural population by more than 15 percent. While its white illiteracy rate hovered around 7 percent, its Black illiteracy rate was almost 40 percent. In the years between 1910 and 1918, however, the county's growth had slowed dramatically, with less than a thousand new residents arriving. The county's literacy rates had moderately improved but remained racially skewed. Lowndes County was larger than Brooks by more than a thousand residents, and Valdosta was the largest city in the region, but other than that, Lowndes County's demographic trends were almost identical to its counterpart. Notably, while the populations of the counties only modestly increased in the years between the 1910 census and the 1918 race riot, the two largest cities, Valdosta and Quitman, both experienced a decline in population, as more and more residents moved to rural outlying areas out of either desire or necessity.[36]

Schooling for Black residents in the area developed in fits and starts based on perceived need. In Lowndes County, for example, whenever a group of Black students from a given area registered for school, the county chartered a new school for them to ensure that integration by way of simple proximity would never be an issue. There were no allowances made for age or grade level of the would-be students. Rural Black schools in Lowndes were one-room, one-teacher affairs, everyone attending together at the discretion of the instructor.

At least four of the schoolhouses in the county were Rosenwald schools, among the more than five thousand funded by Julius Rosenwald, leader of Sears, Roebuck, whose educational philanthropy was inspired by the work of Booker T. Washington.[37] But they were not the only ones. Along with the Rosenwald schools, there were other rural county schools, including Bemiss, Hahira, Jumping Gulley Road, Red Flagg, and Woods Chapel. No less than thirty-four Black schoolhouses existed in the county at some point during the segregation era.[38] Brooks County, with a smaller population and no city the size of Valdosta, had fewer schools than Lowndes, but its schools developed in a similar manner.

Then there was the region's more violent history. Brooks County's legacy of racial violence was long, extending back to the antebellum slave period, when the area was still part of Lowndes County. The county seat in the 1850s was Troupville, but when the Atlantic and Gulf Railroad tracked a route through south Georgia that did not include the town, the locals were angry. One of them, William B. Crawford, responded in June 1858 by burning down the courthouse in Troupville. After being released on bond, Crawford fled to South Carolina, but the controversy lingered, and in August the town voted to divide the county at the Withlacoochee River. In December, Brooks County was officially organized.[39] The new county was majority enslaved, and when the Civil War broke out, those enslaved people took action. In August 1864, led by local white man John Vickery, at least three enslaved men, named Nelson, George, and Sam, planned to take control of Quitman, now the Brooks County seat, destroy it, and abscond to Madison, Florida, where Union forces were stationed. After a local arrest, the plot was discovered prior to its implementation. All four men were tried and executed.[40] There was no wave of white retribution as with other slave rebellions and plots, largely because of the late stage of the war, but white fear and resentment over Black freedom initiatives lingered.

In December 1894, in retribution for an alleged murder, a white Brooks County mob murdered five Black citizens, stopped only by other white citizens after rioters began attacking Black workers on the plantation of one of the county's wealthiest farmers, Mitchell Brice. When a Black woman was beaten, Brice threatened the mob with suppression and prosecution. The 1894 rampage was remarkably similar to the events in 1918, with the lone exception that no prominent citizen stepped forward in response to the violence against a Black Brooks County woman a generation later.[41]

The region's violence was facilitated by a state government that had largely abrogated responsibility for policing such actions. In 1892 Governor

William J. Northen campaigned for reelection on a platform of stopping mob violence in the state, and in 1893 he helped shepherd a bill through the legislature requiring local law enforcement to use posses to prevent violent mobs. Not only could members of the mob be charged with felonies, but county sheriffs could also be charged with misdemeanors for not taking action to stop the violence. Northen's effort was sincere, and he continued to rail against lynching, but his efforts were couched in the abiding white Democratic belief in local control. His assumption that giving local law enforcement the tools to stop mob violence would lead them to stamp it out proved wrong. Attempts to strengthen the law in the years to come all failed.[42] So white mobs understood, even with a state anti-lynching law on the books, that they could act without fear of consequence.

The revolt on the farm of Hampton Smith took place in that context. As Amy Louise Wood has argued, "Lynchings tended to occur in places that were already wrestling with problems of crime and anxieties about moral decay, where lynchings were understood to be just and necessary retributions against abominable crimes, a means to ensure not only white dominance but the larger social and moral order."[43] Rumors spread among whites across Brooks and Lowndes Counties that Black conspirators were holding "secret lodge meetings, gatherings to plot revenge on the whites."[44] The rumors turned out to be false, but the white fear of violence was certainly real. White people feared those who had suffered so much grief under the debt peonage system. The principal players in the Smith conspiracy, as it was termed, were all current or former peonage workers. The story made its way across Brooks and Lowndes Counties that the murder had been committed by Sidney Johnson, a peonage worker Smith had bonded out of Valdosta's Lowndes County jail, conspiring with Will Head, Will Thompson, Eugene Rice, and Hayes Turner; planning meetings were held in the home of Turner and his new wife, Hattie. Johnson went into hiding, but the others turned out to be easy to find.

A mob gathered to exact a perceived justice and to allay broader white anxiety in the region. They also sought to terrorize a Black community that white locals perceived as holding the potential for similar rebellions against virtual slavery on other farms in the region. After the supposed conspiracy of Denmark Vesey in 1822, white authorities in South Carolina arrested more than seventy people and publicly executed thirty-five. After the Nat Turner rebellion in 1831, white vigilantes murdered more than a hundred people in Virginia and North Carolina. Racial terrorism had long been a performative act presumed by white southerners to have preventive and retributive effects.[45] "Mob executions," argues Michael Pfeifer, "were performances enacting what some persons perceived as the values of a community."[46] That performance began in 1918 with Will Head, who was captured first and hanged at the fork in the road at Troupville in Brooks County. Head was originally from Jackson, Georgia, in Butts County. He was the sole guardian of his sons, Edward and Charlie, who were held over to the guardianship of a relative, Sillar Byars, in Jackson after Head's lynching.[47] It was reported that after Head confessed to the mob, one member asked him, "Did you know that you would be hanged and perhaps burned for such a crime?" A stoic Head replied, "Yes, sir, but it's no use worrying about that now." At least three hundred people attended Head's lynching. Before being hanged, he asked to pray, but voices from the crowd shouted, "You didn't give Smith time to pray!" After his death his body was riddled with bullets before "souvenir hunters got busy with their knives and many pieces of Head's flesh were carried away." The crowd lingered at the scene for more than an hour before learning of the capture of Thompson and Rice and moving to the next murder site. Next Will Thompson was hanged from a tree at Camp Ground Church near Barney. Eugene Rice was the mob's third victim.[48]

Then there were the Turners. Hattie Graham was born in Quitman in December 1884, the second daughter of Perry and Betty Graham.[49] She arrived at the Graham house three years after her sister Pearlie, two before her brother Perry, and a full fourteen before her brother Otha, who was soon followed by another sister, Etha, the last child of the family, born in July 1899. In 1910, at age twenty-six, Hattie had a child, Willie Loyd Smith, and when she married Hayes Turner on February 11, 1917, in Colquitt County, her son moved into the house with his new stepfather. (Turner's surviving family lists her as having two children, Ocie Lee and Leaster, as of May 1918.) After her marriage some began to call her Mary, though to most she remained Hattie.[50]

Hayes Turner, according to the *Herald*, had quit Smith's farm prior to the end of his contract, and because of that, when Turner attempted to return to the farm to collect his things, Smith kept him from getting them. Disputes about peonage tenure were common, as lessees often used meal charges and petty fines to extend terms of indenture, almost always without justification or the approval of county officials and often without the knowledge of those who had their terms extended. Turner had planted a crop for Smith in January but abandoned the farm early in May. "He was among the first suspected as having criminal knowledge of the assassination of the farmer," reported the *Moultrie Observer*. In response to being denied the ability to retrieve his property and in an effort to collect thirty dollars owed to him, Turner served Smith on Saturday, May 11, with a possessory warrant.[51] It provided some measure of motive, and to the mob, that was enough.

Hayes Turner was hanged on Saturday, May 18, at Okapilco Bridge, after Smith's funeral. Based on whatever evidence authorities believed they had against Turner, they took him to jail in Quitman, but when Brooks County sheriff Jesse Wade learned that the mob was after him, Wade, county superintendent Francis M. Youngblood, and clerk Roland Knight put Turner in Wade's car and began driving him to Moultrie. Knight drove the vehicle, hoping to make it north as fast as possible. Three miles from the town, however, a mob of about forty men in black masks stopped the car at Okapilco Bridge, some members standing on the sheriff's running boards and covering the officials with rifles and pistols. They took the suspect in one of their several cars and sped off in a cloud of headlights and dust.[52]

A desperate Hattie Turner fled the scene and spent Friday night in the oat field of Charles H. Burton. Burton's farm was at the intersection of Barney and Berlin in Brooks County. Born in 1872, Burton rose to prominence and married comparatively late in life. He met and married Sarah Harrell, seven years his junior, in the second half of the twentieth century's first decade, when he was thirty-five years old. With a prospering farm, the couple immediately began having children. They also hired Black laborers to work the farm. Unlike many white farmers in the area, however, the Burtons tended to act like legitimate employers. The Turners had worked voluntarily for the Burtons previously and had a much better experience than they had with the Smiths. So too had Eugene Rice, another of the lynching victims, worked for the Burtons in the small world of Black Brooks County farm labor.[53]

On Saturday morning Turner told Burton's wife that she was there and began helping her with chores on the property. Charles Burton was not home, as he had been "helping guard the swamp where Sidney Johnson was supposed to be." When he returned from his part in the mob to find Turner there, she told him she "was scared half to death the night before by some one" and so fled to the Burtons. Burton had heard nothing on Saturday night of Turner's complicity in the Smith killing and so let her stay. On Sunday morning he visited Mrs. Smith, "and there were some parties that seemed to think that I was protecting the woman from them." Burton assured them he was not protecting anyone and led them directly to Turner. In his statement Burton could not say as to "the woman being guilty." But "as to lynch law I am in favor of it," he averred, "where they are guilty of the crime" that befell the Smiths. He did not, however, believe "in lynching innocent parties," and "as to the negro Eugene Rice, who was taken from my place and hanged, I think he was an innocent negro."[54] It was the pseudo-moral self-justification characteristic of white racial violence, complete with the paternalism that had defined such justifications since antebellum retributive violence following slave revolts. Many such claims included a nod to chivalry in the protection of the virtue of womanhood, but such statements only applied when the woman whose virtue was threatened was white.

Thus Hattie Turner, also known as Mary, was taken around noon, "without waiting for nightfall," to Folsom's Bridge over the Little River by a mob either punishing her for her part in the conspiracy or responding in anger to her protest over the lynching of her husband.[55] Depending on the account, the mob itself ranged from forty people to between five hundred and one thousand. Turner's clothes were burned off, she was shot multiple times, and she was hanged. Some accounts claim that the mob originally planned to set her on fire, but when her clothes burned off, they decided to hang her instead. Others argue that the fusillade of bullets set her clothes aflame, burning them off unintentionally. The shooting continued after she was hanged, bullets continuing to riddle a now dead body. Crowds thronged to the site all day and into the night. One Moultrie man estimated as many as two thousand cars near the scene later that afternoon. While that was surely an exaggeration, the interest from the surrounding communities was palpable. Such horrific facts, mentioned in multiple local, state, regional, and national accounts in the immediate wake of the attack, have remained undisputed.[56]

Jennifer D. Williams explains that lynching "has exceeded the physical act itself, to become a gendered sign of racial oppression that enables Black men to claim it as a trope of emasculation over time and in varied contexts."[57] It was a role that worked in two different gendered ways. First, it left female victims largely absent from the broader lynching narrative, cordoning off the phenomenon as a male space. Second, it gave female victims that much more contemporary power in the public narrative because such acts of violence were rare. At least 121 Black women were lynched in the half century between 1880 and 1930. They were a small percentage of the thousands of lynching victims, and that relative rarity created an exoticism that amplified the impact of such stories.[58]

Crystal Feimster calculates that at least seven of those women were reported as visibly pregnant at the time of their lynchings. Those numbers are contested in the chapters that follow, but her conclusion about the reports is undeniably true, despite the facts on the ground. "If such brutal lynchings were calculated to make an impression on the black community and underscore its vulnerability, whites succeeded."[59] Maria De Longoria reports, however, that only ten of those female lynchings were the result of "relationships to accused black male suspects." Another six "were accused of being accessories or having knowledge of crimes."[60] It is not clear in which category De Longoria places Turner, but both rationales were given for her murder at various points in the post-lynching justification narrative.[61]

Michael Pfeifer describes a "masculinist perspective" among those who practiced white violence that "saw the collective enactment of violent social control as an extension of masculine prerogative and authority from home and workplace to the policing of a locale and the supervision of its legal institutions."[62] All such elements worked together in Brooks and Lowndes Counties, as home and workplace were fused in the debt peonage agricultural system, a system propped up by the very legal institutions, including policing, that the mob was seeking to extend. And though a masculinist perspective was often concerned with defending white womanhood, Black women fell beyond the scope of such concerns, leaving them vulnerable to extralegal punishment for perceived crimes, or, like Mary Turner, assumed proximity to perceived crimes. Pfeifer, for example, describes the lynching of a Black woman in Catahoula Parish, Louisiana, in November 1892, killed because she was the daughter of a man accused of murdering a local constable.[63] The masculinist perspective, in other words, set up a series of racial lines that Black men continually had to traverse to ensure some modicum of safety; Black women, meanwhile, had to traverse those same lines while also guarding against perceived associative guilt based on relationships with male victims of the mob.

The death of the Turners made five victims of the mob. Authorities brought Sidney Johnson's parents to jail in Valdosta, presumably to prevent them from contacting their son, and kept them under guard for their protection. "Posses were last night looking for other negroes in this section and the feeling among both white and black seems to be growing more intense," reported Thomasville's *Daily Times Enterprise*. It was, if nothing else, a description of a race riot. The paper was describing the work of a mob. In a separate account in the same column, the Thomasville paper reported that "the mob started to burn her and after her clothes were burned off they hung her and riddled her with bullets." In that account the mob killed four victims rather than five. The paper also reported Will Head's confession that the presumed plot was created in the Turner home. According to the *Atlanta Journal*, Head, who worked on the Smith farm, claimed that he had gone into the Smith house to get an early supper, on the pretext that he was traveling to another farm to visit acquaintances but really intending to steal Smith's rifle and bring it to Johnson, whom he identified as the shooter. The *Daily Times Enterprise* claimed, surely with at least a measure of exaggeration, that "between 500 and 1,000 people from Brooks, Lowndes, Colquitt, and Berrien counties were in the mob."[64]

Again the story shifted slightly when the account moved further from the location of the attack. There were also early indications that the white press would attempt to justify the assault. In defenses of the mob's actions, no thought was given to the fact that eight-year-old Willie Loyd Smith would have been present in the Turner house when the plotters were hatching the scheme to kill Smith. Still, the *Butler Herald* was certain that "law-abiding negroes have been in no danger and there has been no hurried exodus from Brooks because of the lynchings." It assured its readers that "leaders among the colored race" felt that the lynchings were justified and had not spread beyond the bounds of the intended targets. Turner, after all, "made unwise remarks yesterday about the execution of her husband, and the people in their indignant mood took exception to her remarks, as well as her attitude." After revenge against Smith, "robbery was a secondary motive" for the original attack, the *Herald* reported. The "assault upon Mrs. Smith" was not part of the original plan but was "evidently decided upon at the spur of the moment." That attack "is what made the white men 'see red.'"[65] Again, white self-justifications followed a long-established pattern.

The account of the early lynchings in the *Chicago Defender* adhered largely to the recognized narrative, but the paper's description of the Hampton Smith killing was decidedly different, as was the broader tone of its coverage. Hayes and Mary Turner were "lynched by a gang of white heathens" after Smith's body was discovered. There was in the *Defender*'s account, as in all of the other initial accounts, no mention of a Turner pregnancy. That, however, was where the similarities largely stopped. The Smiths hired the Turners to work on their farm, the *Defender* explained, but treated them with incredible cruelty. "It is alleged" that Smith "brutally whipped Turner with a cowhide because of her refusal to work longer without pay, there being some difference in the matter of payments due her." Hayes Turner responded by going to the Smith home and demanding an explanation "from the slave driver, whereupon Smith sought his shotgun and fired on Turner." The worker was wounded but managed to escape, and both Smith and his wife pursued him with shotguns. Turner, "half-crazed with the thought of being fired upon," returned home to find his wife, Will Head, and Will Thompson talking to one another in the dining room. No sooner had he told him what happened than the Smiths, "prepared to bombard the residence with buckshot," began firing into the house, ambushing the group. In response the men in the house returned fire, driving "Smith and his wife back to their home." In the general fusillade that ensued, Smith was shot to death through a window. Thompson and Head were found by the resulting mob first, hanged from trees, and shot repeatedly with bullets.[66]

After Hayes Turner was lynched, the *Defender* continued, Brooks County sheriff Jesse Wade was "rushing Mrs. Mary Turner to the county jail at Barney when the mob pounced upon him." The rioters "tied a rope around her body and dragged it to a tree near Folsom's bridge, where it was strung up." Sidney Johnson, according to the *Defender*, "joined the four lynch victims in repelling the attacks of the Smiths" before escaping "the heathenism of the white citizens." His parents and several other close relatives were brought to Valdosta and put in jail "for safe keeping." Lowndes County jailers doubled the guard around the Johnson family. While looking for Johnson, presumed to be hiding near a local swamp, law enforcement was also looking for "a man named 'Julius,' who is alleged to have aided Johnson in effecting his escape."[67] The *Quitman Free Press*, another white local paper, provided a measure of corroboration for the story in reporting that the mysterious Julius was being investigated in Macon, where he was supposed to use several aliases, including "Black Trouble."[68]

"The mob violence has created such an excitement that people are leaving the community in droves," the *Defender* reported. "It is estimated that at least 54 respectable citizens have announced their property for sale and are contemplating abandoning the crime district." Many locals were "still unaccounted for, and it is thought that they have migrated to other sections of the country." Because of the attack on Mary Turner, "women employed at various occupations in the community failed to show up to work following the lynching."[69]

The *Defender*'s account is different from that of its white counterparts in several ways, but the most prominent is that of motive. In the paper's telling, the murder of Smith was an act of immediate self-defense. There was no plot. The mob rampage occurred after the group at the Turner home repelled a violent attack by the Smiths, their only recourse after being confronted with earlier violent attacks. There is no way to corroborate this version of the plantation uprising. The *Defender* had correspondents in Georgia and provided reliable lynching journalism, obviously with an eye to ending the practice. The differences in its account provided a valuable counternarrative to the white newspapers and allowed the subaltern to speak, giving voice to the victims in a way that even broad-minded national white newspapers would not do.[70]

Still, just as important are the similarities between the reporting in Valdosta's, Quitman's, and Atlanta's white newspapers and the *Defender*'s version of the story. The mob was responding to the killing of Smith, and the lynchings were a result of that killing. Mary Turner was not pregnant; she was lynched horrendously but in what can only be described as the traditional manner. And all were describing, in so many words, a retributive act of racial terrorism, whether describing all of the deaths or focusing on one in particular. It was a rampage to stop further rebellions, and ominously, it was not over. The hunt for Sidney Johnson was ongoing.

CHAPTER TWO

Lynchings and Riots

Sidney Johnson was born in March 1900 in Lowndes County. He was the son of Clyattville farmer Richard Johnson and north Florida native Laura Wideman, from Hamilton County, which bordered Lowndes to the south, and raised in adjacent Madison County, Florida. His parents had coupled as teenagers, Richard born in October 1877, Laura in July 1876. They got together in 1896, and four years later they had four children. Vancilene came first, then Lilla. Simon was next, the first boy, followed by Sidney. Months before Sidney's birth, his parents married on September 6, 1899. A decade later in 1910, despite the challenges of Jim Crow and a lack of education, along with a growing family—the Johnsons had nine children by 1909—Richard and Laura managed to own their own farm free and clear just outside of Dasher in Lowndes County. They had three more children the following decade, the last of them, Eulie, born in 1917, less than a year before her brother was killed by Valdosta police.[1]

THE MURDER OF SIDNEY JOHNSON

At the time of his death, Sidney Johnson was nineteen years old. Three weeks prior to the peonage revolt at Smith's farm, Johnson was "caught in a police dragnet while rounding up loafers and gamblers." He was fined, and Smith paid the fine so that he could get labor for his farm. Though the consensus was that Johnson was the shooter in the Hamp Smith murder, he escaped the initial wave of violence. Johnson was "dodging a large posse in the swamp along Knights creek, his feet tied in rags which are saturated in turpentine to prevent the dogs from following his tracks." The *Bainbridge Post-Search Light* reported with apparent confidence that Johnson had reentered Valdosta on the night of May 19 for food before returning to the swamp. Sheriff's deputies from six counties joined Valdosta chief of police Calvin Dampier and a crew of bloodhounds to search for him.[2]

Johnson's shotgun and pistol were known to everyone in Lowndes and Brooks Counties. There had been several reported sightings, and Johnson infamously "emptied his gun at a white citizen of the county who happened to come upon him while out looking for his hogs." In another account, that white citizen, farmer E. C. Guest, had been in Johnson's sights until the men made eye contact and Johnson realized that Guest was alone and not searching for him. In the telling of the *Macon News*, Guest and his family were in town for the afternoon, and Johnson took advantage of their absence to rob their house for food. When Guest returned to find his house robbed, he searched his property and found Johnson hiding behind a log. Johnson fired at Guest, but Guest was able to dodge the attack, jumping behind a tree just in time. He returned fire as Johnson escaped back into the swamp.[3] Thus it is reasonable to assume that Johnson and Guest had some kind of contact, and it is a surety that the contact sparked outrage in the white community. The exact nature of the contact, however, has been lost, as has so much of the narrative, to the uncertainties generated by the temporal and spatial differences in contemporary accounts.

The anger such incidents engendered in white Brooks County residents caused the hunting party to balloon in size, making it too unwieldy to do its work. "Feeling among both the whites and blacks is growing and the situation is threatening," worried the *Tifton Gazette*. It lacked, in the words of the *Valdosta Times*, "the organization and leadership that was needed," and, in fact, "there were so many in the posse, most of them merely lookers-on, that the negro had no trouble in getting his bearings and evading his pursuers." That was when Dampier and other police officers stepped in and pleaded with the rioters to disperse, not because of the lawlessness of their actions but because of their ineffectiveness.[4]

At the same time, the actual search party broke up, as well. On May 21 the group of sheriffs leading the posse called off the search for Johnson, believing that a smaller party would be more mobile and would thus make it more difficult for Johnson to escape in the swamps around Valdosta. "Undaunted," reported the *Macon News*, "and almost without sleep, and only stopping occasionally for food, the posse has maintained its ceaseless chase, and it is sure that capture will follow." Johnson's family was also put in jail for safekeeping while the search was on for him, and, in the words of the *Fitzgerald Leader-Enterprise and Press*, "owing to the increased feeling among the people, the jail is being strongly guarded to prevent trouble." It was assumed that in Johnson's absence the mob might sate its bloodlust with his parents. Meanwhile the rumors surrounding the location of Johnson continued to grow. The *Griffin Daily News* reported that he was part of a shootout at a church "in Line Creek district" just as the church's preacher began his sermon. The *Macon News* claimed that Head, Thompson, and the Turners were all relatives of Johnson. Still, the paper was doubtful of the story: "That this young negro could conceive and execute such a hellish crime against his employer and his wife is almost unbelievable, as Johnson has never before shown more criminal tendencies than loafing and gambling."[5]

That the "hellish crime against his employer" was a response to his employer's own hellish crimes, or that his employer was in fact a peonage contractor and Johnson was bound labor not earning an employment wage, went unmentioned. Local white papers consistently filtered their coverage through a lens of white victimhood and Black aggression, even as white mobs roamed the counties hunting for Black victims. The inversion of the aggression narrative made it possible for many to give credence to false claims of church shootouts and sympathy to officers incarcerating Johnson's family "to prevent trouble." Published concerns about the size of the mob were pragmatic ones about its ability to effectively kill rather than moral qualms about killing per se, because whites in these accounts were victims and thus the killing was a form of retributive justice. That ubiquitous false narrative only further endangered Johnson.

The petrified Johnson eventually emerged from the swamp and crept to the house of John Henry Bryant, at the corner of South Troup and South Pryor Streets. Bryant was so gripped by the fear instilled in the Black population that he decided to tip Chief Dampier to Johnson's location. He was able to distract Johnson by having his wife offer to cook the fugitive a meal, and while she was doing so, Bryant slipped out of the house. So nervous about even being out alone in the tense climate of Valdosta was Bryant that he found a police officer to walk him to the station as if he was under arrest, a pretense to keep an armed white man with him as he traveled.[6]

When Dampier received Bryant's tip, he and several patrolmen, including his son, Emory B. Dampier, surrounded the house. They moved in quickly so as not to let a crowd form, Bryant moving ahead of them so he could call his wife out of the house.[7] They were worried about the mob. It was a policing decision based not on the relationship between the authorities and the policed but instead on the relationship between the policed and the mob. It was, in other words, an action in response to Johnson's hunters, a function of the riot rather than a function of white Valdosta's racialized sense of justice. It was a way of policing the riot by robbing it of its power.

Armed men began congregating in Valdosta between 9:00 and 10:00 at night upon hearing that Johnson had been discovered. They wanted, in the words of the *Butler Herald*, to "give to Johnson the same treatment four other negroes have received in Brooks county although talk of burning the ring leader at stake is heard most frequently, some declaring any other method of punishment entirely inadequate to meet the situation." The police, meanwhile, had "blocked all means of egress from Mud Swamp." The railroad crossings and roads were all placed under guard, with orders to "shoot if any order to halt is not obeyed." The police then snuck "quietly out of the city" to hunt for Johnson.[8]

Before entering the Bryant home, the police realized that they had forgotten their flashlights. There was only a small hand lamp from the Bryants to light their way. In the account published by Thomasville's press, Johnson, soaking wet from the swamp, opened fire as the police entered. He had a shotgun, according to reports, not a rifle, and some of the scattershot tore the younger Dampier's coat collar and burned his face. When Johnson shifted to his pistol after the shotgun, he shot the elder Dampier with that. It was "miraculous that none of the officers were killed as the negro had all the advantage and fired on them first." But the police quickly recovered and returned fire, overwhelming and ultimately killing the suspect. The noise of those shots drew the mob, which then fired "a volley of bullets" into Johnson's dead body. "Men who had for days and nights expected this, seemed to have dropped from the moonlit skies," reported the *Valdosta Times*. "They swarmed in from every direction and automobile after automobile discharged its cargo of human freight." Johnson's coat was later brought to the police station, ripped to shreds by bullets, "and the man's brains almost covered it." The mob tied the body to the back of a car, then drove off with it toward Barney, "the scene of the crime where it was stated by the crowd that the body would be cremated"—burned like the body in the infamous photograph from the Tulsa riot and like the bodies of so many before. After displaying the body in Barney, members of the white mob took Johnson's remains to a campground between Barney and Morven. They placed the corpse on a pine stump, surrounded it with branches and logs, and doused the whole thing in oil. Then "the fire was lighted and the remains of the criminal were cremated and nothing but ashes left of him." The police, meanwhile, claimed to regret having to kill Johnson, as their goal was to take him to the Brooks County jail. "The killing was not done in a mob fashion," Thomasville's newspaper assured its readers, ignoring the paragraphs that explained what happened after the killing. Anyway, "there is no intimation of trouble of any kind whatever, the negroes of the city having already shown that they were not in sympathy with the crime committed by Johnson and many of them have done everything they could to assist in his apprehension."[9]

The *Valdosta Times* echoed that sentiment, noting that Johnson fired the first shot and that "had he surrendered to the officers quietly he could easily have been removed from the house and turned over to the Brooks county officers." The paper made no mention, of course, of the reality that Brooks County officers had been powerless to keep the other lynching victims safe and that surrender meant almost certain death.[10]

Some reports claimed that Hamp's father, Dixon Smith, was shot by Johnson in the raid that ultimately killed him, but they were untrue. It was further self-justification feeding from the white media's victim inversion narrative. Smith "was not only uninjured," the *Quitman Free Press* reported, "but so far as known was not even at the scene when the Valdosta officers attempted to arrest Johnson." It was yet "another of the many sensational stories published about the Smith tragedy which have contributed no little to the apparent impression in the state that people in this section are running wild."[11]

The *Valdosta Times* openly called Johnson a "murderer and rapist." The paper seemed perfectly satisfied that "the dead body was literally riddled with bullets. It was in truth shot to pieces, not figuratively speaking." Johnson's coat contained pieces of the bread on which he had survived the previous days. It weighed more than ten pounds at the police station after the killing because it was waterlogged from Johnson's time in the swamp. Before his body was driven away, police claimed to have observed that Johnson was wearing three pairs of pants, one of them belonging to Hampton Smith.[12]

After the ordeal Dampier praised "the conduct of the colored people of Valdosta," claiming in paternalistic fashion that "at all times he has had the sincere and earnest co-operation of the leading colored people of the city." Calvin Dampier received mail from all over the South wishing him well after his wounding during the raid. The *Times* was also keen to report in its initial coverage of the story that "in no way was the crime for which Johnson paid with his life a matter of direct interest to Lowndes county." Johnson was from Valdosta and so had escaped back to the city, but "this was a series of killings that were under the direct purview of Brooks County."[13]

The *Chicago Defender* described Johnson's death as a "brutal lynching" by "a band of crazed white citizens." His crime, the paper argued, was prompted because "Smith had cowhided a relative" of Johnson, who was seeking to "protect himself from the wrath of Smith when the latter was killed." It was, the paper noted, Georgia's ninth lynching victim in that week. In the *Defender*'s account, Dampier was not acting to stop the mob; he was instead part of the mob itself. The paper placed Johnson in the swamp, not the house, when he was captured. When the mob pounced, Johnson shot to protect himself, "and the cowards scattered like bees emerging from a hive." Soon, however, he ran out of ammunition and was forced to surrender. "Johnson was betrayed by the promise that if he gave up he would not be lynched. Acting upon this advice he emerged from the swamps, soaked to the skin with mud and water, and was seized, his body tied to an automobile and dragged to the city, where it was viewed as a curiosity. Pieces of his bullet-ridden coat were distributed as souvenirs among the mob members."[14]

"Since the lynching of Johnson and Mrs. Mary Turner the city has been in a general uproar. Citizens have sought other sections, where peace and harmony prevail, and from all indications are determined not to return to the mob-ridden vicinity. All methods of redress to law have been suspended, and the mob has run amuck for several days, forcing respectable residents to leave their homes." The assumption among many was that their escape from Brooks and Lowndes Counties would be permanent. They would not return. That kind of ethnic cleansing was an inherent goal of race riots. As early as 1829, a three-day riot in Cincinnati left many Black residents of the city fleeing to Canada. In 1836 and again in 1841, white mobs attacked the *Philanthropist*, the city's abolitionist newspaper, then expanded to attack Black homes and businesses. During all three incidents in Cincinnati, Black residents defended themselves and their property with guns, allowing white assailants to blame them at least in part for the violence. The events were strategically situated to relieve the city of its free Black population. Later, in 1898 in Wilmington, North Carolina, things were tense between white and Black residents. Alfred Moore Wadell, a former Confederate and US congressman, vowed in a speech to "choke the Cape Fear [River] with carcasses." Alex Manly, the editor of the local Black newspaper, the *Daily Record*, responded by writing an editorial reminding white locals that white women often carried on consensual affairs with Black men and then claimed rape whenever the relationships became public. "Teach your men purity," he wrote. "Let virtue be something more than an excuse for them to intimidate and torture a helpless people." A white mob destroyed the newspaper office in response. At least a dozen Black men were murdered. Some fifteen hundred Wilmington residents fled. White people then bought up Black homes and property at bargain rates. Wadell became Wilmington's new mayor. Ethnic cleansing, then, was a core constituent of such uprisings. The *Defender*'s language describing the south Georgia mob running amuck was the language of riot.[15]

In early June the *Atlanta Independent*, Georgia's largest Black newspaper, made the same connection, with author Louis Lautier explaining that the lack of Black political participation "constitutes the Negro's fundamental grievance, to which may be traced to the East St. Louis atrocity, the Houston horror, the burning and torturing of human beings at the stake without the semblance of a trial, lynching, discrimination, segregation and the refusal of an equitable apportionment of public school funds."[16]

Meanwhile, on May 20, a coroner's jury investigating the lynchings ruled them "death at the hands of parties unknown," and any further inquiry seemed in doubt. "Whether there will be any effort made later to definitely establish blame for the four lynchings is a matter for speculation."[17] The same day, Gov. Hugh Dorsey contacted officials in Brooks and Lowndes Counties, asking their opinions about the efficacy of sending troops to quell the riot and offering a $250 reward for Johnson's capture. Georgia law required that in such circumstances, the counties themselves had to formally request troops before the governor could send them, and officials from both Brooks and Lowndes Counties declined. They had things well enough in hand.[18] Two days later, however, according to the *Atlanta Constitution*, "after the stage had been set for the barbaric drama—when the peace and security of the whole community seemed to be at stake—the very officials who had demurred to the governor's original suggestion called on him for help."[19]

Dorsey was a Georgia boy who returned to the state after University of Virginia Law School and married Adair Wilkinson, a Valdosta woman who gave him a vested interest in the south Georgia region. His rise to fame began while he was serving as solicitor general for the Atlanta Judicial Circuit. In 1913 Mary Phagan, a young worker at the Atlanta Pencil Factory, was murdered, and Leo Frank, her employer, was accused of the crime. In a trial tinged with anti-Semitic overtones, and with overtly anti-Semitic coverage in the press, Dorsey secured Frank's conviction. When the governor commuted Frank's sentence, an angry mob dragged Frank from his Milledgeville prison and lynched him. The Frank debacle helped fuel the creation of the new incarnation of the Ku Klux Klan in 1915; the organization's first act was to burn a cross at Mary Phagan's grave. But the case made Dorsey's name and convinced an anti-Semitic population that he would make a more reliable governor. He ran and won in 1916.[20]

Despite the source of his fame, Dorsey was, in the context of the white Democratic South, a progressive reformer, and he emphatically opposed mob violence. "The fury of the population," reported the *Atlanta Constitution*, "has become unrestrained, and ordinary means have become powerless to suppress it." Thus the governor was compelled to declare the area in a state of insurrection. "Posses are still scouring the country," the paper warned, "in the reign of terror." On Wednesday, May 22, Dorsey offered a five-hundred-dollar reward for each of the first five people who apprehended a member of the mob and turned them over to the sheriffs of Brooks or Lowndes Counties with evidence of their participation. It was a message both powerful in its symbolism that leadership in Georgia was serious about eradicating mob rule—the reward was twice what he offered for Johnson—and impotent in its lack of results, as members of the mob would not have been difficult for local law enforcement to find had it been inclined to do so.[21]

On May 23, the morning after Johnson was killed, the Chatham Home Guards arrived in Valdosta on an early train. The mob had quieted after Johnson's perceived comeuppance, and so the unit returned to Savannah that evening. They did not march through the city policing unrest. Instead they spent the day waiting on the train. "The Savannah Volunteer guard organization hopes that when the next battle comes it won't be in a place where they have to stay in day coaches throughout the hot day and then again in the night." Arthur McCollum, acting adjutant general of Georgia, also rushed to Valdosta, where he met with the guard's commanding officer, Maj. Bierne Gordon, the two deciding that the furor that precipitated their arrival had calmed enough to make their presence unnecessary. Another account lists Peter W. Meldrim as the commanding officer, which, though unsubstantiated, would be particularly noteworthy because of the role Meldrim would later play in events in Savannah. Regardless, it was the first time the Georgia State Guards had been called out since the group's founding. Dorsey deployed them after being told by Valdosta judge W. E. Thomas that the sheriffs of Brooks and Lowndes were unable to quiet the mob.[22]

Dorsey had sent the troops to quell the mob through martial law. Benjamin Davis's *Atlanta Independent* appreciated the effort. The governor's "prompt action in declaring that a state of insurrection existed in certain parts of Brooks and Lowndes counties, and the placing of the affected territory under military law," had been the payoffs of a gubernatorial campaign run on a platform of law and order. It stopped the mob violence in south Georgia, but it had even greater potential. Such use of military force "will wipe out lynching, suppress mob violence and guarantee to every citizen, be he black or white, the constitutional right to enjoy life, happiness and prosperity."[23]

"It would have been much less expensive to the state to have called out the recently organized Home Guard of Quitman to quell the disorder in Valdosta incident upon the killing of Sidney Johnson the negro murderer," the *Quitman Free Press* argued in sympathetic opposition to the arrival of troops from Savannah. "The guard here could have reached the scene of the disorder much quicker from this point and would have done just as much good."[24]

White Valdosta was equally "indignant at the presence of a military company," as the crime at Smith's farm and the retributive lynchings that followed were in neighboring Brooks County. The citizens of Valdosta claimed to be taking up a collection to reward the Dampiers with gold medals and to provide both John Henry Bryant and the Black family to whom Bertha Smith originally escaped a monetary reward. It was a gesture, they argued, that proved their own civility, particularly in relation to their Brooks County neighbors.[25] The victim-inversion narrative was firmly in place.

RIOTS, LYNCHINGS, AND THE MEDIA

The victim-inversion narrative was firmly in place among white residents, thanks largely to their press. Black press coverage demonstrated a decidedly different interpretive bent. The coverage of the Black press is significant for its valuable counternarrative and for its notice of the dramatic effect the attacks had on surviving Black residents, many of whom responded by deciding to leave. The country at the time of Johnson's killing was involved in World War I, a fight that President Woodrow Wilson claimed was to make the world "safe for democracy." Democracy, however, seemed far from reality for millions of Americans in the final years of the 1910s. Hundreds of thousands of Black southerners fled the South during the war, continuing the Great Migration into northern and western urban hubs. Meanwhile, Black soldiers returning from the war had been invigorated by the confidence that came from surviving battle, serving with distinction, and experiencing a functional equality overseas. After a war to make the world safe for democracy, the situation at home seemed immanently problematic.

The Great Migration had already begun in earnest at the time of the south Georgia violence, its first major wave coinciding with the onset of World War

I. Between 1890 and 1910, roughly two hundred thousand African Americans left the South for the North and West. There they generally worked outside of industry, as janitors, elevator operators, and domestic servants. Northern industrialists generally refused to hire Black workers, preferring immigrants from Eastern Europe who would work for similarly low wages, and would not risk their products being associated with Blackness. Black workers' only real opportunity for industrial work came during labor strikes, which only drove more racial conflict in northern urban industrial hubs. In 1904, for example, an Amalgamated Meatcutters Association strike led Chicago meatpacking concerns to hire Black scabs to take their place. The strikers pelted Black workers with stones, and after police intervention more than four thousand rioted on Chicago's South Side.[26]

World War I, however, not only pulled able white workers from the factory floor to the battlefield, but it also dramatically eroded European immigration, with the number of immigrants falling from 1,218,480 in 1914 to 110,618 in the year of the south Georgia riot. It was a drop of more than 90 percent and led northern employers to change their attitude about the potential for Black labor. Between 1910 and 1940, more than 1.75 million Black southerners traveled north, doubling the African American population outside of the region. In the decade of World War I alone, roughly 550,000 left, more than all previous decades since emancipation combined.[27]

That migration was an obvious threat to the peonage labor system that relied on the manipulation of Black labor for driving white agricultural profit. Even before the pull factor of wartime factory work, the largest threat to the system relied upon by Smith and others was a group of labor brokers that southern leaders, accustomed to fretting over "outside agitators," referred to as "emigrant agents," recruiters who brought labor from one area and moved it to regions of greater need, even if that labor was already under restrictive long-term contracts or peonage obligations. After Reconstruction, former Confederate states began passing emigrant agent laws to stop the outmigration of Black labor from the region, but those same states actually relied on labor brokers within the area to house and disseminate those in bondage to plantations and public works projects in need of laborers.[28]

Georgia, for example, required license fees for emigrant agents to try to curb the practice, and when one, R. A. Williams, refused to pay, the resulting litigation ended up before the Supreme Court in 1900. In *Williams v. Fears*, the court validated emigrant agent laws as constitutional against the protestations of Williams, who argued that they were an unfair tax that interfered with interstate commerce. "These labor contracts were not in themselves subjects of traffic between the States," argued Chief Justice Melville Fuller, "nor was the business of hiring laborers so immediately connected with interstate transportation or interstate traffic that it could be correctly said that those who followed it were engaged in interstate commerce, or that the tax on that occupation constituted a burden on such commerce."[29] At the same time, however, the court also quoted *Allgeyer v. Louisiana* (1897), which argued that liberty of employment "means not only the right of the citizen to be free from the mere physical restraint of his person, as by incarceration, but the term is deemed to embrace the right of the citizen to be free in the enjoyment of all his faculties; to be free to use them in all lawful ways; to live and work where he will; to earn his livelihood by any lawful calling; to pursue any livelihood or avocation, and for that purpose to enter into all contracts which may be proper, necessary and essential to his carrying out to a successful conclusion" the work he or she chose to do. That liberty, though, was directly connected to contract law, "and this right to contract in relation to persons or property or to do business within the jurisdiction of the State may be regulated and sometimes prohibited."[30] Emigrant agent laws in Georgia were valid, and so too, the court seemed to intimate, were vagrancy laws that punished workers for not having contracts. The *Williams* decision was a victory for Georgia's racialized labor scheme, and in the process served as a validation of similar systems and the project of white supremacy throughout the South.

Williams was a white man, and most of the emigrant agent laws and enticement acts were aimed at white men attempting to take advantage of freedmen who found themselves in a seemingly new system that supposedly monetized their labor. The vagrancy and work contract laws themselves, however, were designed as a check against such behavior by specifically targeting freedmen, criminalizing their desire to participate as equals in the open market. In Florida, just miles south of Brooks and Lowndes Counties, the state's first work contract law, passed in the era of Black Codes prior to the full force of Reconstruction, punished "willful disobedience of orders," "wanton impudence," or simple failure to complete assigned tasks as potential felonies, and while most of the Black Codes fell to federal imposition led by a Radical Republican Congress, Florida's work contract law lasted into the 1890s.[31]

The area's Black outmigration had been directly tied to its brutal peonage labor system since the nineteenth century; the need generated by northern labor shortages during the war only magnified an already established system that intertwined white fears of Black labor removal and white reliance on

Black labor control. By the time of the south Georgia riot, misdemeanor convict labor was also being used by Georgia counties to build roads. So while a budding cosmopolitanism and a desire for some measure of Sunbelt business growth certainly prompted some of the local frustrations with mob violence, motivation for such denunciations also stemmed from a desire to keep vulnerable Black labor in a region where it could be manipulated through the criminal justice system to either work for local planters and turpentine concerns or county public works projects.

While northern race riots like those in Chicago in 1904 or, more immediately, 1919 could be cautionary tales for Black southerners seeking a haven from racial violence, riots and lynchings like those in south Georgia were often a more immediate impetus for convincing reluctant southerners to make the trip. Racial violence was by no means the only factor driving Black outmigration from the South, but specific conflagrations of racialized terrorism did in certain locations drive locals to flee.[32] Of course, as more and more Black southerners moved north, the limited number of jobs available led to both labor and racial unrest, ultimately spilling over into a summer-long wave of race violence in 1919.

On May 10, for example, a group of white servicemen, angered by a supposed attack on a naval officer by a local Black man, stormed a Black neighborhood in Charleston, South Carolina, killing two and wounding many others. Meanwhile, the work of Booker T. Washington's National Negro Business League had given Black farmers in Longview, Texas, a leg up in negotiating lower farm prices. When one of those businessmen was found dead and mutilated, Black leaders demanded justice. After an article in the *Chicago Defender* publicized the lynching, a white mob beat the local agent for the newspaper. The agent and his doctor then defended themselves in July in a shootout with angry white men, which soon led to the burning of Black neighborhoods and other massive racial violence. These were followed by violence in Washington, DC, Chicago, and Omaha, Nebraska. Other incidents occurred in Baltimore, Houston, Little Rock, New Orleans, and New York City, along with dozens of lynchings and more isolated forms of mob-related racial violence. The violence of the Red Summer was, according to David Levering Lewis, an act of "collective barbarism," a massive conflagration that left a death toll that Grif Stockley has estimated to be as high as 856.[33]

But the *Defender*'s involvement in the Longview incident was telling. The Black press had always built itself on a foundation of protest against the prevailing racial mores of the day, even from its initial nineteenth-century founding. On March 16, 1827, John Russwurm's *Freedom's Journal* argued that "we wish to plead our own cause. Too long have others spoken for us. Too long has the public been deceived by misrepresentations." Russwurm, the first Black man to earn a bachelor's degree from Maine's Bowdoin College, founded the country's first Black newspaper with Samuel Cornish, and its mission of correcting white misrepresentations would be carried forward by hundreds of newspapers through slavery, Reconstruction, the Gilded Age, and into the twentieth century.[34] Ida B. Wells, for example, exemplified the continuance of this original mission. She originally reported for the *Memphis Living Way* in the 1880s, before becoming the editor and part owner of the *Memphis Free Speech* and serving as the Memphis correspondent for papers such as the *Detroit Plaindealer*, the *New York Age*, and *Our Women and Children*. She investigated lynchings and railed against them, actively arguing for anti-lynching legislation. In 1892 she exposed one lynching that elicited a violent response from white Memphis. The paper's offices were burned, and Wells moved north to New York.[35]

That reaction, like the white reaction against Manly's newspaper in Wilmington, North Carolina, demonstrated the threat that Black information networks posed to white supremacy and the racial assumptions that undergirded it. Black newspapers remained powerful vehicles of information when legitimate news was underreported by their white counterparts. Nell Irvin Painter argues that the two characteristics of the Black press that most clearly distinguished it from white papers were a racial orientation (as opposed to a "partisan orientation") and "a sense of a supranational racial identity."[36] Writing in 1951, Howard University professor Lewis Fenderson framed the role of the Black press as a "four-purposed social instrument." It informed the Black population about news that involved or affected Black people. It presented a Black position on issues to white society, "thus encouraging interracial understanding." It advocated for Black social acceptance. Finally, it provoked responses from the white press.[37]

Black newspapers also obviously provoked responses from the white citizenry, though those responses were largely the visible wounds of a long-festering disease. Peter Kellogg classifies many white people as having an "atrocity orientation," a phenomenon by which individuals or groups notice racism at the onset of atrocities, like race riots or lynchings, but are unable or unwilling to acknowledge the institutional causes of such violent acts, the subtle racism and discrimination that are foundational for those more overt behaviors.[38] Such was the case throughout the era of World War I. The race riots that dominated throughout the long, hot summer months in the wake of the 1919 Treaty of Versailles were caused by deep, systemic problems in an American society bent on celebrating its success and democracy to a fault. The Black press served as a check against this atrocity orientation.

In Brooks and Lowndes Counties in 1918, of course, the atrocities themselves took precedence, but the atrocity orientation was still there. There were no race riots in defense of the tens of thousands of debt peons forced to work in bondage since the 1880s, and that work was sometimes deadly and almost always brutal. "The skin was beat from my body and the flesh made raw," explained Fanny Jackson of her time at Lowndes County's Kinderlou, just miles from Hamp Smith's operation. "I was beat first on Sunday and then made to sit in salty water, I suppose to cure the wounds." It was the same thing the next day. "I was then put to work, and Mr. George McRee went into the field and made them let me go to the house. I was sick from the beating nearly four months, too sick to work, and a great deal of the time could not rest at all except on my stomach. Mr. Will has my child yet," said Jackson. "He took it from me by force. I have never been paid any wages."[39] In another account from the same farm, Lula Frazier reported, "They made me lie down across a bunk and when Mr. Will whipped me he made Ida Wilson hold my hands and Jim Henry hold my feet. He turned my clothes up and whipped me with a leather strap. Ida and Henry Brown held me when Mr. Ed McRee whipped me."[40] Gov. Joseph Merriwell Terrell had condemned the practice in 1902. "There is no express provision of law anywhere authorizing the hiring of such convicts to private individuals, nor for working them anywhere except on public works. But because comparatively few counties organized chain-gangs to work on public works, it was often found difficult for the county authorities of counties having no chain-gang to dispose of their misdemeanor convicts." In some of the camps, he argued, "convicts have been overworked, poorly fed and inadequately clothed, and that the punishment inflicted on them has sometimes been cruel, and in one instance that has come to my knowledge even brutal." He received many complaints about convicts, "and nearly all of them come from this class of chain-gangs," he said.[41]

Terrell's denunciations went unheeded, however, and the normalization of atrocity continued relatively unabated, ultimately leading Johnson, Head, the Turners, and others to the farm of Hampton Smith, farmhands to white locals but prisoners to those working the farm itself. The violence at Kinderlou, for example, was of so little concern to white locals that Edward McRee, one of the camp's owners, served in the state legislature. His last year serving in that body was 1906, the same year as the Atlanta race riot.[42] White locals in Atlanta, responding to an influx of rural Black migrants seeking work in the new industrial hub and a growing Black elite in the city willing to use its newly acquired political power, rampaged through the Georgia capital, killing dozens, wounding hundreds more, and destroying Black-owned property throughout the city.[43] It was a justly noticed, acknowledged atrocity, but the horror evinced over the Atlanta race riot was not matched by an acknowledgment of the everyday atrocities associated more broadly with white supremacy in the state that created farms like that of Hamp Smith.

There were other race riots in the years surrounding 1906. In Springfield, Illinois, in 1908, a white mob destroyed Black businesses and killed at least nine people after a murder and an alleged attempted rape, circumstances similar to those in Brooks County a decade later.[44] But a consistent litany of race riots come during the era of World War I, beginning with East St. Louis, Illinois, in 1917, Brooks and Lowndes Counties in 1918, the Red Summer in 1919, and Tulsa in 1921.

Lynchings, too, remained ominously present. In 1919 eighty-three people were lynched. Editorials throughout the South decried the practice, accompanying broader calls for cessation in the national media. While national lynching totals would never reach such numbers again, a significant drop in the annual number did not happen until 1923. The murders continued, as did the crusade against them. The NAACP in 1919 defined lynching as a mob of three or more persons, representing the intentions of an entire community. By the end of the decade, the group no longer specified community support as a necessary element of lynching. The change in definition, notes Christopher Waldrep, was not the result of an improvement in white behavior. It had to do with the politics of the continually changing definition of lynching. Waldrep describes the first four decades of the twentieth century as an arena in which various institutions fought to present their own definitions of the word to serve their own various political ends.[45]

The broader region of south Georgia and north Florida was an inordinately racially violent place. None of the counties of the region matched the death count of Brooks County, but all had blood on their hands, as demonstrated by the counts of both the Equal Justice Initiative and the Center for Studies in Demography and Ecology lynching databases.

Both groups' figures are more up to date than those of the early NAACP and Tuskegee Institute, but they are obviously incomplete and inconsistent. The Equal Justice Initiative's county counts not only incorporate more years but also record only totals and not individual information about victims. The Center for Studies in Demography and Ecology's database is far more thorough in its detail, but it too is incomplete. As this account and others make clear, if the victims of the race riot are considered to have been lynched, there were many more than two lynchings in Brooks County in 1918. The database includes three of the victims of the riot, so it is to be assumed that the others would be included as well. Mary Turner is part of the center's list, for example, but is listed as having been lynched in Lowndes County. Turner never made it to Lowndes County. She, like the other victims, was murdered in Brooks County, on the other side of the Withlacoochee River from Lowndes.

That said, the counts are instructive about racialized mob violence in the region. The danger for Black victims metastasized in the 1890s and the 1910s in south Georgia and north Florida, but it was always present. The nineteen counties of the region suffered, even in the dramatically conservative count of the Center for Studies in Demography and Ecology's database, sixty-eight mob killings in forty-three years (the database does not include 1896–99). Those victims were predominantly working-class agricultural workers, many of them drifting in and out of debt peonage or misdemeanor convict labor. Amy Kate Bailey and Stewart E. Tolnay have demonstrated that class played a decided role in creating vulnerabilities to racialized mob violence, as married property owners were less likely to be victims of such assaults.[46] An economic system built on bound Black labor in rural regions ensured that the bulk of the population would remain at least somewhat transient and therefore susceptible to economic, legal, and extralegal forces.

It is true that lynchings and race riots were not everyday occurrences, but they were so normalized that groups of angry white racists felt comfortable enough to take such actions more than once a year on average within the cloistered rural region. Vulnerable Black residents could reasonably expect that even though mob violence did not happen all the time, it was always a possibility hovering over every action, serving as a dangerous exclamation point to the sentence that was the everyday consequence of white supremacy. That white supremacy created a cloistered world wherein collective trauma and the bonds bred by rurality meant that violent acts against individuals were felt by Black communities bound by both kin and susceptibility to similar threats. When those violent acts were against multiple victims, as in the 1918 race riot, the trauma and its community spread were only exacerbated.

North Louisiana provides a productive comparative example to south Georgia, a region heavy with cotton and longleaf pines, with an expansive

Table 2. South Georgia Lynchings

County	*No. of lynchings*		*Center for Studies in Demography and Ecology: Years counted (with no. of lynchings that year)*
	Equal Justice Initiative (1877–1950)	*Center for Studies in Demography and Ecology (1882–1929)*	
		Georgia	
Brooks	20	10	1894 (4), 1901, 1913, 1917, 1918 (2), 1921
Lowndes	4	6	1890, 1894, 1915, 1916, 1918 (2)
Echols	4	0	—
Clinch	2	2	1890, 1895
Cook	1	0	—
Colquitt	7	4	1895, 1909, 1921, 1922
Thomas	8	3	1890, 1891, 1902
Grady	2	0	—
Mitchell	11	8	1894, 1906, 1911, 1917 (3), 1920, 1921
Ware	5	5	1891 (2), 1895, 1908 (2)
Coffee	8	4	1920 (3), 1926

Black labor force vulnerable to white capture, peonage, and overt forms of spectacular violence. The *New Orleans Item* chided Ouachita Parish as the "lynch law center of Louisiana." From the turn of the century to the close of 1918, thirty of the region's Black citizens were lynched. Between 1889 and 1922, Ouachita Parish witnessed more lynchings than any other county in the nation. It was, per capita, the most racially violent place in America.[47] As in south Georgia, labor conflicts between Black and white workers often precipitated mob violence, but those disputes usually came between tenant farmers and landowners or between employers and domestic servants. As Michael Pfeifer notes, more than half of the lynching victims in the northeast parishes of the

Table 2 continued

County	*No. of lynchings*		*Center for Studies in Demography and Ecology: Years counted (with no. of lynchings that year)*
	Equal Justice Initiative (1877–1950)	*Center for Studies in Demography and Ecology (1882–1929)*	
Tift	4	1	1908
Berrien	0	1	1893
Lee	9	6	1916 (5), 1919
Crisp	6	4	1912 (2), 1918, 1924
		Florida	
Madison	14	10	1882 (2), 1884, 1886, 1901 (2), 1903, 1906, 1919, 1921
Hamilton	6	3	1903, 1924, 1929
Jefferson	1	0	—
Leon	4	1	1909

NOTE: — = no lynchings reported by the Center for Studies in Demography and Ecology. In the first column, the counties are ordered in relation to Brooks and Lowndes, the closest in proximity to that center listed first, then moving outward from there.

SOURCE: "Racial Terror Lynchings," Lynching in America, Equal Justice Initiative, https://lynchinginamerica.eji.org (accessed December 14, 2021); Bailey and Tolnay, *Lynched.*

Mississippi Delta region died following allegations of the murder of white planters or merchants.[48] In northeast Louisiana, however, retributive lynchings tended to stop with those accused of crimes; white mobs and powerbrokers used the spectacle of the events to impose fear and order on the population they sought to control rather than, say, rampaging through the county killing multiple victims because of an assumed proximity to the original violent act.

That said, there were exceptions. In Madison Parish in April 1894, a Black laborer named Josh Hopkins argued with his white supervisor and was accused of assaulting him. A white mob assembled ostensibly to arrest him. But a rival group of Black men repulsed the white vigilantes, firing into the crowd and killing a local plantation manager. That act led an even larger white mob to descend on the parish seat of Tallulah, where the members attacked the local jail and killed three Black inmates accused of leading a local "protective association." The mob then moved through the area looking for participants of the original Black group protecting Hopkins, ultimately finding and killing four more men.[49] While the Madison Parish violence could easily be classified as a race riot, it differed from the later violence in south Georgia because the rampage that ensued was not directly the result of the attack on a white employer. It was the clash of mobs that ultimately led to the broader rampage.

In northeast Louisiana, too, there was a semiurban hub, Monroe, surrounded by a rural area largely uninterested in the nascent cosmopolitanism brought by urbanization in the larger city. In south Georgia, Valdosta was that hub, while the rest of Brooks and Lowndes Counties were mired in a Redeemer mindset that sought to control every aspect of Black life as a check against potential modernization and change, a modernization that seemed to rural whites to be imposed by government overreach—which they responded to most immediately by the cattle-dipping bombings that occurred on the eve of the racial violence.

To highlight its 1919 push for legislation, the NAACP held a national conference on lynching at Carnegie Hall in New York. In conjunction with the event, John R. Shillady, the association's national secretary, sent telegrams to southern governors urging them to "demand legal authorities proceed energetically to apprehend lynchers and bring them to trial." Among the proceedings was the signing of a petition calling for federal legislation. Signatories included former senator and presidential nominee Charles Evans Hughes, former secretary of state Elihu Root, Attorney General A. Mitchell Palmer, and former Alabama governor Emmet O'Neal. Governor O'Neal's speech to the conference was one of the event's highlights. His stance was unusual, even among southern white opponents of lynching, most of whom still argued against federal legislation. O'Neal called lynching "a relic of savagery and barbarism unworthy of a self-governing people." Following the conference, the NAACP distributed O'Neal's "Address to the Nation on Lynching," stressing the need for a congressional investigation of the practice.[50]

Activists like Ida Wells believed fully that graphic pictures and descriptions of lynching were necessary tools to fight against the practice. Such depictions served, explains Ursula McTaggart of Wells's strategy, "as evidence of atrocity and admission of White guilt. She forced readers to grasp the reality of lynching violence while highlighting the pleasure that White participants and supporters gained from these atrocities. She put both dead bodies and the violent pleasure of the White mob on display." Descriptions of lynchings in the Black press and from advocacy groups like the NAACP served much the same function. Parading the grotesque was a strategy, a necessary method to wake the consciousness of those unfamiliar with the practice or doubtful of its reality.[51]

But the messages of the NAACP's anti-lynching campaign were fundamentally different from the messages of the broader anti-lynching movement in the South. In 1920, for example, a group of racially moderate southerners created the Commission on Interracial Cooperation (CIC), which assumed the mantle of southern interracial reform for the next two decades. The group attempted to secure better housing and education for the growing Black middle class. The CIC also sought to end mob violence, but it specifically argued against a federal lynch law. Segregation was the southern way of life, as was racial inequality. Any federal legislation directed toward southern race relationships would set a dangerous precedent.[52]

Robert Russa Moton, Booker T. Washington's successor at Tuskegee Institute and a leading anti-lynching advocate, viewed lynching as a distinctly southern problem (and the national figures bear him out). Moton described lynching as "evil," as did the national publications *Review of Reviews*, the *New Republic*, and *World's Work*. *Current Opinion* called lynching a "national disgrace." These national publications, like the speakers at the NAACP's national conference on lynching, opposed the practice on moral grounds. They took their readers' opposition for granted.[53] Herbert J. Seligmann described lynchings as a symptom of a perverted desire to protect southern womanhood. "For the benefit of those unfamiliar with the increasingly popular sport of 'protecting Southern womanhood' it should be noted that the objects of this sport are usually United States citizens of dark skin—Negroes." Acts of racial violence were in their brutality misapplications of southern notions of chivalry.[54]

The horrors of lynching were isolated, however. When events involved not white mobs of three or more expressing the will of the white community through the murder of an individual but rather the whole white community committing mass murder across a broader swath of territory, the horror became something different. Designating racial murder as a race riot acknowledges not only all of the victims of a given atrocity but also a city-wide or region-wide white complicity in the series of violent acts. The use of different designations by both the media and advocacy organizations like the NAACP, to say nothing of the NAACP's own evolving definition of lynching, demonstrated the importance of such labels in both representation and law.

Ann V. Collins diagrammed the basic anatomy of a race riot prior to the conclusion of World War II. First there were structural factors, such as Jim Crow laws, debt peonage standards, and the demography of a given region. Then came "cultural framing," largely facilitated by the segregated media, which validated and reinforced white supremacy, maintained the trope of virtuous and vulnerable white womanhood, and propped up a whites-only model of power and authority that eschewed any kind of complicity or consequence for violent white behavior. Finally, there was a precipitating event that lit a fuse based on those structural factors and cultural framing.[55] The riot in Brooks and Lowndes Counties had all those elements, building a particular form of white atavistic attack during a wartime era rife with such atavism and such attacks.

Such is not to say that identifying a given event as a lynching absolves broader white complicity. Sherrilyn A. Ifill has demonstrated that the conspiracy of silence following many lynchings implicated everyone present, everyone who knew about the attack and remained silent about it, and everyone who benefited from the attack and the white supremacy that motivated it. There was active and passive post-lynching complicity. That was less the case in south Georgia, as the horror of events was wider in scope than a lynching and white locals and media outlets were unburdened by an assumed need for silence, but the larger spread of complicity, both active and passive, emanating from the white supremacy that dominated the region was certainly there.[56]

That horror of events in Brooks and Lowndes Counties imposed the will of the white community in a bloodthirsty series of murders across a broad swath of territory. It developed from larger regional frustrations as well as the more immediate peonage revolt at Hampton Smith's farm. Local coverage of the events, however, varied and came into conflict with coverage in the Black press and in the white state press, leaving a legacy that occupied a liminal space between definitions of lynching and of riot. It was a confusion bred by multiple clarifications, one that would only exacerbate the mythmaking surrounding the atrocity of white violence.

CHAPTER THREE

Memory and Mythmaking

Despite the problems inherent in having one of nearby Valdosta's anchor banks collapse, Brooks County actually did well in 1918. Its taxable values had increased $840,377 over the previous year, the largest such increase in the county's history. "The people of South Georgia are in a prosperous condition," the *Butler Herald* reported, referring only to the region's white residents, "with handsome dwellings, good out houses, with school, church, and public buildings far superior to this, or perhaps any other section of the state. Brooks county impressed me as being the banner county of South Georgia. The people are clever, thrifty, energetic and praiseworthy."[1] It was that generic if uninformed opinion that made the race riot so newsworthy and curious to newspaper editors throughout the state and region.

THE REGIONAL RESPONSE

The most prominent Black newspaper in Georgia was Benjamin Davis's *Atlanta Independent.* Its original account of the riot was interesting for what it included as well as what it did not. "The Independent is a law-abiding journal, published by a law-abiding people in the interest of the peace and harmony of the commonwealth," Davis explained, "and does not in any way approve of crime in Negroes any more than it does in white folk. But The Independent submits that the white man is the greater shielder of crime in that it is absolutely impossible to apprehend and convict a single mob participant. The law is ample enough to apprehend and punish every criminal, but its execution and enforcement is poor indeed." As an example, Davis described "the burning of a Negro in Johnson City, Tenn.," and the white mob's "compelling every Negro in town to march by the carcass as it broiled upon the coals" as a demonstration of "barbarity more revolting than anything in the memory of man." He referred to the murder of Tom Devert, a Black man who grabbed a fifteen-year-old white girl and absconded with her into a lake before locals shot and killed him. It was not enough for them, however. They pulled Devert's body out of the water and burned it.[2]

Davis then turned his attention to the south Georgia mob.

> The outrages committed in two south Georgia counties last week by bloodthirsty mobs are a disgrace not only to our state, but to the white man's civilization. The taking from her home and riddling a helpless woman with buckshot by fifty or more brave (?) and heroic (?) white men, is a piece of cowardice unheard of and unprecedented in the history of our great state. The woman was lynched because she spoke disapprovingly of the lynching of her husband. It matters not of what crime her husband was guilty, she could not reasonably have been expected to give her approval of the conduct of a mob which did not allow her husband a chance for his soul. We make no apology for any crimes the Negroes may have committed; we do not argue their innocence or their guilt, for it will never be known. But, in any event, they were entitled to a trial by a jury. They were entitled to a chance to establish their innocence before a jury of their peers, or the state to have established their guilt.[3]

Davis reminded his readers that Georgia was experiencing a labor shortage. "And black labor must necessarily in self-defense flee from such communities in our state, where life is unsafe, where property is menaced and where Negro women are taken from their homes, strung to the limbs of trees, and shot to death by white bullies." The *Independent* framed its argument patriotically, as driving Black people from Georgia meant that "our fields will lie in waste" and "our soldiers will suffer for food and thus injure the national cause. Every mob is a German agency, and a traitor to American valor and patriotism."[4] Davis's themes were familiar, turning patriotism against those who claimed to be patriots. So too was his emphasis on only one of the deaths and the familiar absence of any mention of Turner's being pregnant, which would only have aided Davis's editorial effort.

A broader nationalism also played a role in the riots of the era. Woodrow Wilson had won reelection by campaigning on his effort to keep the country out of the Great War, but before his second inauguration, the Zimmerman Telegram had infuriated the country with its revelations about German war strategy, and just days after Wilson was sworn in, the Russian monarchy fell in a February revolution that created a provisional government led by Alexander

Kerensky. Less than a month after his inauguration, Wilson made the case to Congress that participation in the war was necessary to make the world safe for democracy.[5]

Those ends were achieved, however, by decidedly undemocratic means. The racial violence of the war era occurred against the backdrop of a segregated military but also in concert with a broader reaction against Germans and German Americans. Libraries removed German books from their shelves. Boston banned performances of Beethoven's works. Columbia University fired two professors for speaking out against US entry into the war. The Immigration Restriction Act of 1917 declared that all adult immigrants who failed a reading test would be denied admission to the country. After the Kerensky government in Russia fell to the Bolsheviks and Lenin pulled his country out of the war, there was also a growing antipathy to communists and a fear that they would try a similar revolution in the United States. The "Red Scare," as it came to be known, created a broad paranoia that culminated in the New Year's Day raids of Attorney General A. Mitchell Palmer, which arrested more than four thousand people, many of them immigrants, on the flimsiest of charges.[6]

In a region like south Georgia, where angry farmers were dynamiting cattle-dipping vats because they had their own suspicions about government overreach, the kinds of intrusion by federal authorities demonstrated by the Palmer Raids were far from motivating factors for their own discriminatory violence. But the broader virulent nationalism that such raids represented helped create a climate of retrenchment throughout the country, bred by fear of losing something fundamental to the American experience. In Boston that fear was German influence. Elsewhere it was communist takeover. In south Georgia it was outsider interference and retribution by a Black population that had been abused and exploited for centuries.

Davis found an unlikely ally in the white *Augusta Chronicle*. "We are still 'lynching niggers' in Georgia—four in Lowndes county and one in Crisp county within the past week," wrote the paper's editor, Thomas Loyless; "but, in the meantime, many negroes are doing their full duty, both on the battlefront and at home." The editorial cited several different accounts of Black domestic and foreign service. Loyless described the rampant outmigration of Black residents to the North to escape such terrors and argued that even putting aside the "humanitarian view" of the situation, the labor shortage was real and problematic for the state. "We wouldn't like it very much if mobs in various counties were engaged in killing the farmers' mules, or running them off. We would soon rise and put down such mobs," the paper reasoned. "Do we value our mules more than we do our negroes? Even under slavery, the latter were held at from five to ten times the price of a mule. And they are much more valuable now."[7]

Brent Campney argues that in post–World War II Georgia, there was a definite tension between more moderate urban white Democrats and rural whites who felt threatened by civil rights gains in the state and preferred the maintenance of violent white supremacy over and against the Sunbelt business imperatives of urban moderates. That effort, however, was a reification of the 1910s and '20s, when "the state's largely urban, white middle class successfully campaigned against lynching, making that tradition a rarity by the Great Depression."[8] Papers like the *Augusta Chronicle* were a part of that effort. By no means an actively anti-racist newspaper, the *Chronicle*, like the *Atlanta Constitution*, was concerned about potential investment and venture capital and the effect such public scandals would have on the potential economic growth of the state.

Another Augusta screed against lynching came in the form of a letter to Governor Dorsey from the Colored Welfare League of Augusta. While the group "deeply deplore[d] the disregard of the courts and the law in all lynchings," it paid particular attention to the killing of Mary Turner, describing themselves as "especially aggrieved in this beastly act against all womanhood, the negro woman in particular." Turner's story was the only one described in the league's petition to the governor, the focal point of the campaign, which correctly placed a spotlight on the brutality of lynching, but in narrowing its focus to one particular lynching, the letter diminished the broad scope of the racial violence in south Georgia.[9]

Either way, Dorsey was uninterested. "Unfortunately," he condescended, "your resolutions and similar protests heretofore emanating from your representative organizations of your race, dealing with kindred subjects, are silent concerning this supreme outrage upon law and civilization, which too often provokes communities to substitute summary vengeance for the form of organized justice recognized by law." He instead chided them for a Black "lawless element" that threatened "helpless women and children," provoking a response. Self-policing that Black lawlessness was "the only practical method" that a group like the Colored Welfare League could use to help "to discourage lynchings and maintain supremacy of our courts."[10]

The *Augusta Chronicle* "is ashamed of Governor Dorsey's 'characteristic reply,' considering the circumstances under which it was made. We didn't expect it, even of a governor who was elected by the 'lynching vote.'" Dorsey's statement, however, was uncharacteristic. His insistence on local control usually trumped his denunciations of mob violence, but the denunciations did exist. In this case his sense of white supremacy and frustration at being lectured by Black women canceled out some of his more helpful criticisms of the thoughtless mob. The *Chronicle* took the lead in calling out the statement "as both a 'lecture' to negroes and an 'excuse' for the mob." The paper acknowledged that Dorsey's advice to limit Black crime would be beneficial, "but its proper place, it seems to us, was not in reply to a respectful appeal from a body of law-abiding negroes to the governor of their state for the exercise of the powers of the state against lynchers."[11] Referring to the Leo Frank case that made Dorsey famous, the *Chronicle* noted that the governor was "swept into the Governor's chair by the lynching sentiment of the state."[12] That was true, and the Northen statute from 1893 gave Dorsey at least some power to act, but the paper's anger at the governor mischaracterized his record and obscured that the real shock of his statement was its inconsistency with other statements on mob violence.

The *Chronicle* was also ashamed of Valdosta. "We recall that Lowndes with its neighboring county of Brooks has been the hotbed of anti-dip-va[t] sentiment; that many of its citizens deliberately dynamited government operated plants for eradicating the cattle tick in that county," the *Chronicle* remembered, "and when we see at this very time that in the published list of deserters under the draft law Lowndes County easily leads all the rest, any forty other counties, in fact with 211 deserters—we are compelled to confess that we fear for the power and influence of its better element and, really, look for little or nothing to be done toward apprehending and punishing the cowardly murderers of Mary Turner." Lowndes County, in the *Chronicle*'s view, was "one of the most prosperous and progressive in the State, with as cultured and noble people in it as are to be found anywhere on earth."[13] But those of culture and nobility had been shouted down by a lawless mob that led its citizens to hang and shoot a woman.

White southern newspapers often played on respectability politics to justify the behavior of lynch mobs. It was a common tactic of those newspapers to tout the respectability of the citizens engaged in the lynching as a form of legitimizing the event, drawing a contrast between the good guys doing the punishing and the bad guys being punished. But the language of respectability, of warranted or unwarranted lynchings, was rarely coded to signal class differences, making the *Chronicle*'s account fundamentally unique. As Susan Jean has argued, white southern defenses of lynching could not afford to pawn off bad behavior on lower-class white people, because such would signal that the practice itself was somehow problematic and lower class. It would be an admission that lynching itself was a problem rather than certain lynchings that fell beyond the bounds of what propriety and respectability politics had deemed appropriate.[14]

To the end of respectability politics, the *Chronicle* also took the *Valdosta Times* to task for lamenting the Hampton Smith murder without openly condemning the mob violence that followed. The editor of the *Times*, C. C. Brantley, who played a prominent role in a later dispute involving the violence, responded to his Augusta counterparts, arguing that it was easy for them to criticize when the heinous crime against Smith happened so far away from the South Carolina border. It was easy for them to forget the events that caused the mobs to form: "Absence from the scene and ignorance of the details makes a very great difference." Brantley seemed to want to have it both ways in his response to the *Chronicle*. "As we have intimated before, we are not sorry that determined men were plentiful enough in Brooks county to swing up the perpetrators of the fiendish crime against Hamp Smith and his family," he wrote, referring to those like the *Chronicle*'s editor, Tom Loyless, who castigated the violent mob as "sob-blubberers." But just paragraphs later, he argued that the *Times* "does not like to appear as condoning mob violence, because we do not. We are aware that mobs make mistakes and that it would be better for the lawful methods to handle all forms of crime." Still, "we are not going to throw any stones at the friends of Hamp Smith for the spirit of revenge which rankled in their bosoms against the human hyenas who shot him to death in the dark and then made a savage assault upon his wife."[15]

In response to Brantley's attack on the *Chronicle*'s position, and his blaming the paper for Dorsey's decision to send troops to Valdosta, Loyless repeated the basic argument that he had been making all along: "Lynching is a crime against the state and against society, whether the individual victim of it be innocent or guilty." He questioned Brantley's motives as "studiously offensive or obviously stupid." The paper refuted the *Valdosta Times* point by point. The *Chronicle* had not excused the attack on the Smiths, it had not made excuses for Black crime, and it had not personally attacked Dorsey. The paper's fight was not with the governor nor with Lowndes County. It was "a fight on mob violence in Georgia and elsewhere."[16]

The *Atlanta Independent* again agreed. "You do not know whether a single one of the six Negroes lynched in Brooks county . . . was guilty or not," the paper scolded Dorsey, ripping apart his evasion of the lynching question by putting the onus on the Black community. "The presumption of innocence always goes with the accused until the State proves to a moral certainty the contrary." The paper could be just as condescending as the governor. "You forgot to condemn lynching in your zeal to place the burden upon a race of people, the majority of whom are law-abiding, industrious and respectable." What was more, Dorsey was fundamentally wrong. "In each case in Lowndes county, a Negro put the officers of the law next to the culprits shot and burned," the paper explained. "Who is shielding the two hundred white cowards and assassins who shot Mary Turner to death in Brooks County? Are Negroes protecting them from the strong arm of the law, or is it white men?" The writers of the *Independent* usually supported Dorsey, "but we can but hang our heads in shame when we observe your apparent surrender to mob law in your reply to the Welfare League."[17]

The *Savannah Press* was indignant that the violence "when the wife of the murdered Hayes Turner was hanged to a tree and lynched because she made 'unwise remarks' must assuredly have brought a chill of horror and a suffering sense of shame to every decent and self-respecting citizen of this state." Turner's murder "topped the record of shameless atrocities" in Georgia's history. "Poor Mary Turner was a victim to the lust for blood which the lawless killing of her husband had awakened." The *Press* quoted Maj. Joseph B. Cumming, a former Civil War officer from the Fifth Georgia Regiment who settled in Augusta after the war and wrote a frustrated lament to the *Augusta Chronicle* painting a picture of a devastated Mary Turner. She did not have at her disposal "the high-sounding phrases of the fine old pagan philosophers," so she made instead an "'unwise remark.' Away with her to the nearest limb! Break her neck and then manifest the calm, righteous and judicial judgment of her executioners by riddling her body with bullets. Were these human beings or fiends hot from hell?"[18]

"Mob law is no better than anarchy," said one editorial in the *Cordele Dispatch*. "What will the outside world have to say? Do we care? Yes, indeed. Those who meted out justice to the fiends they caught might for a day say they did not care, but they do." In another piece the paper lamented the crimes committed by those fiends but maintained that "lynching lowers our respect for the dignity of the law and the maintenance of peace and good order." You could, the paper implicitly argued, believe in racial superiority and oppose lynching. "We cannot afford to lynch our beasts, brutes and culprits, because it would make it possible for us to find too many of these."[19]

The *Tifton Gazette* also denounced the lynchings, making the case that a belief in racial superiority actually required an opposition to lynching. "A race claiming mental superiority must learn to govern itself before it can with justice assert its right to govern others," the paper admonished. "No one is better for the lynchings while two of the state's most representative counties and the white race as a whole is incalculably injured." While the paper clearly believed in white supremacy, it differentiated that from "race prejudice," upon which, it argued, lynching was built. It was race prejudice, for example, that led the mob to forget that a Black family gave Bertha Smith succor after her ordeal, or that a Black man finally located Sidney Johnson. "Mobs do not catch criminals," the paper concluded. "They only handicap officers of the law in their efforts to catch them."[20]

The *Atlanta Constitution* was similarly appalled. "Now that the mob law debauch in two south Georgia counties seems to have come to an end, through the intervention of the governor, it leaves the state disgraced and humiliated before the world," the paper described. "What is Georgia going to do to put an end to this constantly recurring disgrace of mob violence?"[21] The paper denounced the lynchings, arguing that it was theoretically possible that those killed were guilty of complicity in Hampton Smith's murder, "but none was accorded his constitutional right to a chance to establish his innocence by lawful dispassionate trial." Despite the masculine pronouns, the paper singled out Mary Turner's lynching, as had the others, as particularly egregious because of her sex. Such behavior was "humiliating to decency and a harmful disgrace to the state."[22]

Still, the *Constitution* supported Dorsey's statement to the Colored League of Augusta, reversing its earlier disgust with the violence and arguing that Black citizens wanting to avoid the lynch rope needed only to follow the law. It was that sentiment that made Mary Turner's lynching so problematic for the paper. "Even the broad latitude of the jury in Judge Lynch's court would have found excuse, if not justification, for the lamentations of a widow, white or black, suddenly bereaved of her husband, however unworthy he might have been, and, with time for consideration, would have tempered crude justice with moderation, adjusting the punishment in accordance with the offense."[23]

The *Constitution*'s indignation existed outside of its position on lynching in general, making any further excess in its enactment all the more beneficial to the paper's case that traditional lynching for a crime was somehow legitimate. Not only does such a formulation push against later claims about Turner being pregnant, but it also clearly shifts, even in the white press, the narrative away from the race mob in the region, justifying its behavior with a wave of the hand, to an almost exclusive emphasis on the attack on Turner, as not only as the most horrific attack but also the only unjustifiable one. In so doing it brought together all the threads of the problematic coverage and historical interpretation that have dominated the south Georgia riot narrative, namely, emphasizing the gruesome nature of the Turner lynching to the detriment of the broader culture of terror in the region and its context in the national white backlash.[24] Like its local counterparts, the *Constitution*'s coverage was also an attempt to marshal white supremacy and the patriarchal benevolence that supposedly supported it as an argument against such barbarism. In structuring their cases to prop up white superiority as the principal arbiter of legal justice, white newspapers in the state were able to denounce both murderers and murdered, to protect their own reputations against support for riots while ensuring white readers that they would never abandon the racial line upon which that legal justice was premised.

Descriptions in white southern newspapers, Susan Jean explains, "may obscure from us the full truth about lynching as it was manifested in the South, but they reveal volumes about lynching as it was manifested in the white southern imagination."[25] The *Camilla Enterprise*, itself the paper of record for a town that was the scene of an infamous Reconstruction-era race riot, appreciatively printed Dorsey's statement in full, titling it "Negroes Must Not Overlook Crime." The newspapers of nearby Waycross and Cairo also endorsed the governor's statement and, by extension, the lynchings themselves.[26] So too did the *Macon Telegraph*, which trotted out the typical call to protect white womanhood and the damage done to the Black population by agitators.[27]

It was a failed effort. In describing the Turner saga in 1920, British journalist Stephen Graham typified the emphasis on Turner by arguing that lynchings were almost universally explained away as a defense of white womanhood against Black male sexual aggression.[28] Turner's story was important to Graham and others because it gave lie to that flimsy excuse. The other victims were male. The story of the attack on the Smiths included that traditional justification, claiming that Smith's pregnant wife was raped after her husband had been shot and killed. Those claims seem unlikely given the common false justifications used for lynching, but they were consistent with the general justificatory theme of white defenses for mob violence. Turner's story took precedence partially because of the violence practiced upon her, but also because she was a woman and because she was not present for the alleged attack on

Bertha Smith. Hers was the one case that could not be tied even tangentially to a defense of white southern womanhood. She was the exception that proved the rule.

Meanwhile, the *Valdosta Times* was also keenly attuned to the vitriol leveled at the city for the riot—or in some Georgia press statements to the scapegoating of the city as not representative of the state's racial behavior more broadly—and pushed back against the narrative. "While the reports of the affair and the attendant lynchings have been sent out from Valdosta, because this city happened to be the news-distributing center for this section, there have not been the slightest symptoms of lawlessness upon the part of the people here." In the *Times*'s telling, even when Johnson escaped into hiding in Lowndes County, "he was followed by posses composed mostly of people from the scene of his crime—friends and neighbors of Hampton Smith." When Valdosta's police took up the hunt for Johnson, their success hinged on a tip from a member of the city's Black community. "We mention this phase of the case to show that there was no strained relations between the whites and blacks." There was no reason for Dorsey to send troops save the exaggerations of those outside of the region. "There has been no crime here—no lynching here," and if Johnson hadn't fired on officers, "he would have been turned over to the constituted authorities for such punishment as the people in the county where the crime was committed might decide upon." That being the case, the *Times* closed, the people of Valdosta and Lowndes County "do not care for the notoriety which certain newspapers are trying to give them."[29]

Thomasville's paper also reprinted a *Valdosta Times* editorial on the turmoil. "While The Times believes that little more than even-handed justice was done to the black brutes who met summary punishment for their fiendish crimes in Brooks county last week," went the editorial, "the Times regrets some of the acts of barbarism which accompanied the execution of these men." In addition, importantly, "we also regret the lynching of the negro woman, who though apparently deeply involved in the plot against Hampton Smith and his wife, might have been allowed to face a jury in the court house and answer for her offense. That she would have been punished, if the facts warranted it, goes without saying."[30]

Such claims accompanied a lecture on "madness," on anger as a motivating factor for mob action. Members of the mob "lost control of themselves. They became like a machine without a governor—a ship without a rudder, or a high explosive without the appliance to control it and direct its energy." If the mob had shown "calm determination all the way through, stopping with the execution of the victims much of the sting which accompanies mob violence would have been removed."[31]

In this formulation the destruction that followed the lynchings was the problem, not the lynchings themselves. The exception to that claim was Turner's lynching. While she was "deeply involved" in the plot, she deserved a jury trial before her killing. Such pronouncements worked in several ways. First, by denouncing the "madness" of the mob, the paper simultaneously reported on the riot and used its existence to justify the original violence. By regretting the killing of Turner, the paper sought to defend the common dignity of the white majority in the region while also diminishing the existence of the other Black men who were killed. Their lives ceased to matter in the equation. Instead the *Times* found problematic the way their bodies were treated after death. If the lynching of the woman was the only actual miscarriage of justice, then the men could all be assumed to be guilty without second thought and riot actions could become tertiary to madness and the specific lynching of Turner above all others. The Black male victims and the white male mob disappeared, the event reduced to the bad behavior of those who participated specifically in one act on one day in response to one event. It was not a riot or mass murder. It was the unjust lynching of one woman.

MEMORY AND MYTHMAKING

In response to the publicizing of the Turner lynching, hundreds of letters flooded the offices of President Wilson and his attorney general, A. Mitchell Palmer. The Negro Womanhood of Georgia asked "that you use all the power of your great office to prevent similar occurrences and punish the perpetrators of this foul deed." Palmer responded to all of the letters with same stock reply, reminding correspondents of the Supreme Court's ruling in *Hodges v. United States* that lynching was a state crime like other murders and that the federal government had no jurisdiction to prosecute it.[32]

Tuskegee leader Robert Russa Moton also wrote to Wilson telling him "something ought to be done" about the growing unease among Black Americans over lynchings and riots. "The recent lynching in Georgia of six colored people in connection with a murder, and among them a woman who it is reported was a prospective mother, has intensified tremendously this attitude of colored people." Moton believed that "a strong word, definitely from you on this lynching proposition will have more effect just now than any other one thing."[33]

The president responded positively, telling Moton that he had been "seeking an opportunity to do what you suggest and if I do not find it soon, I will do it without an opportunity."[34] Though Wilson was himself a firm believer in white supremacy, the national outcry compelled the president to condemn lynching. "We proudly claim to be the champions of democracy," he proclaimed in late July 1918. "If we really are, in deed and in truth, let us see to it that we do not discredit our own. I say plainly that every American who takes part in the action of a mob or gives it any sort of countenance is no true son of this great democracy, but its betrayer."[35] It was a surprising statement, putting Wilson into lockstep, if briefly, with the anti-lynching advocates of the Black press.

J. W. Davidson, associate editor of the *Atlanta Independent*, described the specter of mob violence as a "great pall which hangs over us like a mighty cloud." He asked authorities to "make every black man feel that he is presumed to be innocent until he has been proven guilty. Give him due process of law as you do white citizens, and all will be well." It was a remedy, but it was not a likely one.[36] The *Independent*'s publisher, Ben Davis, was even less optimistic. "If we are to judge from the barbarity practiced in Georgia by white mobs," he wrote, "there are hundreds and thousands of Georgia Crackers that are more concerned about annihilating the Negro race, who are fellow citizens with them under the law, than they are putting down the kaiser and kaiserism in the world." As mob violence exploded in the South and the nation, there were Black voices who suspected a German influence. Davis's *Independent* was frustrated that the *St. Louis Argus* "discounts race prejudice as the main cause of the recent epidemic of lawlessness, and suggests a widespread German propaganda to incite the races one against the other."[37]

The *Argus* credited Hun treachery with inciting white violence, but local white papers also saw a German connection in Black criminal behavior. Those who participated in Smith's murder, according to Bainbridge's *Post-Search Light*, were "either directly or indirectly urged to crime by German agents who have been working secretly among the Negroes in this section," part of a broader "German south-wide plot to stir up the negroes and cause a race war."[38] The *Atlanta Journal* claimed to have "unmistakable sources" claiming that "persons have recently gone through this section talking to the colored people and inciting them to crime against the white people." Those persons were nowhere to be found, but there was "evidence of a reliable nature" that "German influences have been behind it."[39]

The *Memphis News Scimitar* went even further, claiming that "some of the best-known negroes in the community are declared to have reported to their employers that German agents have been trying to bring about trouble between the races." In this telling it was white officials who "were reluctant to believe" that German agents had anything to do with Smith's murder.[40]

The notion became a well-worn rag for the region's papers. News outlets in Butler, Augusta, Bainbridge, Macon, and Nashville all repeated a version of the story.[41] The one local paper that treated the German influence accounts with derision was Brooks County's *Quitman Free Press.* "Who these pro-Germans are or where they came from remains a mystery which even the correspondents seem unable to explain," the paper observed. "In the meantime the farmers north of Quitman and in the community where the Smiths lived were astonished at the pro-German phase as they all knew the real causes underlying the tragedy."[42] It was, to the paper, yet another outcome of sensationalized reports from out of town.

The claims forced W. R. "Roland" Knight, clerk of Brooks County Superior Court, to announce that "no German plot to provoke an uprising of negroes is in the least indicated by any developments." In fact, it was "American citizens determined to keep sacred the honor of American women" who "revenged the fiendish attack" on Smith's wife. "Just as long as there is a drop of American red blood in an American, attacks upon our women by brute negroes will be resented," said Knight.[43]

That kind of commentary also went the other way. The *Memphis Commercial Appeal* lamented that "the leaders in Germany announce to their people that we are barbarians" when word of mass killings like that in south Georgia became part of the news cycle. "In Germany there is a government by kings and war lords. In other countries there is a government of uncontrolled public opinion, but in America there is a government of law. The law written in the books is the Ark of the Covenant of our whole American scheme of liberty and justice. If the law fails we are a lost people."[44] The *Baltimore Daily Herald* did similar work when it titled its coverage "Georgia Huns Lynch Negro Woman and Three Men."[45] It was an intentional attempt to reverse the white southern narrative. After the Brooks and Lowndes attacks "comes the ridiculous, stupid and reckless lie that German agents are fomenting trouble among Negroes in the section where the savages have been indulging in their pastime of mob murder." It was a common and false trope. "For several months after this government entered the world war lying news dispatches were sent out almost daily from different points in the South that Negroes were being incited to disloyalty and treachery against the government by German agents or sympathizers. Negroes by their splendid exhibition of loyalty and devotion to the government clubbed those lies to death."[46]

"We do not like to accuse anybody of pro-Germanism, but it strikes us that the lynchers, both North and South, are doing precisely what the Kaiser would like to have them," the *New York Post* explained. "Every fresh lynching degrades us to the Prussian level and makes it the more difficult for Americans to hold the Germans up to scorn for their crimes against humanity."[47]

"Running true to form," a frustrated *Pittsburgh Courier* complained, "the relentless cracker element here [in south Georgia] is now trying to place the responsibility for the lynching of the four colored people on some species of German propaganda."[48] The conspiracy thinking was a reification of the anti-immigrant paranoia prompted by the war effort, the same paranoia that led to banning German books, soon to be replaced in the wake of the Red Scare by charges that those acting in defense of their rights or of civil rights more broadly were under the influence of communism.

For local newspapers in south Georgia, meanwhile, it was a welcome respite from defending against German rumors, but the papers instead usually found themselves defending the region more broadly against outside attacks. And the outside attacks were legion. The *New York Post*, in an early, stern denunciation of Turner's lynching, described a Mississippi lynching several years prior wherein members of a mob took a woman, "filled her skin full of pine splinters and set fire to her; hence we have something to be thankful for," the paper wryly concluded, "that yesterday's lynching was at least not quite so barbaric as it might have been." Such was no consolation to the five who were killed prior to Johnson's capture, nor to those who remained, terrorized by the mob. And each new incident put many of those terrorized survivors on the railroad north, leaving southern agricultural work depleted as a result. "If the argument of humanity and decency will not prevail, perhaps that of self-interest will."[49]

There were similar laments by the *New York Tribune*,[50] the *Brooklyn Eagle*,[51] the *New York Age*,[52] the *New York World*,[53] the *Baltimore Daily Herald*,[54] and the *Bridgeport* (CT) *Telegram*. An editorial in Connecticut's *Telegram* lamented "the lynching of a woman." The paper was not surprised at such barbarity from "the sovereign state that hounded Leo Frank to his death at the hands of a mob," but attacks on women were a new low. "Georgia makes it harder for America to beat the Hun."[55] The coverage was one of dozens of national screeds against the Turner lynching, all of them proclaiming it horrific. In so doing, however, those contemporary accounts foreshadowed what the historiography of the event would do, diminishing both the racial furor of south Georgia and the multitude of victims it created in aid of seeking justice for the most horrific of those cases.

Southern authorities and journalists pushed back against the derision of northern newspapers in several ways. One was far more pragmatic than argumentative. On June 5, local authorities in Griffin, Georgia, seized seven hundred copies of "a recent issue of a well known Chicago newspaper" that had been shipped south and put them "at the disposal of the department of justice," claiming that the issue was "in violation of the espionage act." The discovered paper described the south Georgia lynchings in detail, "with photographs of some of the victims," and featured "long editorials criticizing state and federal officials. The whole paper seems to be made up of matter designed to create racial strife in the south and to weaken confidence in the government." Though the *Chicago Defender* did not feature pictures of the victims, the accounts almost surely refer to the country's most prominent Black newspaper. Griffin police discovered the editions after they were delivered to one of the Black employees of a local garage. The garage's white owner was there when the papers were delivered by express mail and notified the authorities.[56]

The *Quitman Free Press* adamantly pushed back against the narrative developing outside of Brooks County. There were only four people lynched, the paper claimed. They were lynched only after a small and dedicated group of Smith family and friends had determined their guilt. "There was absolutely no disorder, no hunting of innocent negroes, none of the wild mob outbreaks." Reports of racial tension and "intense feeling among white and black" were wrong. "This is no apology for lynch law," the paper claimed, "but the sensational stories originating in other towns nearby make it appear that the situation was worse than it really was."[57] Of course, it was, in fact, an apology for lynch law, promoting white judgment of Black guilt as equivalent to legal judgment of guilt, a conflation that ensured that innocent Black people would always need to fear being hunted.

Brooks County sheriff Jesse Wade was also frustrated by what he saw as sensationalized coverage of the violence, arguing that "beyond the actual fact of the four lynchings there had been no disorder in the county, no mob hunting negroes." He claimed that the local vigilance committee made sure the victims "were involved in the crimes or had previous knowledge of them" before lynching anyone and that the only real mobs were the crowds of people coming from out of town to gawk.[58] Again civilian and legal decision-making were conflated in defense of white supremacy. The everyday atrocities against Black lives and bodies were so ingrained in the minds of leaders like Wade and local media outlets that extrajudicial killings were simply signposts of vigilance.

The *Free Press* argued that the search for the Black criminals was conducted by "serious men" from a local "vigilance committee" who "obtained a detailed confession" from Will Head and "counselled not lynching him until the negroes he implicated were caught and details verified." Instead the paper mimicked Wade, blaming "the mobs of curiosity seekers . . . who flocked afterward to the scene of the lynchings and mutilated the victims in their gruesome search for souvenirs" for the uglier parts of the rampage that made the press. The *Moultrie Observer* understood its neighbor's criticism of the incursion into Brooks "by citizens of other counties" and disapproved that the mobs "found delight and entertainment in looking on at the lynchings and playing pranks with the lifeless bodies of the victims as they hung in the air." But the paper noted that the attack on Smith "occurred very close to the Colquitt county line and some of the acquaintances and neighbors of Smith were citizens of Colquitt county," a justification tantamount to defending accessories after the fact, those white citizens who sought to vicariously participate in the killings by rubbernecking at the scene. The paper also noted that county lines would not have been noticed had the hunt for the lynch victims taken the mob into Colquitt and that the Smith family did not resent the help of people from Colquitt. In the aftermath of violence, everyone was defending their turf.[59]

The *Observer*, however, did come to its Quitman ally's defense. The paper was "opposed to lynching as a general proposition, and especially opposed to lynching those who are not the leaders in the crimes the lynchings are intended to avenge," but discussions of eliminating lynching were useless "until something has been done to prevent the unspeakable crimes committed by negro brutes on helpless white women and children." In response to northern commentators asking "how much longer the American people are to tolerate lynchings, we will answer it frankly: As long as they have to tolerate rape." It was the typical white southern deflection. "The real problem that confronts our civilization is to get rid of the degenerate negro (and the degenerate white man, to[o], as for that matter) and to prevent the perpetration of these crimes which stir quiet, peaceful citizens to violent action." After all, "you cannot tame a mob and organize it into a prayer meeting or an aid society. A mob is a cyclone, and goes where it will and devours all that comes in its path." Thus the only way to stop lynching was to police the Black population. "The negroes who murdered Hampton Smith in Brooks county were nondescripts who had been picked up around Valdosta. Their character probably unknown to the man who employed them." A similar problem had occurred in nearby Crisp County, the paper claimed. It seemed like an argument against debt peonage, but the *Observer* went the other way, suggesting that "we might have a detention camp where they could be interned before they commit these crimes."[60]

The *Observer* had no interest in hiding or cloaking any information pertaining to the events. "Lynching is a deplorable thing," the paper's editorial page explained, "but we will have to evolve to a point where we are rid of such heinous crimes as that committed in Brooks county last week before we can get away from lynching."[61] The paper did mention Turner's clothes being burned in a way that other immediate accounts did not. "Reports as to the cause of the lynching of Hattie Turner vary," the *Observer* explained, parsing the excuses of her involvement in the conspiracy and her protests that drove the mob crazy. There was also a variance in accounts of Turner's burning. Some claimed that the mob first decided to burn her, but after her clothes burned off, they decided to hang her. Others denied that there was a plan to burn Turner and claimed that after she was hanged her clothing caught fire "from pistol shots fired at close range" after her death. "At any rate the woman's garb was burned."[62]

It was a statement of fact as the paper interpreted it, but that very effort demonstrates the contingency of such news reports. "Remembering and forgetting are not dialectical opposites," explain Jessy Ohl and Jennifer Potter. Acts of cultural forgetting in relation to elements of lynching are "contingent on the rhetorical invention of lynching as impassioned acts by limited individuals beyond the social orthodoxy." In the case of Mary Turner, Walter White was the limited individual whose impassioned act was an effort to find the truth about violence in south Georgia. The will to believe his report was another impassioned act, because he was unquestionably one of the good guys in the lynching narrative. "The interplay between dominant and counter-memory suggests that public memory of traumatic experiences resists removal in favor of ideological revision as a method for coping and control."[63] Or as Bradford Vivian suggests, remembering and forgetting, whether in relation to lynching or anything else, are densely "interwoven dimensions of larger symbolic or discursive processes."[64] In that spirit, this account is a discursive engagement with the public remembering of the lynching of Mary Turner.

Ohl and Potter's study examines lynching imagery, but their claim that "rhetors often tailor and adjust images to accentuate, to perpetuate, or to contest public memory to gain and maintain political dominance" can easily be transferred to storytelling.[65] With no photographs emanating from the Turner rampage, rhetoric does the work of spectacle to affect public memory and political strategy.

The public memory of lynching, Ohl and Potter argue, manifests itself in three ways. It relegates lynchers to certain segments of society, it creates a melodrama of good and evil, and it implicates mob rule in taking over a group and eliminating the better judgment of the individuals involved.[66] The first and last of these assumptions are generically intended to absolve people of individual responsibility. Case histories over the past two decades have given lie to such efforts of public memory. The second manifestation is the one that presses on the memory of the lynching rampage in south Georgia, since creating that melodrama in aid of political activism ultimately led to mistakes along the way.

As a result that memory, particularly in the form of the "writing of the history of lynching," has been, in the words of historian Joel Williamson, "strangely disjointed and discontinuous." In a jarring 1997 essay, Williamson admitted that he "learned about white people massively lynching black people only as a scholar in the middle years of the 1960s," because white southern history, which he had made a distinguished career of studying, never included it in the grand narrative that set the parameters for the subject.[67] The narrative that does include lynching has gained currency in the decades since Williamson's lament (and his interpretation was challenged vigorously at the time of its publication),[68] but one of the ways it has continued to develop is through rational analysis of newly available data to draw the most reasonable conclusions. The second generation of lynching scholarship, in other words, is entering a period of historiographical critique and revisionism that inevitably follows early historical efforts.[69]

Similarly, Karlos K. Hill has argued that "the lynched black body in the black cultural imagination is best understood as a floating signifier that could be fashioned for various rhetorical purposes." That fluidity moves in space between a variety of interest groups, white and Black, North and South, and in time within those groups, as the semiotic use of Black bodies changes based on the needs of the communities learning about that history. Hill uses a variety of categories for those representations, but all of them depend on representations of the lynched victim rather than the victim him- or herself.[70] That dependency places a burden on the representations to do the work of consolation, victimization, or resilience in the given communities who find identity in the narratives, which makes countering them a fraught endeavor.[71]

"Lynching was always intended as a metaphor for, or a way to understand, race relations," argues Jonathan Markovitz. It was an understanding, however, that was "inevitably partial, and the particular aspects of southern race relations that were meant to be invoked by lynching or by references to lynching were the subject of heated battle." And those battles had stakes: "The dynamics of lynchings worked to construct basic ways of conceptualizing the world that are still relevant today."[72] Nothing could be more true in the case of the Mary Turner story. As Julie Buckner Armstrong has described, the memory of Turner has played out in a variety of cultural forms.

Lynching, according to Emma Coleman Jordan, is "a contemporary civic metaphor for the black experience within the American legal system." Many African Americans "incorporated the violence of lynching into a coded family cautionary tale about survival in a universe controlled by hostile whites."[73] Meanwhile, white members of the community repress the memory of lynching. At an official level, they seek to erase it from popular conceptions of a community's history.

French theorist Maurice Halbwachs argued in the 1940s that individual historical memory was dependent upon collective thought and constructs: "It is in society that people normally acquire their memories. It is also in society that they recall, recognize, and localize their memories." These memories become ritualized as a kind of thought policing. Or, as Halbwachs's countryman Roland Barthes claimed, memory "purifies" human groups. "It makes them innocent, it gives them natural and eternal justification, it gives them a clarity which is not that of an explanation but that of a statement of fact."[74]

Modern authors like Jan Assman and John Czaplicka have challenged Halbwachs's notion of contingency in the creation of memory. Memory has a "fixed point," they argue. Still, they do not challenge contingency entirely, particularly in relation to collective memory. "One group remembers the past in fear of deviating from its model, the next for fear of repeating the past," claim Assman and Czaplicka. "Which past becomes evident in that heritage, and which values emerge in its identificatory appropriation, tells us much about the constitution and tendencies of a society."[75] The work of Barbie Zelizer endorses such thinking only in describing the stakes game present in memory negotiations: "Collective memory is always a means to something else." It "is evaluated for the ways in which it helps us to make connections—to each other over time and space and to ourselves."[76]

All such memory studies emphasize the powerful role that symbols play in reinforcing social memory standards, and there could be no more powerful symbol than a tortured and brutalized pregnant woman. "The traumatic effects of lynching tend to transpire through acts of secondary witnessing,"

Jennifer Williams explains—acts such as oral narratives and journalism that set the trauma in place as part of the cultural standard of a community. That continued reinforcement creates, in the words of Elizabeth Alexander, "a traumatized collective historical memory which is reinvoked at contemporary sites of conflict."[77]

The traumatic collective memory of the facts of Mary Turner's lynching, in other words, was and is all too real. That memory does its own important work, helping to shape both local and national identities, whether the historical facts match actual events. It is also important to note that Turner's story is told in the context of what Elsa Barkley Brown has called "the erasure of women from contemporary assessments of the Black condition" and from historical accounts of African American political struggles.[78] The symbolic meaning of Turner is only magnified in the face of that broader omission.

The semiotic power of that memory and the work that it has done, however, is something fundamentally different than the factual recounting of events. Mari N. Crabtree tells the story of J. Charles Jones, founding member of SNCC and later a civil rights lawyer, who recalled growing up in the 1940s in South Carolina, his father telling him a story about a white mob storming the house of a Black man who had "said something" to a white woman. The mob took his wife, eight months pregnant, and strung her up, cutting open her abdomen and pulling out the fetus. It was a conflation of a local South Carolina lynching and that of Turner. As Crabtree explains, "The disturbing details of Mary Turner's death had so deeply made an impression on Jones's mind that, even though her lynching happened a few hundred miles from where Jones grew up, he subconsciously made that violent story local and personal."[79]

But that conflation was not yet possible in those early days after the rampage. Whether castigating lynching or supporting it, whether local press or national, there was one element of the story that was never part of the narrative. The *Valdosta Times*, the *Quitman Free Press*, and the *Moultrie Observer* never mentioned a Turner pregnancy. Nor did the *Chicago Defender*, the *Augusta Chronicle*, or the Associated Press. It was clear that Hattie Turner, sometimes known as Mary, was lynched, either for protesting her husband's lynching or for hosting a planning meeting for Hamp Smith's murder—again demonstrating the inherent contingency in the interstitial spaces of white newspaper accounts. She was taken to the Little River in northern Brooks County, hanged, shot repeatedly, and, either intentionally or accidentally, had her clothes burned from her body. It was a brutality matched only by that practiced on the mob's other victims. Through the variations in the coverage, such remained the consistent narrative both for those who defended what had occurred and those who were horrified by it.

And then came Walter White.

CHAPTER FOUR

Lost in Translation

On May 20, 1918, NAACP secretary John R. Shillady sent an open letter to Governor Hugh Dorsey, the Atlanta Chamber of Commerce, and the Savannah Board of Trade urging that members of the mob that killed Mary Turner and other victims be brought to justice and that steps be taken to protect the life of Sidney Johnson upon his eventual capture. Shillady noted that "eleven Negroes have been lynched in Georgia since September 15, 1917, all charged with crimes for which the law provides ample remedy." That no mob members had been charged with crimes marked the region as hypocritical. "The eyes of the nation are now fixed upon Georgia to see whether your state will vindicate her laws and insist upon legal punishment of those who have defied her courts and flaunted their disregard for law in the faces of Georgia's law-abiding people."[1]

THE INVESTIGATION AND ITS LEGISLATIVE OUTGROWTH

Shillady had taken over as executive secretary of the NAACP in 1917 after a career in public service that had led him, most recently, to head the Mayor's Committee on Unemployment in New York City. Shillady's tenure with the association would be comparatively short. He was white, which, it was assumed, would give him a measure of protection when venturing south. But when he traveled to Austin, Texas, in August 1919, just over a year after the rampage in south Georgia and months after the NAACP's national lynching conference, he was attacked by a mob, with the endorsement of the Texas governor, that included a county judge and a constable. Shillady never fully recovered from the assault and resigned the following year; his tenure was succeeded by the more notable one of James Weldon Johnson, who would in turn be succeeded by Walter White.[2]

In early June 1918, White received a letter from an acquaintance in Atlanta who claimed to have been in Valdosta at the time of the rampage. The correspondent assumed that Hampton Smith was "killed over trouble following a crap game" and rehearsed the by-then common assertion of "pro German influences." That was obviously untrue, but it piqued White's interest in the case, so when Shillady sent him down to investigate, he was ready.[3]

White was a Georgia native, born July 1, 1893, in Atlanta to an upper-middle-class family. In 1906 he lived through the city's harrowing race riot. It was a defining moment for the boy: he and his father witnessed a man beaten to death and helped rescue an elderly woman from the mob. The Atlanta race riot was also a moment of awakening for the young, light-skinned White, who found in the horror of mob violence his identity as a Black man in a white country.[4]

The family survived the ordeal, and after high school White attended Atlanta University, where he graduated in 1916. After college he took a job with Standard Life Insurance and simultaneously became involved in activist work. He helped form an Atlanta chapter of the NAACP and petitioned Atlanta's school board to improve standards of education in the city's Black public schools. His work got him noticed by James Weldon Johnson, who invited him to move to New York to join the NAACP as a secretary assistant serving mostly to investigate lynchings and other racial violence. Despite his youth and inexperience, and over the protests of some because of those qualities, White agreed. Early in 1918 he left Georgia to work for the NAACP in New York. He would not, however, be gone from the state for long.[5]

When White was charged to travel back south to investigate the race riot in south Georgia, he had just recently returned to New York from a similar investigation in Estill Springs, Tennessee. There he investigated the brutal lynching of Jim McIlherron. McIlherron was from a family of relative wealth in the area, a fact poor white locals resented. He had threatened the sheriff early in his life before moving away and finally returning. He was notorious among poor white people for his willingness to push back against racial assaults and the stifling white supremacy in the area. The white residents had a practice of throwing rocks at the Black locals, and McIlherron had once threatened a group that attacked him. On February 8, 1918, a confrontation with another rock-throwing group ended with McIlherron shooting at three men and killing two of them. He was caught three days later. A large mob gathered, tied its victim to a tree, then tortured him and burned him alive. No one was charged with the murder.[6]

The story of McIlherron's torture appeared in the May edition of the *Crisis*, just as the retribution for Hampton Smith's killing got underway in Brooks and Lowndes Counties. McIlherron, in fact, was lynched twelve days after White began his work with the NAACP. As he did in many of his later investigations, the light-skinned White passed as a white man to give himself an easier range of motion in Estill Springs. "Publication of the facts I had uncovered created a modest sensation," he later remembered, a sensation that was repeated when he made his second investigative trip for the association. During his time in Tennessee and his first trip to Quitman, the rookie investigator was just twenty-four years old.[7]

While he was in Estill Springs, White had used press credentials from Oswald Garrison Villard's *New York Evening Post* in the event he was questioned as to his presence in the town. He still had those credentials when he made his first venture to south Georgia and used them to claim he was a journalist to present his findings to Dorsey. White's biographer Kenneth Robert Janken notes that "his freelancing style and his unauthorized use of Oswald Garrison Villard's press credentials dismayed secretary Shillady, who tried to rein him in." Still, "it was precisely this display of . . . derring-do that increasingly came to define his investigative work." White intended that while in the "process of shaming the white South, he could also make it look inept by infiltrating its inner sancta." White's Tennessee and Georgia lynching exposés "earned the NAACP more publicity than it had received for past investigations," precisely because of the sensational nature of the investigator's coverage.[8]

White spent several days in Barney, Quitman, and Valdosta, speaking to everyone he possibly could to learn about the ordeal. His principal informant, however, was George U. Spratling, an assistant to white undertaker Samuel McGowan, whose mortuary had taken care of Hamp Smith's body. Spratling was a Black man "of small education but of considerable intelligence." McGowan was one of the two ringleaders of the mob, along with Quitman cotton broker W. A. Whipple, and he had forced Spratling to accompany him, promising his assistant that he would not be attacked in any way. White's other two sources were indirect. Dr. Athens N. Grant and Dr. Maurice H. Cobb, two Black physicians in Quitman, provided secondhand knowledge from sources of information that they knew.[9]

Athens Nathaniel Grant was born on February 12, 1886. Unlike many in the region, Grant was intent on an education, but he would get a late start. He married Bertha Henderson early in the twentieth century. Their first child was born in 1903, when Grant was just seventeen years old. Two other children followed, but Grant was determined, eventually traveling to Meharry Medical College in Nashville and returning to Quitman to start a practice. His success allowed him and Bertha to provide a home not only for his children but also for his elderly father. Like so many others in the saga, Grant had a one-year-old at home, Athens Jr., born July 31, 1916. He was a man with a lot at stake, but one who had demonstrated his willingness to go out of his way to make things better for his family and community.[10]

Maurice H. Cobb was born in 1868 in Jefferson County in north Florida, bounding Georgia's Brooks County to the south. The son of the formerly enslaved J. W. Cobb and Rosa Beard, Cobb was determined to make a better life for himself. After medical school he originally settled in Valdosta, where he established a practice for the city's Black residents. Maurice had married early only to find himself a widower by the time he moved to Georgia. In the 1910s, however, he married his second wife, Florence, and moved with her to Quitman.[11] Cobb was, however, an unreliable witness.

In December 1903 Cobb was arrested by federal marshals on a peonage charge after claiming to be a girl's legal guardian and selling her to Lowndes County's Kinderlou. Lula Durham was fifteen years old, on her way to White Springs, Florida, from her home in Vienna, Georgia. She stopped at a Valdosta boardinghouse run by Cobb and his mother-in-law. Seeing an opportunity, Cobb accused Durham of sleeping with a local man and blackmailed the girl, telling her that he would forgive the affront if she paid him twenty-five dollars. She did not have the money, so he and a partner, George Hart, called Kinderlou's Frank McRee and claimed that Durham had been a patient of his medical practice who owed him for his services. Cobb, Hart, and McRee then pressured the girl to agree to serve time at Kinderlou to pay her supposed debt, keeping her in bondage for three months. Durham's mother hired a lawyer to attempt to free her, but they were forced to fight not the blackmail charge but instead the manufactured claim of restitution for medical services. Ultimately Mrs. Durham had to pay the McRees three-fourths of the "debt" before her daughter was released.[12] It was not Cobb's first offense, as he had previously been implicated in selling young Black women to Kinderlou on supposed debt peonage charges. He was convicted in 1905 in federal court in Savannah.[13]

Another of White's sources was a boy whose last name was Miller. Grant later told White that he had "seen the Miller boy['s] father and he was too afraid to tell the names of those parties that he knows of in that affair [the lynch mob] but if anything can be had from either of them I will let you know as soon as I can get it from them." He could not. The Millers had nothing more to say in that paranoid and violent climate. But the young Miller was a less prominent—and less comprehensive—additional source for White's investigation.[14]

Regardless, the sources White was able to cultivate identified McGowan and Whipple as the mob's leaders. William A. Whipple was born in 1875, the second son of Quitman farmer Thomas F. Whipple and his wife, Martha. Whipple bounced around in his career, operating a livery stable in his mid-thirties while continuing to live with his parents. But in the 1910s he changed careers, opening a dry goods store and cotton brokerage. Whipple too had a child in 1917, his only daughter, Elizabeth, despite still living with his parents.[15] The fact that the mob's ringleaders both had young children at home demonstrates how little risk angry white men felt when deciding to mete out their own form of justice or to commit acts of violence against Black bodies.

McGowan and Whipple's co-conspirators, according to White, were Brown Sherrill, who worked for Whipple, and several members of the Smith family, including Hamp's father, Dixon, and three of his brothers. Ordley Yates was a clerk in the post office. Frank Purvis worked for Griffin Furniture Company, and Fulton DeVane for Standard Oil. Farmers Richard and Ross DeVane, Lee Sherrill, and Jim Dickson were also part of the group. Two additional men, last names Chalmers and Van, were also involved. Spratling claimed to have heard McGowan boast about the killings, saying, "If the Germans were as thick as the grass in the courthouse yard the same thing would be done again."[16]

Spratling's testimony, and White's retelling, presents a picture of a mob dominated by three Brooks County families, the Smiths, DeVanes, and Sherrills, with several of their acquaintances included in the group. Richard Wiley DeVane was born on December 9, 1857, in Quitman. In the 1880s he married his first wife, Allice, and the couple settled into a life of farming and children. They had eight by 1900. Among them were Charles Ross, the first child, and Fulton, the fifth. It was a regimen that took its toll on Allice, who died in the early twentieth century. In November 1914 DeVane married Florence Parker, thirteen years his junior. With Richard in his late fifties and Florence in her early forties, the couple had no more children. Russell, the youngest of Richard's children, was sixteen when his father remarried and was out on his own soon after. In 1918 Ross was twenty-eight years old and Fulton twenty-two.[17]

On February 9, 1910, four years prior to his father's second marriage, Ross married Emma Susan Patrick and began his own farm and family. The couple had three children prior to 1918. Fulton remained unmarried until the 1920s and wanted to escape the family business, instead moving into Quitman to become a livestock dealer. Still, he and the Devane family were close with the Smiths and other farming families in rural Brooks County.[18] It was a world of continued opportunity for family and financial growth, all facilitated by whiteness and a white supremacy that the Devanes and others would do anything to protect.

With his sources sparse but his investigation complete, White concluded his trip to south Georgia and wrote a detailed report of the events as he had learned them. The NAACP press release summarizing White's report from the scene described May 17–22 as a "five days lynching orgy" wherein eleven verified deaths occurred. White submitted his report to Governor Dorsey on July 10, simultaneously mailing a copy to President Woodrow Wilson.[19]

White's report explained that along with Will Head, Will Thompson, Eugene Rice, Sidney Johnson, and the Turners—those lynchings reported in the press—there were five additional verified victims: Chime Riley, Simon Shuman, and three unidentified persons pulled from the Little River just below Quitman roughly one week following their lynching. White explained that one local minister had put the total as high as eighteen, but there was only evidence to verify eleven.

Riley, in White's telling, was lynched near Barney, his body disposed of by tying clay turpentine cups (used to collect sap from turpentine trees) to it and sinking it in the Little River. The body was not recovered, but White's informant claimed to have found one of the turpentine cups when the river was low. A white mob called Shuman from his house on the Moultrie Road near Berlin. Everything in the house was destroyed, and Shuman had not been seen since.[20]

White reported that more than five hundred local Black residents had fled the area despite threats from the white mob that those choosing to leave would be assumed to have been complicit in the Hampton Smith plot. "Hundreds of acres of once productive lands are now overrun with weeds and dozens of farm houses and cabins deserted by their former occupants."[21]

Hampton Smith, in White's telling, ran his farm, Old Joyce Place, with an iron fist, beating his farmhands and often refusing to pay them. His reputation kept him from hiring voluntary labor, so he began bonding out those who could not pay their fines, taking advantage of the racially motivated and long-established debt peonage system in the region. Sidney Johnson's fine for gaming was thirty dollars. Smith paid it, and Johnson was forced to work at Old Joyce Place. Though the report does not mention the duration of Johnson's tenure and records of the sentence no longer exist, similar peonage cases in the area suggest that Johnson would have faced a term of at least six months of virtual slavery for the thirty-dollar fine, and Smith would have had options to extend the term based on manufactured fines and food costs. When

Johnson claimed one day to be sick, Smith beat his new employee, and Johnson responded by threatening Smith. Johnson then shot and killed Smith. White acknowledged that Smith's wife was shot, as well, but argued that there was no evidence that she was raped. Johnson, meanwhile, never went to the swamp, instead staying at his house until the posse came for him. He told anyone who would listen that he was the only one to blame for the attacks at Smith's farm.[22]

Regarding Mary Turner, White explained that his account was "related to the investigator by men who affirmed that they were present at her death." Because the lynching itself was not in question, he did not rely on evidence for verification, as he had with the additional five victims, instead emphasizing the testimony of at least two Black residents who claimed to have been present at the event. White reported Turner as "approaching confinement," the final stage of pregnancy. She was tied by the ankles and hung upside down. Members of the mob pulled cans of gasoline from their vehicles, poured them on her, then set fire to her clothes. She was then disemboweled; "her unborn child fell from her womb and while still alive, was crushed by the heel of a member of the mob." Turner was then riddled with rifle bullets. After the killing she was taken down and buried ten feet from the tree where she had hung, her headstone an empty whiskey bottle with a cigar shoved into the neck. The report also claimed to have a photograph of the grave.[23]

It is a horrifying story, and Turner undoubtedly suffered mightily as the victim of a gruesome lynching by a rabid mob. Two holes in the story exist, however. First, White's report is the first time Turner was described as pregnant, even among other denunciations of the event. His account is made more problematic by the fact that White used hearsay of an unnamed number of people claiming to have been there instead of maintaining the same evidentiary standard for the claims of additional victims. While unwilling Black attendants certainly accompanied the mob, they likely would not have been front and center at the lynching tree. So even if those who claimed to have attended were attempting an honest account, theirs was one conditioned by fear, an obstructed view, and a lack of understanding of human anatomy. It was also conditioned by temporal distance from the trauma, wherein the horrors grow in the mind of those affected.[24] The second problem with the evidence, related to the first, is that the photograph of the grave White originally claimed to have was never produced. Instead he used in his report an image of the Brooks County lynching tree, assumed to be the place of Hayes Turner's death. As the focus of White's story, the emphasis of the entire encounter, was Mary Turner's death, one would expect that image to accompany the report. But it never appears in the NAACP's files.[25] Again, that does not mean that such a grave did not exist. It very well could have. But it demonstrates instead evidentiary problems from White's time in south Georgia, considering that he presented as fact details not noted in any previous account temporally closer to the actual event.

"Though the conquest of Georgia by the mob has been accomplished with a fair degree of thoroughness throughout the state, the law-abiding elements are in general restive, and at times able to prevail even against the might of the hated oppressor," went one draft of White's report. "But in South Georgia the grip of the mob is secure, the sentiment is firm; and the law writhes in agony as it is torn to shreds by the all-powerful lynchers. The 1918 atrocities in Brooks and Lowndes Counties but serve to accentuate the awful blood lust to which the neighboring counties are subject." The report explained that of the 386 documented lynchings in Georgia between 1889 and 1918, 119 had occurred in south Georgia, a very high number for a sparsely populated part of the state. More than 4 people per county in the designated 28-county region were lynched, as compared to just over 2 people per county in the remaining 115 counties. And Lowndes was the leader among them all, with 16 lynchings, almost 4 percent of the state total happening in and around Valdosta. In a span of 7 counties that the NAACP classified as south Georgia, more than 25 percent of all lynchings in the state took place. "And nowhere have lynchings been accompanied by more gruesome features and horrible cruelties than in South Georgia," the report stated. Though this account did not mention Turner's pregnancy, it did mention Turner, and the "mutilation of the body and the erection over the grave of a scurrilous headstone" as part of the indignities shown her. "Is it any wonder that salesmen refuse to do other than a cash business in South Georgia, that they openly condemn the people of that section as untrustworthy, as lacking in every instinct of business honesty?" the report asked. "In the thrill of the man hunt, they forget the value of the man; as long as it is a pleasure to kill Negroes, they toss carelessly aside any stray thoughts concerning the necessity of Negro labor."[26]

It was a damning report, with a power of its own to provoke a moral outrage counter to the provocation of the mob itself. And the NAACP knew that it had in the provocation a valuable tool against the scourge of lynching. NAACP secretary Shillady made the case that White's report was an indictment of regional law enforcement. "The facts disclosed by our investigator were not difficult to acquire and could have been ascertained by the criminal authorities of Georgia whose business it is to vindicate her law and prosecute offenders against it, had they been so minded." White criminal authorities in Georgia were almost universally loath to prosecute white offenses against Black lives and bodies, so beginning in August the NAACP began using Turner's story in its fundraising materials. "Join the National Association now," went one such release, after a summary of White's report on the Turner lynching, "and help break up these acts of violence and cruelty."[27]

And they worked. After White published his account in the *Crisis*, letters and donations began coming into the New York office. The goal of anti-lynching activism was "to play on the empathy of national spectators and engender in them feelings of outrage and disgust toward lynching," argues Amy Louise Wood, and the Turner story engendered an outpouring of outrage and disgust. For example, Memphis banker Bolton Smith, a white man, donated ten dollars to the NAACP's anti-lynching fund after reading the account. "I do not agree with the position of your association in many respects," he wrote, but he was struck by the account of the south Georgia riot. He asked for ten copies of the story so he could share them with others who would not normally read the *Crisis*.[28]

White's report was sent to Woodrow Wilson under a cover letter from Shillady, urging the president to make a statement against lynching based on, among other reasons, the lack of action by local authorities and the brutality of the attack on "a woman eight months pregnant" who was hanged "by the heels, disemboweled, and in the process giving birth to an eight months old child which was crushed under the heel of one of the lynchers."[29]

Though Dorsey had been seemingly uninterested in White's initial report, the NAACP did not give up its effort to convince the governor to act, sending him a telegram in August. "All patriotic America awaits with interest your action in seeing that perpetrators of these most barbaric lynchings are brought to justice." Dorsey's reply was vague, at best. "So far as I am able to ascertain no definite results have been obtained in the effort to apprehend the guilty parties," wrote the governor. "I shall take pleasure in advising you in the event any developments take place." Dorsey was a vocal critic of mob violence, but he also, like Governor Northen before him, believed in local control. He had campaigned for the office on keeping governmental intervention out of local judicial proceedings. His response to White, then, was not inconsistent, but it was frustrating to the NAACP's representative.[30]

At the same time, the NAACP began discussing national action with C. P. Dam, a lawyer with the Washington firm Servan and Joyce, in the weeks after White's account of the Turner lynching appeared in the *Crisis*. Dam's family employed a Black housekeeper who showed him White's Turner exposé. He was dramatically affected by her story and wrote to Shillady in mid-September, "I am in position to reach influential members of Congress, men, who I believe would be prompt in demanding that these criminals be brought to justice even though it would require the power of the Federal Government to bring it about."[31]

White sent Dam his report from Brooks and Lowndes Counties, a full version that had not appeared in the NAACP's magazine, emphasizing the members of the mob who had not been held to account. "These names have been withheld up to this date, for the purpose of aiding the Governor of Georgia in corroborating the evidence which was given him," he wrote. "Although over two months have elapsed, the governor has apparently taken no action whatever." That being the case, the NAACP was looking for other avenues. "We are still on the case in the hope that some of the men may be punished, and it may be that we can co-operate with you and your associates in working towards such an end. With no implication intended you will appreciate our position when we state that we are anxious to put the names and evidence only in the hands of those persons whom we know will use it to an advantage." White was worried about "promiscuous distribution" of his evidence, as it would "defeat the ends towards which we are working."[32]

Dam was interested and drew connections between the murders in south Georgia and the race riot in East St. Louis. Along with proofs of White's *Crisis* account, the NAACP also sent Dam its report on the East St. Louis riot, hoping that the lawyer could use his influence with congressmen for a federal intervention into such lawlessness. "If, through your efforts, men of influence in Congress are interested in the cause, an important step forward will have been taken." Dam was moved by the accounts, wanting desperately to "bring these American Huns to justice." He told White that he would lobby various senators who might be willing to take action.[33]

Meanwhile, down South, a bill "embodying Governor Dorsey's recommendations" was introduced in the Georgia legislature by Representative Joseph Law of Burke County. On July 23 Law presented "a bill for the prevention of lynching in the State." It was given a second reading the next day but died soon after without even going to committee. Burke County was just to the south of Augusta; its dominant news source was Tom Loyless's *Augusta Chronicle*, which had taken such a strong stance against mob violence. Law's proposal was a symbolic gesture with no real hope of passage, but when taking on an act soaked in symbolic significance, the doomed law was at least a representational start. In Dorsey's statement on lynchings, he denounced the practice but demurred, "There is already pending in the Federal Congress a bill conferring upon Federal tribunals jurisdiction to punish those participating in lynchings."[34]

There were actually three bills in Congress: one introduced by L. C. Dyer of Missouri, one by Merrill Moore of Indiana, and one by William C. Mason of Illinois. In reporting on the events in south Georgia, however, one national newspaper expressed its pessimism that any would make much progress. "In the opinion of several constitutional lawyers," the paper explained, "the federal government has no power to protect the life, liberty and property of citizens except against any possible encroachment *by the states*."[35] The constitutional lawyers were right. Dyer's bill, the most prominent of the bunch, did not make much progress. Dyer continued to introduce the bill until it finally achieved success in the House in 1922, only to be stopped by filibuster in the Senate.[36]

Dam was also interested in White's source of information. White declined to give Spratling's name, citing the overwhelming danger an informer would find himself in were his identity to be publicly known, but promised that the NAACP could present the informant if required for meaningful testimony.[37] White's effort to shield Spratling was understandable and important, but it also demonstrated that White's evidence was coming largely from one witness, an assistant to an undertaker in the background of the proceedings. It was a good vantage point from which to recognize people in the crowd, particularly from families with whom one might be familiar, but not to determine the specifics of what was taking place at the front of the group.

Regardless, Dam had the most luck with William Kenyon of Iowa, who agreed to look into the matter but refused to promise protection for Spratling or to spend any money on the operation. "I feel outraged as a citizen by this lynching proposition and I would like to go to the bottom of it," he wrote, "but the evidence will have to be furnished me without my going to any expense."[38] It was questionable whether outrage without expense was really outrage at all, but the interest of at least one senator was a foot in the congressional door.

And so White made a second trip to south Georgia, traveling to Jacksonville, then Thomasville, then Quitman on a mission to attempt to convince Spratling to come to Washington. He arrived in Quitman for his second visit on Tuesday night, November 12, where he met Spratling with both Drs. Grant and Cobb at the informant's home. Spratling was laid up with Spanish flu, which was then spreading across the nation. White consulted with him for more than an hour, explaining that the NAACP would pay his expenses, find him a job up north, and support him until he was able to support himself in return for congressional testimony. Spratling, however, was unconvinced. He had four children and a stepchild, the youngest only eight months old. His wife had died since White's July visit, and only his mother was there to help him care for the children. Going north, he feared, would expose the children to a climate change that would be detrimental to their health at their ages. Furthermore, all of his relatives lived in and around Quitman, and he knew that his public testimony, despite his absence, would ultimately get them killed. Spratling's was a legitimate fear, a recognition that the atrocity orientation surrounding mass racial violence was an outgrowth of the everyday atrocities of white supremacy that stifled Black dissent in all its forms. Finally, Spratling owned three pieces of local property, one with a building that cost more than $1,100, and they would not be easy to sell. Everyone in town had read White's *Crisis* article on the lynchings, and one of them, a white ex-policeman named D. W. Walton, confronted Spratling, showed him the article, and told him ominously that such lies were a shame. White countered that Spratling could fill out an affidavit delineating his testimony or testify in the Senate anonymously. He could send his children to live with his brother in Jacksonville. The witness told White he wanted time to consider his options before uprooting his life. White, in turn, convinced Spratling's pastor, Samuel Scott Broadnax, and the doctors to continue to pressure him to testify in some way, shape, or form.[39]

"We apprehended some reluctance on the fellow's part," Shillady admitted to Kenyon. But the NAACP remained confident, assuring Kenyon that they would cover Spratling's expenses and would shoulder the financial burden if the Iowa senator moved to procure justice in the south Georgia case. Back in Brooks County, White claimed that "this region has been in a virtual reign of terror since I was here. Eight negroes, relatives of the persons lynched in May, have been lynched, or have disappeared, since I was in Quitman."[40]

Dam, meanwhile, was still lobbying three additional senators whom he felt might take a similar interest in the south Georgia case. He felt they were coming around and told Shillady that he might have good news on that front by the end of November. To that end, and mindful of the long game that was the potential Senate process, Dam suggested that White and the NAACP "not display too much activity in that vicinity for the present. The main thing is to guard against the witness being tampered with."[41]

And so White left the effort to convince Spratling to testify in the hands of physician Athens Grant, who was similarly stymied by the potential witness. Spratling "still hold[s] his same old stand he has not decided to let us have any more information nor have we yet succeeded in getting him to accept the terms that you tried to so forciable [*sic*] show him the night that you were here with us." Nor had Grant any luck with "the Miller boy" who also claimed to have been present at the Turner lynching.[42]

A frustrated White pressed Grant to work with Cobb and Broadnax to persuade Spratling to testify about what he saw. Grant had been the one who told White that eight additional lynchings had occurred since his last appearance, and White also pressed him to provide those names. No case could go forward without names and testimony. It was another set of claims that proved fruitless for White.[43]

In lieu of Spratling's cooperation, the NAACP began discussing the idea of sending a group of white undercover detectives down to Quitman to settle there for a while and create a report from white sources about what happened. "This would be a pretty expensive process," Shillady admitted, one that might push past the NAACP's budget.[44] Shillady also continued the organization's effort to press Governor Dorsey to act, though Dorsey maintained that he had not "had opportunity to learn the facts concerning the lynchings to which you refer." It was his common answer, the common answer of many southern leaders. He was opposed to lynching, he told Shillady, but he did not have enough evidence to prosecute anyone for the crime.[45]

White then wrote to Broadnax, hoping to convince him directly to apply pressure to Spratling. He reminded the minister that Spratling's testimony in front of the Senate investigating committee was vital to the effort for a federal anti-lynch law and that the NAACP would pay for Spratling's transportation, find him a job, and "do all in our power to see that he is free from any loss because of his making the change." White was soon heading to Washington to confer with allies like Dam, Kenyon, and the other senators who Dam had been lobbying and "would be glad to have something definite to tell them."[46]

Dam, for his part, was certain as of mid-December that he had four senators willing to take up the fight, providing they "have the strongest proofs of our cause that can be obtained." That meant "the matter of that witness." The Senate had to deal with a revenue bill for much of December, but come the new year, Dam promised, "I will crowd the matter as much as I possibly can." Presuming, of course, there was a witness. The NAACP assured him they were continuing to work on Spratling.[47]

Meanwhile, in the House, the NAACP focused its attention on Illinois congressman Martin B. Madden and Missouri congressman Leonidas C. Dyer. Madden had dinner with a group of Black representatives seeking his support for lynching interventions, including James A. Cobb, lawyer and chairman of the legal committee of the Washington, DC, NAACP branch. Madden was game and promised Dyer's support, as well, and suggested Chicago politician Oscar DePriest as another potential ally.[48]

In February 1919, however, Shillady sent Dam another letter with two enclosures, additional letters from "colored men" in south Georgia providing information about the lynching rampage that "varies from that given Mr. White in the beginning." Shillady had "assurance that the information contained is reliable." The new testimonies, both unsigned, "were sent to me by a reliable colored man, head of a life insurance company in the South."[49] Shillady's letter offers no proof of intentional duplicity by White, but it does demonstrate that Shillady and the NAACP no longer believed that his account could withstand congressional scrutiny.

There is also no specific reason to think that White was told about this contradictory evidence. There is no specific evidence that these letters took the same form or substance as a series of affidavits that later appeared from leading members of Black Valdosta (see chapter 6), but it is reasonable to assume that they did, considering that the NAACP's senatorial effort brokered by Dam stopped as of that letter. The organization did not give up on a federal antilynch law by any means, but the particular effort built on the atrocities in south Georgia died quietly with that correspondence. While Shillady's cover letter survives in the NAACP's records, the accounts that it enclosed do not. There is no specific evidence that the NAACP intentionally kept those letters out of its official record or that the organization intentionally covered up the "reliable" evidence that contradicted White's original report, but it is reasonable to assume that they did. White's story of the Mary Turner lynching remained the NAACP's official version, the one that made it into the historiography, the one that was embellished upon over the years, becoming more and more gruesome in the retelling. The NAACP had much to lose if it was determined that their account had been inaccurate. No matter how horrible the actual rampage was, opponents would accuse them with some validity of sensationalizing the deaths for the group's political ends. And so Shillady shared the new information with Dam, then quietly stuck to the organization's original story, despite the new evidence that it was not true.

White's willingness to exaggerate the truth had roots that extended back to his childhood trauma in experiencing the Atlanta race riot of 1906. In his memoir he describes his father and himself bringing a shotgun to the house at his mother's insistence. The only two men in the house, Walter and his father hid his sisters and his mother in the back of the house then took up posts at the front windows. The mob reached their house, led by the son of a local grocer that he knew. As the mob moved closer, young Walter pointed his gun at the crowd, but shots from a nearby house broke up the mob and spared him from having to shoot anyone.[50]

This story changed many times over the years, embellished further in each retelling. While the experience was unquestionably harrowing, there was in reality no gun in the White household. In earlier versions there were noises from the crowd, but later White specified they were racial epithets from the mob leader. That leader was originally not identified but later became the son of a grocer whose store the family frequented. His motives for the embellishment, his biographer explains, "lie properly in his adult efforts to raise his national profile. He wanted to show whites that black men (including himself) were just like white men in their determination to be brave protectors of the family, and he wanted to stifle the rumblings of his black critics who questioned his race loyalty."[51] This kind of compensatory fabrication, done with purpose, was ostensibly for a version of the greater good, but it was fabrication nonetheless. It was the exaggeration most engage in at some point when recounting their own life stories, and it does not diminish the actual terror that the young White surely felt in the face of violent white rage. Important for White's later account of the Brooks County violence, however, is that the terror he felt and the duplicitous, racist insanity of white Atlanta in 1906 did not need embellishment. An accurate account of the Black experience of the white mob was enough to demonstrate barbarous terrorism, but White chose instead to pass a fictional account as fact, as he did again twelve years later.

MORAL PANICS AND URBAN LEGENDS

The narrative power presented by the story of the lynching of a pregnant woman was demonstrated two years prior just over a hundred miles from the site of the Turner attack. In Newberry, Florida, just outside of Gainesville, a 1916 incident had remarkable similarities to the rampage in Brooks County. When a white constable attempted to serve a warrant for hog stealing to a Black man named Boisey Long, an ensuing fight led Long to shoot and kill the constable. A white mob, organized by the Alachua County sheriff, killed one of Long's friends, supposedly for resisting arrest. Five others, two women and three men, were taken to jail, and on the morning of August 18, a white mob took them and hanged them all from the same oak tree.[52] A coroner's jury covered for the lynchers by ruling that the two women fell from the tree and choked to death. The three men climbed the tree to save them and also fell to their deaths. There were no arrests.[53] Contemporary newspaper reports gave no information on the status of the women.[54] It was another in a long line of southern horrors made possible by the pervasive racism of the region that seeped into every aspect of social, legal, and political life. Mary Dennis and Stella Young were mothers, to be sure, but neither was reported to be pregnant until the results of an NAACP investigation appeared in the *Crisis*. The exhaustive report provided a detailed account of the region and the attack; toward the end of the long article, a short paragraph noted that "Stella Long [Young] had four or five children. Mary Dennis had two children and was pregnant. The other Dennis man had a family also." The information was not sensationalized or emphasized as a cornerstone of the story. It was simply another terrible fact in a terrible case of white southern "justice."[55]

Two years later, the lynching of Mary Turner made pregnancy a vital part of such coverage. A 1919 NAACP report described another lynching rampage that took place six months after the Turner attack at the end of 1918 in Shubuta, Mississippi, claiming that two of the women killed in that case were pregnant, as well. The violence in Shubuta resulted from the murder of E. L. Johnston, a failed dentist living on his father's farm. Johnston was shot while in the process of milking a cow, and his death was assumed to be caused by a nineteen-year-old debt peonage worker on the farm named Major Clark. After what was likely a forced confession, investigators also arrested Clark's younger brother and two young women, Maggie and Alma House, aged twenty and sixteen, respectively. They were taken to the local jail, from which a white mob took them to a bridge over the Chickasaw River and hanged all four of them in another gruesome act.[56] Again the NAACP investigated and produced its own report. The group did not send White. At the time of the actions in Shubuta, he was back in south Georgia, trying to convince his witness, George Spratling, to give testimony of his account of the Turner lynching to the Senate. Instead they hired a white private investigator from Memphis, Robert Church, who discovered that both of the House sisters were pregnant as a result of sexual contact with, and possibly rape by, Johnston. When Major Clark got to the farm, he and Maggie commenced a relationship, and consequently he confronted Johnston, ultimately leading to the latter's murder, though Church could not attribute the act to a specific individual because all the principals had been killed. In the NAACP's version of the account, twenty-year-old Maggie was five months pregnant, and sixteen-year-old Alma was eight months pregnant, due only two weeks later. "Alma Howze was so near to motherhood when lynched," the NAACP report stated, "that it was said by an eye witness at her burial on the second day following, that the movements of her unborn child could be detected."[57]

Again the NAACP was the only source for the claim. In an article about the lynching, the *Baltimore Afro-American* explained that Shubuta was rural and disconnected from the civilized world. "There is only one argument that bears weight with them and that is force," the paper lamented in its outrage, a lament that could have been made about similarly rural Brooks and Lowndes Counties. "They constitute our American Huns, to whom everything else is a 'scrap of paper' except cold steel."[58] It described the lynching of two men and two women from the Shubuta bridge. But it did not mention pregnancy, as no contemporary report did, despite the fact that the victims were left to hang from the bridge for a full day and night, and the image of a young girl two weeks from childbirth would certainly have been part of any story that expressed frustration with the incident. In addition, it is scientifically impossible for an unborn child to be alive two days after the death of a mother, making the most sensationalistic and moving part of the investigative narrative demonstrably untrue. Though there is no corroborating evidence to make a case that the NAACP got the pregnancies of Maggie and Alma House wrong, the timing of the event and the similar disconnect in coverage suggest that such is the case.[59]

This is significant, because as the Shubuta lynchings were taking place in December 1918, White was desperately working to convince George Spratling to testify about the Mary Turner lynching before the Senate, an effort based almost entirely on the horrors of the lynching of a pregnant woman. Immediately the NAACP had the possibility of featuring two more pregnant women, one a teenager eight months pregnant like Turner, even though there were no corroborating accounts of visible pregnancy. In February 1919 the Georgia-based lobbying effort ultimately failed; John Shillady told Dam that contradictory information from White's report made the Turner narrative and the potential Spratling testimony unhelpful for the effort. After canceling the campaign in February, however, Shillady continued publicly endorsing White's account, even though he had new evidence that it was not true. And so in April 1919 the NAACP published *Thirty Years of Lynching in the United States,* which featured the stories of Mary Dennis, Mary Turner, and the House sisters. The next month, in May 1919, the story of the pregnant House sisters, taken advantage of by an overbearing sexual predator, was featured in the *Crisis*—a story with a familiar ability to horrify, particularly in its impossible description of a fetus still moving in the womb two days after its mother's death.[60]

These women were resisting white oppression, engaging in what Patricia Hill Collins defends as "Black feminist thought" in pushing back against racist actions, and the reaction proved deadly.[61] Black women, dispossessed by both race and gender, found themselves suffering differently from their Black male counterparts, their voices subsumed into a largely male public sphere and their femininity disregarded as inauthentic in a white South that used the protection of white womanhood as a common justification for its violent acts. Representations of Black women as lynching victims played on conceptions of their vulnerability, giving them a political audience they were never able to have in life. But because that audience was built from assumptions of vulnerability, their strength was diminished even in death. The creation of pregnancy narratives for some of those women placed a new actor in the narrative, one perceived to be even more vulnerable, further diminishing the role of the female victim at the same time that it elevated her presence. The ubiquity of the Mary Turner story, for example, is based almost entirely on her pregnancy, elevating her death while diminishing her life to a particular vulnerability. Of course, pregnancy is a distinguishing marker of femininity, and the use of her death as a tool against racialized mob violence was designed, at least in part, to push back against the narrative of the protection of white womanhood constantly paraded by white vigilantes, but such was not an example of Black feminism in the service of contradicting white chauvinism. Mary Turner and the other supposedly pregnant victims of racial violence were reduced to symbols marshaled, at least with respect to the structural leadership of the NAACP, by male actors to convince other male actors to pass a law to curb the violence of other male actors. As bell hooks has explained, "When black people are talked about the focus tends to be on black men; and when women are talked about the focus tends to be on white women."[62] The power of those symbols was rooted in pregnancy rather than gender, as hundreds of other female victims were not elevated to Turner's status. "Appropriation of the marginal voice," hooks reminds us, "threatens the very core of self-determination and free self-expression for exploited and oppressed peoples."[63]

The act of Black women "speaking as an equal to an authority figure" was "a courageous act—an act of risk and daring."[64] Audre Lorde has described "the transformation of silence into language and action" as an act that "always seems fraught with danger."[65] Turner's act was both courageous and fraught with danger, to be sure. She existed in what Frances Beale famously described as Black women's state of "double jeopardy": "As blacks they suffer all the burdens of prejudice and mistreatment that fall on anyone with dark skin. As women they bear the additional burden of having to cope with white and black men."[66]

"The importance of any one factor in explaining black women's circumstances," argues Deborah King, "varies depending on the particular aspect of our lives under consideration and the reference groups to whom we are compared. In some cases, race may be the more significant predictor of black women's status; in others, gender or class may be more influential."[67] For Turner race was the determinative factor in the last moments of her life, and gender was the determinative factor in her life after death. It was a modification of the traditionally understood intersectionality between the two dispossessions, as the tangled cord of race and gender discrimination was pulled taut and knotted at the point of her murder, race dominating on one side of the cord, gender on the other.

"After World War I, rather than explaining lynching as an outcome of deeply rooted racist structures and institutions," explains Amy Louise Wood, "African American activists increasingly attacked lynch mobs, in their primal savagery, as disgraces to democracy and modern civilization," and nothing could be more disgraceful than the lynching of a pregnant woman.[68] The Tolnay-Bailey-Beck Database of Southern Lynch Victims at the CSDE Lynching Database lists seventeen female lynchings in the 1910s. The four victims the NAACP claimed were pregnant, all of whom were central to the push for anti-lynching legislation, were 23.5 percent of the total, a percentage that disappeared in the decades before and the decade after.[69] It is possible that this spike is a coincidence, but when combined with the evidence available for the Turner lynching, that possibility seems less than likely. To be sure, white lynch mobs likely never took pregnancy into account when violently attacking Black women, as the Gainesville attack demonstrates. Bloodlust was not abated by such concerns, and Black women remained extremely vulnerable to white assaults, whether sexual violence or mob murder. This particular spike, however, demonstrates that in this case, something is amiss.

A contextual framework for this kind of development can be found in the literatures of urban legends and moral panic. Moral panic, as first described by sociologist Stanley Cohen, is an explosion of fear or broad concern about a threat from a specific source. Cohen's study involved a perceived epidemic of violence among British youths in the mid-1960s. Media coverage targeted Mods and Rockers, two dominant factions of English youths, for violence and vandalism. Stories were exaggerated. Some were fabricated. Cohen's formulation included the signaling of "folk devils," deviant stereotypes that become the focus of public concern and anger.[70] Typically the fear of such devilry is exaggerated and takes on a life of its own beyond the reality of whatever threat might actually exist. When threats are culturally constructed, they only really become problems when there is a consensus or collective group agreement that concern is warranted.[71]

While the epidemic of lynching, and the revulsion surrounding the lynching of pregnant women in the 1910s, was very different from England's teenage violence in the 1960s, they were both certainly moral panics. There are several elements that tend to define moral panics. First, there must be an increased level of concern, and corollary to that concern, there must, within at least one segment of society, be a functional consensus that the problem is real. The level of public concern in such situations is disproportionate to the actual threat, and the cited figures by those generating the panic are, in the words of researchers Erich Goode and Nachman Ben-Yehuda, "wildly exaggerated." Finally, moral panics are inherently temporary. Panics either become institutionalized or they disappear. They emerge suddenly and vanish just as quickly.[72]

Moral panics can begin because of genuine sentiment or because one of the actors has something to gain. They can start from the top down or the bottom up, or from representatives and groups in the middle—such as, for example, the media. The problem with that interpretation, however, is that organizational entities like the media do not have a moral status. There must be a preexisting latent fear to foster the development of a moral panic, but that fear must find a directed expression by a moral agent and must be carried by a facilitating entity such as the media or politicians. In the words of Goode and Ben-Yehuda, "All the organizational efforts in the world cannot create public concern where none exists to begin with. At the same time, concern needs an appropriate triggering device and a vehicle to express itself in a moral panic, and for that, interest group formation and activity are central."[73]

The interest group in this particular scenario is the NAACP. It might be difficult to view any campaign against lynching itself as a moral panic, particularly as lynching was just one in myriad forms of violence—physical, economic, emotional, sexual—practiced on the Black population in the early twentieth century. That difficulty remains even though public fascination with and revulsion over the practice created a definitional moral panic. It is less difficult, however, to see the lynching of pregnant women as a moral panic. As Amy Kate Bailey and Stewart E. Tolnay have explained, the percentage of lynching victims who were women was relatively constant and never constituted more than 5 percent of the total during any time period.[74] In the decade of the 1910s, that percentage was the lowest of any corresponding decade, at only 3.7 percent. The percentage of supposed pregnant women lynched was 0.8.[75] And yet a pregnant woman, and pregnant women more broadly, pushed by the NAACP became the symbol of the monstrosity of lynching in the effort to convince Congress to pass federal anti-lynching legislation in 1918 and 1919.

They became such semiotic representations, if this account is correct, through urban legend. A legend, as social psychologists Richard LaPierre and Paul Farnsworth explained in 1936, "is a rumor that has become part of the verbal heritage of a people."[76] They are "specific propositions for belief" that are passed from person to person "without secure standards of evidence being present."[77] They are a form of apocryphal folklore whose source is always at least one person removed. Market analysts like D. Todd Donovan, John C. Mowen, and Goutam Chakraborty have interpreted urban legends as "morality plays that socialize consumers by providing warnings to others about what may happen if one misuses resources."[78] Marco Guerini and Carlo Strapparava describe urban legends as a form of folklore "just plausible enough to be believed." They are "marked by a tension between the credible and incredible," a combination of the informational qualities of the news and the emotional qualities of a fairy tale.[79]

Perhaps the most authoritative voice on urban legends is folklorist Jan Harold Brunvand, who interprets them as a "subclass of folk narratives" that, unlike fairy tales, are believable and, unlike myths, are set in the recent past and concern only human beings rather than, say, gods or spirits. To stick in the cultural mind, urban legends need "a strong basic story-appeal, a foundation in actual belief, and a meaningful message or 'moral.'" When they do have those elements, and they do stick in the cultural mind, they become "folk history, or rather quasi-history."[80]

The pregnancy narrative in the federal anti-lynch law fight falls well within the urban legend paradigm as established by folklorists. And Mary Turner unquestionably became part of the verbal heritage of the lynching narrative. There was no secure standard of evidence for the story of Turner's pregnancy or the attack on her fetus, and the information on which the tale was based was secondhand when White reported it and at a further remove when it spread. The NAACP presented it as a morality play, plausible enough to be believed, to help bolster its push for federal legislation. In addition, it was not the only urban legend in this regard. The narrative of the Shubuta lynchings several months after Turner's death also traded in pregnancy rumors, at least part of which were demonstrably untrue. More important, such stories were important tools for Black parents teaching their children about the dangers they faced in a southern apartheid state beset by racial violence. They became visceral representations of what could happen to those who traversed the racial line, demonstrating how dangerous white people could be and the all-too-real threats they could pose at any moment. The pregnancy claims, then, can be interpreted as exclamation points on dispositive educational sentences that amplified the problems faced by a group who lived in a constant state of trauma and danger that was oppressive in its ubiquity.

In that sense, elaborations on the stories of lynchings can be seen as versions of Henry Louis Gates's motivated signifying, which "functions to redress an imbalance of power, to clear a space, rhetorically. To achieve occupancy in this desired space, the Monkey rewrites the received order by exploiting the Lion's hubris and his inability to read the figurative other than as the literal." Such signifying "alters fundamentally the way we read the tradition, by defining the relation of the text at hand to the tradition. The revising text is written in the language of the tradition, employing its tropes, its rhetorical strategies, and its ostensible subject matter, the so-called Black Experience."[81] If Turner's violent and horrific death serves as the original text, the development of urban legends about the nature of that violence and horror becomes the revising text, written in the language of the tradition of the Black Experience, reading the figurative power of the violence to redress an imbalance of power.

That being the case, such disconnects between public discourse and actual fact were not, in the main, nefarious; most were borne of well-intentioned confusion or specific instructional intent. It was also a common issue in the formal reporting of lynchings, because the perpetrators themselves often stayed quiet about their experiences and actions. In the reporting of female lynchings, that confusion was even more common. Of those seventeen women lynched in the 1910s, for example, the story of many was disrupted, incomplete, or wrong, and no such disruptions were about pregnancy in particular.

Take, for example, the lynching of the Barber family in Monticello, Georgia, two hundred miles north of Brooks County, on January 14, 1915. The local police chief, J. P. Williams, had attempted to arrest Daniel Barber and his wife, Matilda, for bootlegging liquor; the Barbers resisted arrest, and Williams shot and killed Matilda. That led Barber, his son Jesse, and his two daughters, Ella and Eula, to attack Williams and beat him violently. All four were arrested, and once word spread, a mob of angry whites coalesced at the jailhouse, overtook the guards, and dragged the family out. They were taken to a large tree in the center of the Black section of town and hanged, another overt, violent display intended to reinforce the line of white supremacy and traumatize Black citizens.[82]

In the account of historian Maurice C. Daniels, both Ella and Eula were married adults. Barber was forced to watch as his three children were lynched before he joined them in death on the same grotesque tree.[83] It is an interesting comparative case, as Ella and Eula Barber, like Mary Turner, were lynched after white action against a family member. Though there was never a pregnancy claim about the two sisters, information about them varied based on the source. Daniels's version of events mostly jibes with that of the white *Atlanta Constitution* and the Black *Baltimore Afro-American*.[84] The *Chicago Defender* added that both Ella and Eula Barber were raped before being lynched.[85] In the *Atlanta Independent*, they were described not as adults but as young girls.[86] The *Augusta Chronicle*, a white newspaper with a strong anti-lynching reputation, gave the most attention to the attack. While providing far more detail about the event, the paper turned the order of lynching on its head, claiming that it was the father who was lynched first, followed by his children. There was no mention of marital status.[87] The *Denver Star* listed Eula as Bula, as did several other sources, and added further specificity. Bula/Eula was twenty years old and was lynched first. She was then cut down, and her sister was hanged with the same rope and shot repeatedly as she swayed from the branch. Other sources listed their last names as Barker.[88] Such variances in reporting only demonstrate the ease with which urban legends can develop in light of such informational disparities.

As another example, women lynched in the 1910s often were described as "demented," as in the 1917 case of Emma Hooper in Louisiana. For Anne Beston, lynched in Pinehurst, Georgia, in 1912, "her disposition was warped and she took on the animal nature of her surroundings." (Not only was Beston considered warped, but like the Barbers and Turner, her name was often confused. She was Anne Beston, Baston, Boston, and Barksdale, depending on the source.) Similar claims were made regarding Rosa Richardson, who killed a young white girl in her charge in 1914 near Orangeburg, South Carolina.[89] Such confusions were hardly intentional, and those spreading them were justifiably outraged at the atrocities, but when white racial murders occurred in areas where white-controlled media dominated, and the closed society of the South stanched dissemination of the full accounts of racial murder, speculation was often part of the journalistic effort to fill in gaps in the stories.

There was one other pregnancy claim in an infamous Georgia lynching, one that happened at the close of World War II, just as the Turner lynching had happened at the close of World War I. In July 1946 two married couples were killed near Moore's Ford Bridge just outside of Monroe. Roger and Dorothy Malcolm and George and Mae Dorsey were working as sharecroppers on the Walton County farm of J. Loy Harrison. After Roger Malcolm was arrested for the alleged stabbing of a local white man, Harrison brought Dorothy and the Dorseys and drove to Monroe, Walton's county seat, to bail Roger out of jail. As the five of them drove back to Harrison's farm, they were stopped by a white mob at Moore's Ford Bridge, which spanned the Apalachee River. Harrison claimed to have protested, but the mob took his four Black passengers, tied them to a nearby tree, and shot them. It was a generation after the Turner lynching, but there were legitimate similarities. The governor, Ellis Arnall, claimed to disapprove but conducted no investigation. At the same time, the Moore's Ford lynching spurred attempts at federal anti-lynching legislation that ultimately failed in Congress. This time the effort was spearheaded by President Harry Truman, but white southern legislators were able to stop passage of a bill. The main similarity with the assaults in Brooks County, however, was the persistent rumor that the victims were pregnant. Some said that both of the female victims were in a state of pregnancy, and that their fetuses were ripped from their wombs and killed in a vicious repeat of the Turner saga. Eventually the pregnancy claims focused on Dorothy Malcolm, who was rumored to have been seven months pregnant at the time of the attack. The rumors were not true, but that did not make them any less persistent, despite the fact that in 2,790 FBI interviews spanning thousands of pages, Malcolm's pregnancy appears in only eleven lines of transcriptions. When the NAACP produced its report on the later tragedy, it did not include a pregnancy claim in the document. "There was no proof of these things," argues historian Laura Wexler. "Yet those who told the stories and those who listened to them didn't need proof. The history of lynching made the stories believable, even if they weren't true."[90]

Perhaps even more pressing to the instability of lynching narratives, the lore of the Moore's Ford attack also appeared similar to its Brooks County predecessor. The FBI investigated the lynchings but constantly received mixed messages, often from the same witnesses over time, about what happened that night. Even the stabbing victim, who expressed seemingly genuine remorse about the killings ostensibly enacted in his name, changed his story when the FBI came calling, claiming not to know who the guilty parties were. The communist *Daily Worker* reported without attribution that Georgia governor Eugene Talmadge had met with the stabbing victim's family, insinuating a racist coverup at the highest state level. The NAACP leaked two supposed eyewitness accounts that it had discovered through its own investigation, but the statements did not even have the right location for the lynchings. Still, normally reliable news outlets like the *Chicago Defender* ran with the story when a local preacher claimed to have found two eyewitnesses, even though they were the two unreliable NAACP narrators. Harrison was the only known witness, and his changing story about the events soon made him a suspect in the case. In 1991 a man came forward claiming to be an eyewitness to the crime, accusing Harrison and three other men of the killings and two local law enforcement officials of threatening him to keep quiet. All of the accused were dead, but people wanted to believe the story because it provided a measure of closure to the case. But as Wexler has demonstrated, the 1991 version of events does not hold up to scrutiny. Throughout the 1990s the self-identified witness told his story, but the story continued to change. Toward the end of the decade, during a 1998 memorial for the victims, the supposed mother of one of the dead was brought on stage, and yet she was not actually the victim's mother.[91]

The lore of the event developed in its immediate aftermath, and in the decades that followed, even those closest to the violence were unable to relate in any kind of uncontested way what really happened, beyond the reality of the deaths themselves. Instead each was forced to choose the story that sounded most reasonable based on individual preference and claim it as truth. That kind of confusion of multiple clarifications is the soil from which panics and legends grow, creating an unstable narrative that can never be validated with certainty.

The presentations in both white and Black newspaper accounts clearly play a role in maintaining moral panics and spreading urban legends like those in the cases of Turner, the Houses, and Dorothy Malcolm. Historian Susan Jean describes a particularly ugly scene in Polk County, Florida, in June 1900, where a Black man killed a white man with an axe, and as a result the Black man was lynched. In different newspaper accounts, the reason for the axe murder and the way it happened were completely different. The lynching itself was completely different, as well. In the local newspaper, the murder happened as the result of an unnamed disturbance. The Black man then hid in the local Black Mason lodge until a sheriff's posse found him and took him into custody. Officers tried to protect the man, but eventually the mob had its way, absconding with the assailant and shooting him. In the white *Tampa Tribune*, as the story spread farther and to a larger market, the narrative changed. The Black man was "a notorious negro" who chopped off the head of a respectable white citizen for apparently no reason. When the white man's fellow upstanding white friends found his decapitated corpse, a group went and confronted the Black man, who confessed to the crime. The group then brought him back to the scene of his grisly act and shot him. The story had grown so much in transit to Tampa that it was barely recognizable. Even the names were different. In the local paper, the axe murderer's name was Sam Smith. In Tampa it was Bob Davis.[92]

This kind of spread, with stories growing in both severity and white justification through time and space, is the hallmark of urban legends. Everyone, however, white or Black, had something to gain in the stakes game of representing lynching. And as the stories of female lynchings in the 1910s demonstrate, the sensationalism related to such storytelling was only exacerbated when gender became part of the paradigm. Portions of the stories of the lynchings of Mary Turner, Maggie and Alma House, Ella and Eula Barber, and Ann Beston were demonstrably wrong, and for Turner and the House sisters, that wrongness was directly related to claims about their pregnancy, stories that changed in time and space. As the story changed in Tampa. As it did in white and Black newspaper coverage. As urban legends did when driven by a broader moral panic stoked by the specific exigencies of gender and potential pregnancy.

CHAPTER FIVE

Institutional White Supremacy

In the same edition of the Thomasville newspaper that reported on the killing of Sidney Johnson, the paper reported the killing of Jim Cobb, a Black man lynched in nearby Cordele. Cobb had been taken from the county jail by a white mob after being accused of murdering Lillie Mae Tyson Simmons, the young wife of local planter Roy Simmons, a white woman who, along with a local Black farmer, had recently paid off Cobb's debt and pulled him off a chain gang. The murder of Simmons was brutal. She was beaten to death with an iron crowbar and stabbed repeatedly with a silver table fork. When another of Simmons's workers discovered her, she had been dead for hours, her two-year-old son crying on the kitchen floor beside her, tugging on her to try to wake her up.

THE MURDERS SPREAD

Cobb was pulled from the Cordele jail by a mob of more than four hundred people and taken in a procession of more than seventy-five cars seven miles to the site of Simmons's death on Tremont Road to be hanged for his alleged crime, his body then riddled with bullets. Before the makeshift execution, leaders of the mob tried to convince Cobb to confess, but he remained steadfast until the end that he was not guilty. So frightened was the Black community by the mob that no family member would claim Cobb's body and no Black undertaker agreed to handle it. Thus, in the words of the *Atlanta Constitution,* "it was finally burned as the only way of disposing of it." A coroner's inquest of Simmons's death placed blame for the killing on Cobb, giving a kind of official sanction to the lynching.[1] No one from the lynch mob was prosecuted or even mentioned in coverage of the attack.

In this situation, too, Dorsey wired Crisp County sheriff John Henry Ward, asking if he needed additional support in the form of a troop presence. Ward, however, declined, arguing that local authorities could handle the brief but deadly uprising. The mob in this case acted despite pleas from the murdered woman's father not to lynch Cobb, and Roy Simmons, her husband, was in November arrested for committing the crime, making a mockery of the original coroner's inquest, laying bare white racist rage, and indicating Cobb's innocence.[2]

The Cobb lynching demonstrated that the general state of race antagonism that accompanies a riot creates aftershocks that reverberate throughout the region. The day after the Smith murder, for example, on May 17, Mitch Williams, a Black man caught in Florida the month prior and extradited to Macon County, Georgia, for murdering a white man, Foster Deal, thirteen years prior, was convicted on very little evidence and sentenced to die on June 14.[3]

Just four days prior to the murder of Hampton Smith, a Black man in Dublin, Georgia, southeast of Macon, was killed after himself killing a white man in a knife fight. Bubber Fullwood had received wounds in the knife fight against Arthur Kinchen, but Kinchen took the worst of it, and in retribution his son chased down and killed Fullwood. It was not a lynching per se, but it was the retributive murder of a Black man by a white man, and the younger Kinchen was not arrested for the attack.[4]

On May 19 Will Anderson, a Black worker, was hiding in the Alapaha River swamp, on the run from a white Turner County mob after being accused of striking the farmer he was working for, Robert W. Pope, after Pope refused to pay him for his time on the farm. Reports claimed that he struck Pope's wife, as well, and though neither of them were seriously injured, the breach of etiquette and the assault, however minor, carried an obvious death sentence in the racially charged climate of south Georgia.[5] It is possible, though unproven, that Anderson's could have been one of the unidentified bodies later pulled from the river in Walter White's account.

Slightly farther north in Barnesville, on May 21, Black farmworker Ed Calhoun was assumed to have murdered farmer John A. Willis. Calhoun had recently arrived in Barnesville from Jacksonville, Florida, and had disappeared after a local mob formed to find and kill him in retribution. The mob in Barnesville was led by the town's police chief, Z. T. Evans. The group found the frightened Calhoun, whom they cornered in an old house. He got a couple of shots off in his defense, one grazing Evans's shoulder, but the mob set the house on fire, forcing their prey to jump from a window and run. That was when "dozens of guns were turned on him and he fell dead." The mob then carried the body into town on the running board of a car and dumped it in the local park for residents to view, spreading trauma throughout Barnesville's Black population.[6]

At a special meeting of the Colquitt County city council on May 27, ten days after the Smith murder, white heads of industry and employers of Black servants met to decry "alleged intimidation of negro labor by a small element of white men." They claimed that Black workers were being terrorized, threatened with violence, and in two cases even assaulted. It was, in reality, a small-town attempt to end what the governor of Florida had already taken action to stop, the recruitment of Black labor out of the notoriously brutal and racist region, to provide Black workers the opportunity to escape debt peonage and Jim Crow. It was an understandable threat to both the economy and social well-being of the region's white elite, and they were willing to use violence to maintain their hegemony.[7]

On Saturday, June 1, Moultrie policeman David I. Murphy shot and killed Earnest Monroe. The officer attempted to arrest Monroe for drinking, which was one of many flimsy excuses white police used to arrest Black suspects, to create a fine they could not pay and ultimately force them into peonage. Monroe jerked away and told the officer to "stand back." He did not point a pistol at the policeman, but he had one, and a frustrated Murphy shot and killed him. An all-white coroner's jury ruled unsurprisingly that the killing was justified.[8]

Also in early June, four Black prisoners broke out of the Lowndes County jail. They were able to cut and bend part of the cell's metal wall and crawl through to freedom. They had found a wrought-iron bar and sharpened it into a saw. Their charges ranged from burglary to selling whiskey, but the escape reinforced to white Brooks and Lowndes Counties that lynch law for violent crime was justified as a form of swift and responsible justice. Black prisoners could escape from jail. Mob violence would eliminate the possibility by removing bureaucracy and guaranteeing a finality to the event.[9]

In mid-June another mob formed and found a victim in nearby Moultrie. This time, a Black man named Sam Brown was drinking and "walking up and down the road," causing "quite a little disorder and excitement." Locals responded by calling the sheriff, who tried to convince Brown to come to the station. Brown refused, and the argument ultimately led the two into a shootout, wherein both men emptied their guns but neither managed to hit his target. Brown ran into a cornfield and disappeared. Despite the fact that no one was injured, a white mob formed nonetheless, goaded in part by the racial animus driving much of the white rage in south Georgia. The sheriff, W. W. Boyd, urged the mob to disperse, telling them that he would get Brown the following day. To no avail. The mob continued to grow in size, and "spread out over the country looking for Brown." One of the mob factions was stationed near the Bethel School and saw a man walking down the sidewalk, who they thought was possibly Brown. The mob called out to him to hold up his hands. He refused and, assuming he was going to be attacked, pulled his own gun. The crowd responded by gunning him down. The man was not Brown, however. He was H. T. Jones, a white Thomas County farmer who died as the result of his wounds. In response his family swore out warrants against three members of the mob, Bill Radney, John McCracken, and Dave Knott, each of whom were indicted on a manslaughter charge. It was a fiasco, but one endemic to the mob mentality. When white men were killed, charges followed. "The negro," the media reminded its readers, "is still at large."[10]

The *Moultrie Observer*, which had defended mob violence over and against the criminality of the Black population when describing the Turner case, changed its stance in response to the accidental Jones killing. "The negro should have been apprehended and punished" by law enforcement, the paper reasoned. "When the best is said of the mob it cannot be justified," went one editorial. "And where the mob takes the enforcement of law in hand there is bound to be mistakes made." It was yet another example of the variable positioning of local accounts of violence. Brown was eventually arrested. He pleaded guilty to carrying a concealed weapon, but the superior court charged him with assault with intent to murder.[11]

Meanwhile, Black soldiers were heading off to war. On June 22 seventy-four Black draftees from Lowndes County departed for Camp Gordon, northeast of Atlanta in DeKalb County. Hundreds gathered at the train station to see off the troops, crying and hugging and celebrating service to the country. Women of the "colored auxiliary" of the Red Cross were there to provide the men a bagged lunch for the trip. The following month, another eighty-five Black draftees repeated the ceremony en route to Camp Gordon. It was a blatant, overt reminder that real citizenship was being denied to those who were making national sacrifices during World War I.[12]

Still, white paranoia did not dissipate easily. In August a Black man named Ike Radney was charged with assault in Colquitt County and was being taken to Albany for fear of his safety when a mob took the prisoner, hanged him from a tree, and repeatedly shot the body. "Two wrongs don't make a right, and the person who took part in the lynching only committed a greater wrong than that which the Negro was charged with having committed," the white Albany press inveighed. "Every one of them is a murderer and ought to be tried and convicted as such." But they were not tried, of course, much less convicted. The names of the murderers were never even publicly disclosed.[13]

None of these attacks prompted Dorsey to send troops as he had in May. In August, however, a strike of both streetcar workers and employees of the Swift Spinning Mills in Columbus led the governor to send two companies of soldiers from Camp Gordon to take control of the city and place it under martial law.[14] Meanwhile Dorsey quietly watched as the state's racial violence continued without using the force at his disposal to quell it. And so there was more.

In early September a white Macon mob lynched John Gilham, a Black man accused of an assault on two white women in Jones County and a murder in Ware County. He had escaped from a chain gang and after hiding in the swamps for ten days was discovered by two Black men who immediately turned him over to police, surely knowing what was to come. Later that month seventeen-year-old Sandy Reeves was accused of assaulting a young white girl near Blackshear. He was taken from his arresting officers on their way to Waycross and lynched just outside of town.[15]

In September 1918 in nearby Fargo, just outside of Homerville, a white man robbed and murdered Jim Jones, a Black man who had just earned $2.50 for some work for the owner of the local mill store.[16] Meanwhile, in Colon, just below Fargo, a drunken Black man, Preston Riley, ran through the town's Black neighborhood with a shotgun, shooting two residents and leaving others fleeing into their cabins. Though no one died, it was a mass shooting of rural Black residents in the midst of an overarching period of racial violence. The *Valdosta Times*, less concerned about the incident because of its Black victims, wryly explained to its readers that "it was the quality of booze that makes a bad negro worse."[17]

Just days after the rampage, citizens in the small Colquitt County town of Funston ginned up their own lynch mob after rumors spread that a local Black child had attempted to enter the house of a nearby prominent farmer. The mob caught the boy and planned to lynch him until cooler heads convinced the mob to allow an investigation of the charge. It turned out that the boy had walked by the house and put his hand on the fence gate. The white children playing in the yard were so upset that a Black boy would touch the fence that they ran inside and cried to their parents, which began the rumor that ended in the capture of the boy. The mob released its captive.[18]

In December 1918 four Black prisoners in Bainbridge, another south Georgia town in Decatur County, were murdered on a chain gang by a white guard. The guard claimed that when he dropped his gun, a Black convict picked it up and tried to shoot him. After he recovered his gun, he killed the prisoners who were Black, leaving two white convicts alive.[19]

As Leon Litwack has noted, lynch mobs were relatively unconcerned about proof of guilt or innocence. The lynching spectacle was about providing African Americans in a given region with an example, "knowing full well," as one Black southerner explained, "that one Negro swinging from a tree will serve as well as another to terrorize the community." It was an important point, one that distinguished race riots from the lynch mob. The actions of the white people of Brooks County, and to a lesser extent Lowndes, as well as those of whites in Thomas County and Berrien County, spreading across a wide regional swath, demonstrate that this was not a group in search of the lynch mob's "one Negro swinging from a tree." Instead they carried with them the white rage and body count of the riot mobs that were endemic in the country between 1917 to 1921.[20]

Through the remainder of 1918, the region was, in the words of Stewart E. Tolnay and E. M. Beck, a festival of violence. But lynching was not the only violence afoot. On May 21, with the lynching rampage still ongoing, the Milltown Manufacturing Company, just outside of Valdosta, went up in flames, doing $45,000 of damage and temporarily putting between four hundred and five hundred workers out of a job. While the plant's planing mill and dry kiln were spared, the company lost roughly $4,000 worth of lumber. The fire did not start at the plant's boilers, leading many, particularly in the heated climate of the race riot, to assume foul play. The two watchmen on duty, however, claimed to have seen no suspicious characters. The plant was owned by J. A. J. Henderson of Ocilla and was valued, when timber rights were included, at more than $200,000.[21]

The *Griffin Daily News* placed the blame for the Milltown fire at the hands of an "incendiary who fired" the plant. The *Valdosta Times* agreed. The plant "was engaged, almost entirely, in cutting lumber on government contracts," the *Times* reported. "This, together with the mysterious origin of the fire, has suggested sabotage to the minds of many, although there is nothing else, so far, to bear out this theory."[22]

The race trouble was such that Valdosta officials, worried about continued violence, closed the city's pool rooms and skating rinks as places where nefarious machinations might occur. On July 12 police chief Calvin Dampier issued an order requiring all domestic servants to carry work permit cards on them at all times. White workers were exempted, of course, but Dampier ordered his officers to arrest any Black woman without a card. "Several respectable women have been the object of insulting remarks hurled at them by burly white policemen," reported the *Chicago Defender*. Dampier was "known as the 'cock of the walk' in this city," and was responsible for "lynching a woman, Mrs. Mary

Turner, her husband and two other members of our Race."[23] As the *Defender* alluded to, it was a decidedly gendered move in the short time after the Turner lynching had brought such ignominy to the region. It was also an effort at intimidation during a time of intense racial tension. Requiring work permit cards was, to many at the time with a living memory of the practice, a version of the slave passes dispersed in the region and throughout the antebellum South that allowed the Black population to move from plantation to plantation and place to place.

Dorsey was eventually overwhelmed by the glut of racial violence and finally felt compelled to speak publicly. On July 3 he gave an address to the Georgia legislature denouncing lynching. "Mob violence should be suppressed," he said, "and by state authorities." The governor's office needed authority to act immediately upon hearing of potential lynching scenarios rather than "having to await a call for military assistance from local authorities." He argued for indictments of mob members by state grand juries and trials held in counties away from where the violence took place. "While this is drastic, still I submit that the nature of the offense against the sovereignty, peace, order and dignity of the state is such as to warrant these measures."[24]

It was a bold statement, one that gave many the false impression of an executive crackdown on mob violence. Mobs, riots, and unlawful assemblies, after all, were already illegal in Georgia, as was lynching. "Death as a result of lynching is murder and punishable as such," said the Georgia Code of 1914. "Riots, routs, unlawful assemblies, etc., are criminal," as well. In September, then, the NAACP again wrote the governor, this time about the murder of John Gilham, attempting to demonstrate that the aftershocks of the rampage were still felt in the region. "We urge, indeed, we implore you to exercise all the powers of your office and call to consultation leading men of Georgia in a determination to remove this foul blot of unpunished lynchings from the fair name of your State."[25]

For all that talk, however, no members of any of the era's Georgia mobs met justice in a court of law. Prosecutions for the crimes in Brooks County, in fact, actually went the other way.

SHORTY FORD

One of the great pending questions of the Hampton Smith murder was the identity of the mysterious "Julius," said to have been a participant in the killing but since seemingly vanished into thin air. He loomed like a specter over white locals who wanted further recompense for the original crime. Known as "Black

Trouble" or "Black Terror" in the local press while he was still at large, the press knew of the would-be suspect only that he possibly came from Macon. "The negro Julius, 'Black Terror' and other scary names applied to him, is not believed to exist," the *Moultrie Observer* reported at the time of Johnson's killing, "only in imagination." If he did exist, officials were determined to find him.[26]

In late May, Ed Scott was arrested for burglary in Callahan, Florida, and shipped to Brooks County on suspicion of being "Black Trouble," by this point identified as either Julius Brown or Shorty Ford. He was not recognized, however, by anyone in the Smith family. Fearing the much deeper trouble in which he found himself in Quitman, Scott openly admitted his actual crimes as alibis for the Barney crimes. He confessed to robbing "a number of freight cars of large quantities of meat, hams, flour, lard and sugar," as well as a series of freight car robberies of "hand bags belonging to conductors and flagmen." He told his captors where he hid his finds in various locations in Waycross and Jacksonville and even outed some of his accomplices. Authorities rushed to find the stolen goods, then returned the prisoner to Fernandina on May 31 to stand trial for a Nassau County burglary.[27]

On May 31 the Associated Press reported that a Black man calling himself Rounder Ford, but who authorities believed to be Julius Brown, was arrested in Jacksonville on suspicion of his involvement in the Hampton Smith murder and held in Duval County jail. The report stated that officers were "prevented" from bringing Ford, né Brown, to Brooks or Lowndes County. Dixon Smith, Hampton's father, traveled to Jacksonville, realized that Rounder was not the perpetrator, and watched as he went free.[28]

In early June another man was arrested in Jacksonville. Edmund Nicholls, as he was originally called in the local press, was known more popularly as Shorty Ford. After being arrested he reportedly confessed to his role in the crime, and in response Dixon Smith again traveled to Jacksonville to assess the new defendant's identity. Smith was confident that this was not "Rounder" Ford, already released, and that it was, in fact, the perpetrator of the crime. His ability to identify anyone was suspect, as he was not present for the original attack, but "he did not want an innocent man brought into the trouble." Besides, the new prisoner, according to authorities, confessed. "He even told the color of the mules on the Smith farm," the *Valdosta Times* assured its readers. He described the attack and claimed that after Bertha Smith regained consciousness, the conspirators attempted to chase her as she fled to the swamp. Ford, according to the *Times* report of the confession, was from Valdosta and had worked in various garages around town. He left Valdosta on Tuesday, May 14, arrived at the Smith farm on Wednesday, and was pulled into the plot that took place on Thursday night. His confession also reportedly implicated another man, Charles Reese, from Macon, as taking part in the crime, a character who, "until the confession made by Ford, was not known in connection with the crime."[29]

The man's name, it turned out, was not Edmund Nicholls. It was Leamon Wright, known to some as Shorty Ford, who had been arrested by deputy sheriffs Mallory Jones and Frank Edwards after being pointed out by "a negro spotter from Valdosta." Wright, né Ford, was born on June 16, 1904, to Will Wright and the former Hattie Hatch in Greensboro, Georgia, far closer to Macon than to Quitman. At the time of Hampton Smith's killing and the resulting riot, he was fourteen years old.[30] Still, officials argued that he had been in Valdosta as a "for-rent automobile driver." When he first entered the local jail, he denied any involvement in the crime in south Georgia, but after several hours of interrogation, "he is declared by the officers to have made a confession which was reduced to writing and signed by him." In his confession Ford claimed that one of the men crawled under the house during part of the crime, and the *Moultrie Observer* validated the detail, reporting that "the investigation showed signs where someone had been under the house at the exact spot he described." But the officers, according to the *Times*, still had doubts about the sincerity of the confession and so waited several hours before returning to Ford to get his story again. It was the same, so again they put it in writing and had Ford sign the statement. He had "intimate knowledge of the entire tragedy," claiming that he was "one of the six or seven men who plotted the crime." At another point he claimed that there were only five conspirators and three who actually participated in the event. He claimed, according to the *Times*, "that the negro known as Head, and Hayes Turner, were in the plot, but that the negro Will Rice [*sic*], who was lynched, had nothing to do with the crime." And so the Jacksonville authorities contacted locals in south Georgia. Ford, however, knowing the racial animus in south Georgia, protested and asked to be kept in Duval County.[31]

Southern District Superior Court judge W. E. Thomas ruled on May 15, 1919, that "if the defendant be brought to Brooks County for trial in either of these cases he will be lynched, which fate, as is well known, came to others alleged to have been engaged in the same criminal acts of which the defendant stands charged." He ordered the venue for Ford's trial changed to Chatham County.[32]

In response Solicitor General Hay signed requisition papers in the name of Lowndes County officers, then sent them to Georgia governor Hugh Dorsey asking permission to remove Ford from the Duval County jail to somewhere as yet undetermined in Georgia. Dorsey agreed, but there were "complications entering into the case." There was no way Ford would be extradited to Brooks County, and it would be generally unsafe for him to go to Lowndes, as well. If he was taken to another county, that would essentially be the fault of the Brooks mob, leaving "some question about Brooks county paying the bill. And of course," the *Valdosta Times* protested, "it cannot be collected out of Lowndes county, as the prisoner does not belong here." Though rumors that Savannah would be the most logical choice were in the air, ultimately the governor would make the call.[33]

The decision was ultimately made to move Ford to Savannah, the largest south Georgia city in relatively close proximity to both Quitman and Jacksonville. The *Valdosta Times* reported that Ford had an aunt in Valdosta, Daisy Lambert, who according to authorities admitted that her nephew was the one for whom authorities had been searching, "although it has not been stated how she knew this." She was, according to the *Times*, "very glad that the boy has been caught" and wanted him to be "properly punished. However, she says she desires it should be done in a legal way." Lambert's claims were suspicious, to be sure. A poor woman who moved through several jobs from cook to laundress, and through several addresses around the city, she had no reason to lie about the relationship but also no point of reference for the man caught, particularly with the number of people already captured who had been known as "Shorty Ford."[34]

The NAACP had quieted on the case after February 1919 when it realized that White's original report had been in error, but it was still interested in outcomes related to the south Georgia rampage. "Will you be good enough to keep us informed of developments in the case of 'Shorty Ford'?" Shillady asked Dr. L. C. Crogman, secretary of Atlanta's NAACP branch. He had heard Ford was being transferred to Brooks County and was worried about the possibility.[35]

Unsurprisingly, there was error in the Ford investigation, as well. As early as March 1919, officials in Valdosta knew that Leamon Wright was not the Julius Brown or Shorty Ford known to them. "The negro known here by that name was born here and is well known to the officers. He is short and black, while the person under arrest is of much lighter color." Ford made his first confession on June 13, 1918, to Frank A. Edwards, but he never mentioned Sidney Johnson, the crime's principal actor. "Just why Lemon [*sic*] Wright made the alleged confession to the officers in Jacksonville cannot be understood," the *Valdosta Times* admitted. But it seemed false. Johnson was not mentioned probably because he was not caught until a week after the crime; he was not included in the initial body count, not someone who a reader of the initial lynching coverage would recognize. "There is a story here to the effect that when he was placed in jail at Jacksonville a negro spotter was locked up in the same cell and told him all about the crime, and it was from this source that he obtained what information he had as to the details which he gave his confession." Either way, local officials did not know Wright and did not understand his confession, but "officers and others in Valdosta are much interested in the habeas corpus proceedings instituted in Savannah."[36]

By April those hearings were over, and the *Times* assumed that Shorty Ford would stay in Chatham County and be tried in Savannah. Bertha Smith, Hampton Smith's widow, would travel to the coast to see Ford and attempt to identify him.[37]

Two weeks prior to Ford's December 1919 trial, the *Savannah Tribune*, a Black newspaper that had been an institution in the city since 1875, published an editorial on trials, mobs, lynching, and justice. "While it may to some little extent subserve the interest of law and order," the paper's editor, Sol Johnson, wrote, "the practice of rushing a wretch charged with crime through a mock legal proceeding called a trial contravenes the theory of court trials, public hearings in fair and impartial atmospheres, and justice." Johnson used the long year of mob violence as a comparative foil, focusing in particular on the massacre at Elaine, Arkansas. Individual lynchings were just as destructive, adding up to Elaines by a thousand cuts. Both were appalling tragedies, but the southern court system could not be considered a viable solution to mob violence. It was, instead, another version of it. "It is coming to the point where a thinking Negro cannot conceive the thought that any white man can be perfectly fair and impartial to any Negro when the issue at stake is as between the Negro and a white man." Not only did court trials offer a "slim chance" of actual justice, but the paper went even further, arguing that "a speedy trial is a positive and acknowledged concession to the mob."[38] Ford's trial bore out the *Tribune*'s prediction.

Ford's original attorney quit the case only a week before the trial was to begin, leaving the judge to appoint Major A. Pratt Adams and Colonel Alexander R. Lawton as his counsels. Lawton's and Adams's voices presumably held weight in Savannah's courts. Alexander Rudolph Lawton was the son of lawyer and Confederate general Alexander Robert Lawton and was prominent in legal circles of the city and the nation. Adams was from another prominent Savannah legal family, a second-generation lawyer from the University of

Georgia. Both served Ford not as advocates of racial equality or as opportunists seeking a payday but instead as part of a regular public defense rotation. Their intention was to argue that the case rested on mistaken identity, but they were new to a case that had been in the works for well over a year. The prosecution was led by Clifford S. Hay, solicitor general of the Southern Circuit, which encompassed Brooks and Lowndes Counties, and Walter C. Hartridge, solicitor general for the Eastern Circuit, headquartered in Savannah.[39]

The judge in the case was Peter Wiltberger Meldrim. Born in 1848, he had joined the Civil War effort at age sixteen to defend Savannah from General Sherman. From a wealthy Savannah family, he attended the exclusive Chatham Academy then the University of Georgia before becoming an attorney, politician, and ultimately a judge. Meldrim was moderately progressive for his time and place. He chaired the Georgia State Commission on the Education of Colored Persons from its inception in 1891. He was in the Georgia State Senate and was the mayor of Savannah. He became a superior court judge in 1917, where he would stay until his death in 1933.[40]

The trial took place on December 16, 1919. Ford was not tried for the murder of Smith but instead for criminal assault upon a white woman. Valdosta's Oscar T. Hill, a special railroad officer for the Georgia Southern and Florida Railroad who also worked in the area as law enforcement, and Bertha Smith traveled to Savannah to participate in the proceedings. Hill had been part of the sheriff's search party looking for Sidney Johnson and described the hunt in court.[41] But when Smith took the stand, she did not recognize Ford. She told the jury, however, that despite not recognizing the defendant, she was satisfied that he was guilty. The prosecution excused her inability to identify Ford by reasoning that "after being in jail for more than a year it would be hard for an inexperienced person to be absolutely sure about identifying a negro." Ford testified that he knew nothing about the crime except what he had heard of the infamous case. He argued that his Jacksonville confession was not legitimate, as he "simply signed his name to a piece of paper and that others afterwards wrote the alleged confession." In Savannah it was claimed that he made another confession to reporters, but he repudiated that statement as well. His defense claimed that the original man arrested as Shorty Ford was actually the culprit. That man had drowned in the interregnum and could not be called as a witness. On Tuesday, December 16, 1919, Shorty Ford, alias Julius Brown, alias Leamon Wright, was found "guilty without recommendation of mercy" in Chatham County Superior Court, despite his supposed victim not recognizing him, and was sentenced to be executed on February 6.[42]

Hill claimed that the real Ford had drowned near Jasper in north Florida and that he had seen the body. Calvin Dampier also testified in the trial and could not positively identify Ford. The only person willing to identify Ford as part of the cabal was Dixon Smith, Hampton Smith's father, who was not present at the time of the crime. The key to his conviction was the second supposed confession that Ford made to a Savannah reporter, in which he reportedly claimed to be from Valdosta. The white reporter testified that Ford denied being part of the murder but apparently admitted that he had driven with the conspirators to the Smith home for a potential robbery, thus leading to his implication in the crime. The defendant, however, repudiated all such claims. Thus despite the fact that Bertha Smith, Oscar T. Hill, and Calvin Dampier all essentially cleared him, a reporter's hearsay and Dixon Smith's testimony condemned the young man to death. Ford "received his sentence without a word or perceptible quiver." When asked if he had anything to say before the sentence, "he uttered two or three syllables which were not understood."[43]

The body to which Hill referred was that of a Black man fished out of the Withlacoochee River near Valdosta in May 1919, said to have been a prisoner taken from the jail in Jasper, Florida, killed, and dumped in the river, "thus," as one report put it, "adding another victim to the Hamp Smith tragedy near Barney, in Brooks County, last May."[44]

Meanwhile Brooks County was charged for the trial. Even though it was taking place elsewhere, the charge for Brooks for the Chatham County trial was three hundred dollars per day. The trial was supposed to take place on Monday, December 15, but delays in bringing witnesses from the southern part of the state delayed it until Tuesday, costing Brooks County another three hundred dollars. It was the kind of expense, along with the extensive delay in the trial, that only bolstered white rural arguments for lynch justice.[45]

In response to the guilty verdict, attorneys Lawton and Adams submitted a motion for a new trial, claiming that there was new evidence that gave Ford an alibi—he was actually in Atlanta at the time of the crime—and therefore exonerated him. Meldrim delayed the execution and ultimately, on June 23, 1920, granted Ford a new trial. Ford's lawyers presented that new evidence on July 1, claiming again that the whole ordeal was a case of mistaken identity. Mary Dozier of Newington, the defendant's aunt, identified him as Leamon Wright and said that she had never known him as "Shorty." Two additional witnesses testified at the new trial to Ford's presence in Atlanta at the time of the crime. Oscar T. Hill returned to state conclusively that the defendant was not who he had known in Valdosta as Shorty Ford.[46]

Evidence of Wright's innocence seemed overwhelming, but the prosecution, led by Walter C. Hartridge, solicitor general for Savannah's Eastern District, had the advantage of white supremacy and its assumptions in communicating to the white jury. Hartridge was a Savannah native, educated in the city's public schools. He learned law as an apprentice in the office of Charlton and Mackall before being admitted to the bar in 1890. He was, unlike many other attorneys, relatable to a jury. When he questioned Smith's father, Dixon Smith testified as to Ford's guilt, despite the fact that he was not present at the crime. That testimony, combined with a rehashing of the dual confessions from the first trial, was enough to convince the white jury that Ford's alibi evidence was inadequate. The jury deliberated only ten minutes before convicting him again. Ford "sat calmly during the hearing of the testimony and for the first time since the beginning of the trial the prisoner betrayed perceptible signs of nervousness as he was escorted into the court room" to hear the final verdict. He "looked directly at the clerk as the verdict was announced and a moment later became trembly with a melancholy look on his face." Meldrim again sentenced him to death.[47]

In August 1920 Ford was scheduled to be executed, but his lawyers got the execution postponed through another motion for yet another trial, arguing again that there were alibi witnesses from Atlanta. Meldrim had run out of patience, however, and denied the request for a new trial. Still, the effort managed to keep Ford alive a little longer.[48]

Then another delay spared Ford yet again. His lawyers managed to get his appeal heard by Georgia's Supreme Court. The court, however, was unconvinced. Presiding justice Marcus Beck ruled that "no error is assigned upon any of the court's rulings made pending the trial." He described the appeal as relatively pedestrian in its claim that the evidence was contrary to the verdict. "Upon examination of the brief of evidence contained in the record it appears that the verdict is not unauthorized by the evidence." He affirmed the lower court's ruling. Shorty Ford was to be executed.[49]

His lawyers appealed to Governor Dorsey for a commutation of the sentence, making again the mistaken identity argument that they attempted at trial. Dorsey, however, argued that if the evidence was not compelling enough for twelve jurors, it would not be compelling enough for him. In December 1918 he had taken some criticism for not commuting the death sentence of a white Milledgeville man convicted of murdering his wife. The *Macon Telegraph* saw the execution as problematic because the man, they argued, was mentally ill. (The *Valdosta Times*, however, deeply committed to justifying racial killing, defended the governor. "All murderers are crazy to a certain extent," the paper claimed, dismissing the criticism.) Dorsey couldn't be seen as denying a white man clemency then giving it to a Black man supposedly involved in the scandalous events in Brooks County. He denied Ford clemency.[50]

Finally, on May 11, 1921, Ford was officially scheduled to be executed on June 3, the birthday of Jefferson Davis. The former Confederate leader's birthday was a legal holiday in Georgia, but Chatham County scheduled the execution of Ford and another man, Israel Water, for the day. Water was to be transferred to Bryan County before his execution, leaving Ford to die alone in Savannah. Dorsey refused to "interfere in any way" when asked to postpone the execution past the state holiday.[51] The symbolism associated with the execution was just as important as the execution itself, as it was the final Confederate-stained exclamation point on the tragic sentence that was the 1918 south Georgia race riot.

Brooks County paid for Ford's board in the Chatham County jail for the duration of his time between 1919 and 1921, "but the last check will be paid next week and this item of expense will be ended," the *Quitman Free Press* gratefully reported the day of the execution.[52]

The night of June 2 was agonizing for Shorty Ford. Chatham County sheriff M. W. Dixon scheduled his execution for the following morning and supervised the preparation of a gallows that was in full view of the prisoner. He was visited on his last day by his lawyer, but also by religious leaders, a reporter, his aunt Mary Dozier, and his girlfriend. It was when his girlfriend finally arrived that Ford broke down. Officials covered the gallows behind him as he wept in her arms, knowing that the long, drawn-out process of his legal lynching was almost at an end.[53]

His attorney had changed by 1921, his case now led by C. Graham Baughn. Baughn was a young lawyer, recommended for bar admission in 1918 by A. Pratt Adams when the latter was head of the Georgia Bar's executive committee. Baughn again announced his client's innocence on the day before his execution. He had traveled to Atlanta to corroborate Ford's alibi and discussed the case with his client. "I said to him: 'Shorty, you know you will have to die tomorrow. If you want to meet your Maker right, you must confess that you have been guilty of this crime.'" He promised his client that if he confessed, attorney-client privilege would ensure he never revealed it. Still Ford "repeated over and over again that he would die an innocent man." Ford told a reporter much the same thing. "I'm innocent, as sure as there's a God in heaven," said the sobbing, condemned man.[54]

Sheriff Dixon told the press that he had received "hundreds of applications" to be the official executioner, despite the fact that "only a sworn deputy sheriff can fulfill this duty."[55] It was a testament to the willingness of local southern white men to participate in the hangings of Black men.

On June 3, in honor of the Davis holiday, a refurbished First White House of the Confederacy was dedicated in Montgomery, Alabama, by the Sons and Daughters of Dixie. Mississippi senator Pat Harrison spoke at the dedication, calling Davis "truly the Oliver Cromwell of America." He "never want[ed] to see the glories of the South forgotten in the maelstrom of industrial strife," he told the assembled crowd. "The sentiment of the South is too dear, its heritages too priceless, its sacrifices too great, its principles too precious and enduring to be bartered, however large and alluring the price." Several living veterans of the war were on hand to celebrate the occasion. In Savannah public schools, banks, and all city and county offices were closed in honor of Davis and the former Confederacy.[56]

A crowd started gathering at the Chatham County jail early that morning. The vast majority of the early risers were Black, but soon white onlookers joined the gathering as well, an integrated group there to bear witness to a rare Savannah execution. By 10:15 the city's Habersham Street was packed for blocks down to its intersection with Liberty Street, so much so that six local police officers had to clear a path in the road for traffic.[57]

Ford, meanwhile, was waiting in his cell with a white minister, John S. Wilder of Calvary Baptist Temple, and two Black ministers, N. H. Whitmire of Mt. Tabor Baptist Church and W. F. Underwood. All three encouraged him to confess his crimes, reminding him of the danger of going to his death with unconfessed sins. Ford, however, was adamant. He had done nothing wrong. His conscience and his soul were clean. He left his cell shortly after 10:00 AM, walked to the gallows, and calmly stood as officials bound his hands with ropes and affixed the noose around his neck. Ford asked his ministerial companions to pray for him and to sing a hymn. Officials then put the death mask over his head, shielding his vision for what was left of his short life. As the preachers began to sing, the muffled sounds of Ford's singing came from inside the bag covering his mouth.[58]

The crowd had fallen into a hush just after ten o'clock in expectation of the grim denouement. All could see the killing from their position on the street, but everyone also wanted to hear the opening of the trapdoor that would signal the hanging of the convicted man. Meanwhile, inside, the two Black ministers completed a prayer. Sheriff Dixon then read the death warrant, closing with

"May God have mercy on your soul." At 10:24 the trap was dropped, the clanging of the iron door heard in the street by the hundreds of witnesses. It was three years after Hamp Smith's murder. Leamon Wright was seventeen years old.[59]

His death was not a quick process. It took attending physicians thirteen minutes to declare that the prisoner had died. He was then cut down and taken to the undertaking parlor of Andrew Monroe on Savannah's Charles Street, where the body lay all afternoon and evening. Hundreds of Black residents of the city made a pilgrimage to the facility, keeping "an unbroken line" of visitors all afternoon and evening. The procession demonstrated that white and Black spectators came to the jail that morning for two different reasons. White spectators were, for the most part, curious about a rare event in the city. Black spectators interpreted the execution as a legal lynching.[60]

The funeral was held the following day at Whitmire's Mt. Tabor Baptist Church, organized by his devastated aunt, still in town from Greensboro, before the prisoner was buried without headstone or remembrance in the strangers section of the southern portion of Savannah's Laurel Grove Cemetery. It was an ignominious end to a case dramatically affected by racist assumptions. And the racist assumptions continued. The summation of Ford's claims of innocence until the moment of his execution were portrayed in many white Georgia newspapers as a brief last statement by the accused: "Bos, I'se shore innocent."[61]

When Ford was finally executed, E. H. Griffin, editor of the *Bainbridge Post-Search Light*, saw it as a justification of the lynch mob. "It was a most horrible crime, yet the law moved so slow that he was all this time paying the price. Yet people wonder at the impatience of the public at times."[62]

CHAPTER SIX

Memory and Media

In September 1924 Beatrice Morrow Cannady wrote a letter to the editor of the *Portland Morning Oregonian* comparing the sensationalistic trial of Nathan Leopold and Richard Loeb that had just concluded to lynchings in the South. She was frustrated that the life sentence for the thrill killers was not good enough for many who wanted to see them hanged and who claimed that they had "never heard of a crime more atrocious and revolting." Those commentators must never have heard of southern lynch law, she argued, and in particular "the case of Mary Turner down in Valdosta, Ga." She recounted the general White narrative. Turner protested her husband's lynching, and for that she was strung up by her feet "and ripped open with a butcher knife, much after the fashion of dressing a beef—and her prematurely born infant cried out in protest only to have its little life stamped out under the heel of one of the mob." Based on that unpunished murder, Cannady argued that though she made no apologies for Leopold and Loeb, "I do not believe they should be hanged so long as other murderers older and worse than these boys are permitted to go free."[1]

OREGON

Cannady was in a position to know. She was Oregon's loudest voice for civil rights in the early twentieth century, editor of the state's only Black newspaper, the *Portland Advocate*. Born in 1889 in Littig, Texas, Cannady graduated from Wiley College before doing graduate work at the University of Chicago. She arrived in Oregon in 1912 to marry Edward Daniel Cannady, founder and publisher of the *Advocate*, where she almost immediately began working. A tireless advocate for Black rights, she was a founding member of the Portland NAACP chapter and was leading it at the time of her letter to the editor. Two years before her *Oregonian* editorial, she became the first Black woman to graduate from Portland's Northwestern Law School.[2]

Somehow Cannady's letter to the editor found its way to C. C. Brantley, editor of the *Valdosta Times*, who wrote to the *Oregonian* to respond to Cannady. He was either unaware of or unimpressed by Cannady's credentials. The Georgian claimed that Turner was lynched because she was part of the conspiracy to kill Hampton Smith. She "was taken out by Smith's neighbors and hanged by the neck to a tree, but there was no other act of brutality committed." In mentioning Smith's neighbors, Brantley was placing the act in Brooks County rather than in Valdosta. "We have our bad element just as Oregon has," he reasoned, but people would go to great lengths for swift justice in cases pertaining to the sanctity of white womanhood. "When lynching is resorted to in the case of an outrage against womanhood, it is not so much the spirit of lawlessness or frenzy that stirs the populace, but it is the desire of chivalrous men to get rid of an enormously bad case without making it more public," explained Brantley in defense of lynching, conveniently forgetting that Turner's death was itself an outrage against womanhood. "It is a bad system, but it is no worse than exists in other states, and is existing as the colored man carries his problem into other sections."[3]

Brantley's is an interesting document. He admitted that Turner was lynched. He defended lynching as a practice in the defense of white womanhood. He even openly expressed his racism, that it was the Black man carrying "his problem" who created race violence. His is a defense of lynching in the common southern journalistic style. It was not the equivocation of one who is claiming virtue. He made clear that the lynching did not take place in Valdosta, and in his letter took pains to explain that Sidney Johnson was the only person killed in the city, and only by police returning fire after being shot by the suspect. With that exception, however, his was an open, if ham-fisted, defense of lynching. His reason for writing was to deny that Turner's lynching happened in the manner described by Cannady, which was simply a repetition of the manner described by Walter White. For someone openly defending lynching and racism, writing this kind of letter to a far-flung newspaper to deny a particular circumstance had an unmistakable ring of truth, precisely because he did not deny the other parts of the Turner story. It is Brantley, in fact, who mentioned that there were additional lynchings that took place as a result of the Smith attack. He did not apologize for them, because he was not sorry they happened. He wanted only to clarify that they did not happen in Valdosta and that they were not comparatively different from what he assumed to be garden-variety lynchings.

Charles C. Brantley was born in Georgia on June 16, 1874, and began working for the *Times* in his early twenties. He became the active editor in the mid-1890s and the official editor of the paper in 1898. He stayed in the role until his death, with two brief interludes. In 1909 he served as secretary for Georgia governor Joe M. Brown, and for seven months in 1914 he served as associate editor of the *Macon Telegraph*. In 1929 he was part of a group that purchased the *Times*, becoming both editor and owner of the paper. Brantley was a prominent citizen, on the board of the first Valdosta Board of Trade in 1912. He was a charter member of the Rotary Club, founded the year after the tumult of 1918. His wife, Florence, was among the twenty-five founding members of the Valdosta chapter of the United Daughters of the Confederacy in 1901 and later served as the group's president.[4]

Brantley, however, was not so invested in Valdosta that he would refuse to criticize it. In June 1917 he launched a series of editorials critical of law enforcement, in particular calling into question the behavior of Lowndes County sheriff J. F. Passmore. After a series of critical articles, Passmore told Brantley that he had to stop publishing them. He refused. The harangues were such that a frustrated Passmore went to the offices of the *Times* to confront the editor. When he found that the editor was out of the office, the sheriff sought him out in the street and attacked him with a cane until concerned bystanders stopped the assault. Valdosta police arrested Passmore, and Brantley overzealously swore out a warrant for assault with intent to kill. The grand jury settled instead for an assault and battery charge, and in December the superior court fined the sheriff $250 for the attack. The controversy, taking place just months prior to the lynching rampage in May, demonstrated that Brantley was certainly willing to criticize his own and to use his local paper for more than civic boosterism.[5]

After Brantley's response, Cannady wrote to W. E. B. Du Bois to explain the situation. She wanted to verify the information in the NAACP's pamphlet on the south Georgia affair so that she could confidently respond to the Valdosta editor. Du Bois referred her letter to White, who assured Cannady that "this man has either through ignorance or dishonesty lied."[6]

Thus, White wrote his own letter to the *Oregonian* in response to Brantley, telling the story as he had been telling it since 1918, with a few changes. The mob, this time, did not respect Smith but reasoned, in a quote provided by White, "niggers must be taught that they must not touch any white man no matter how worthless the white man may be." He claimed this time that his sources were the actual members of the mob who openly bragged to him about Turner's murder and that he "corroborated all the evidence." He explained that Dorsey "made the confession to me that he was absolutely powerless even to make an investigation," that "the laws of Georgia made it impossible." Still, White remembered that an investigation "was made by certain officials acting in an unofficial capacity and the facts corroborated."[7]

It is possible that the story changed in White's mind over time, as such stories often do, but the quote was a direct contradiction of the evidence that several members of Smith's family were part of the mob. Claiming to have heard from proud members of the mob was very different from trying to coax George Spratling to testify in Washington. Georgia law did make an investigation possible, though there was no record of an unofficial investigation taking place to corroborate White's version of events. The problems in White's account seem understandable considering the temporal distance from actual events, his desire to defend his original story, and the possibility that he never knew about contradictory evidence received by John Shillady. On the other hand, it seems unlikely that Shillady would not have informed White, meaning that an interpretation that assumed a willful exaggeration of events to maintain NAACP claims would also be reasonable to make.

Brantley saw similar problems with White's account. He responded, he claimed, by making an inquiry over much of December 1924 and writing yet another response to the *Oregonian*. He began by invalidating White's evidentiary claims. "The very idea that a strange negro could talk on such intimate terms with the mob who did this lynching is preposterous," wrote Brantley, apparently not understanding White's ability to pass. He explained that Turner was known there as Hattie and that he talked with "every white man and negro who lives in that immediate neighborhood." Everyone acknowledged the lynching, but everyone also denied the pregnancy, the knifing, and the mutilation of the fetus. There was also no liquor bottle marking Turner's grave. It was a water bottle "placed there by some negro women and flowers were put in it." Turner was buried by the Black community, not the lynchers. Those to whom he spoke did not even remember her being officially married. (She was, but she had not been married in Brooks County. Turner and her husband were married the year prior in Moultrie, the seat of a neighboring county.) "She was the lowest type of negro strumpet, and was about as much entitled to be called 'mistress' as a she-bear."[8]

Brantley argued that Will Head's confession put the conspirators at Turner's house, admitting that Smith bonded out criminals to work his farm but explaining that the practice was normal in the South, that "they were not held in involuntary servitude, but were at liberty to go where they pleased." The flint that sparked the incident was the attack on Smith's wife: "It stirred the blood of the people in that section, and that they went to excess in their eagerness to avenge that brutal murder is not denied." Turner, when confronted by the mob, "flew into a rage and uttered such vile curses upon the white women of Brooks county," which in turn enraged the mob and led them to drive her down to the river and hang her. He claimed that the men knew it was a "ghastly sight" and so returned and covered the body with a rubber coat, using a gold scarf pin to keep it attached. "The report that she was in pregnancy grew out of the condition in which Mrs. Smith was when the outrage was perpetrated against her," wrote Brantley. "There was not a word of truth in the statement regarding the alleged 'Mrs.' Turner."[9]

Brantley then described the trial and execution of Shorty Ford, claiming without any evidence that it was Ford's parents who had arrived in Savannah and established his identity. That, however, was not something he could investigate in Brooks County. "I do not deny that there was a reign of lawlessness there then," he said, "but I do deny that there was no reason for it." He also openly denied that there was any similarity between what happened in south Georgia and events in East St. Louis and other locations of Red Summer race riots. "A Georgia mob goes after some particular individual and gets him, while most of the victims of the Pennsylvania and Ohio mobs have been innocent bystanders." Not only that, but "it is only the bad negroes who are ever molested" in Georgia. That was clearly untrue, as the mob in response to the Smith killing ranged far afield beyond any specific conspirators and did, in fact, act as a modern race riot. But Brantley countered with examples of contemporary punishments for white assaults of Black victims and judicial mercy for Black defendants, as if there was a one-to-one comparative ratio or that white behavior in 1924 governed white behavior in 1918.[10]

It was another in a long line of lynching justifications that used mistrust of the legal system as a valid condition for action. Christopher Waldrep places the genesis of such mistrust at least in part on the legal formalism demonstrated in early state jurisprudence through a series of inferior courts established after emancipation. "Formal procedures and customs allowed Black defendants and victims opportunities they had never had under the slavery regime," Waldrep argues, thus providing a racialized pseudo-justification for extralegal methods of control.[11] As Michael Pfeifer has explained, "Lynchers failed to assimilate conceptions of an abstract, rational, detached, and antiseptic legal process that urban middle-class reformers wrote into statutes," and the Brooks County mob and its defenders were decided exemplars of that failure.[12]

But Brantley's was also the common white southern form of argument by deflection, fitting into the mold described by Susan Jean and other historians of the lynching phenomenon. Conflicting accounts of lynchings in white mainstream newspapers, as Jean has argued, are efforts "by white southerners to control the representation of lynching." She explains that southern editors who supported lynching often attempted "to impose their own boundaries on the phenomenon," to distinguish what counted as a legitimate lynching from one that went beyond the bounds of propriety. When events did fall beyond those bounds, they demonstrated their disapproval.[13]

Brantley, however, was engaged in something different. He was not defending the lynching itself but was instead contesting the facts as presented in another account. His disapproval of lynching a pregnant woman was not, for example, a legitimation of lynching a nonpregnant woman. He was not attempting to impose his own boundaries. He was correcting the record. It was an act of civic boosterism, to be sure, but one that drifted beyond the boundaries imposed by most southern editors.

It is significant that Brantley's defense happened when it did: "Following World War I," Jean argues, "a fundamental shift occurred in the way southern whites publicly discussed lynching."[14] Prior to this period, stories of protecting the virtue of white womanhood upheld the practice in white southern journalism, but as more and more lynchings moved beyond the boundary of that particular trope, newspapers took a different tack. "White southerners sought to exert a measure of control over the practice and the representation of it through disapproving accounts of lynchings that fell outside the bounds of respectability."[15] Pushed to do so by pressure from groups like the NAACP and the exposés of investigators like Walter White, they attempted "to suppress negative publicity by at least making a show of condemnation after a lynching."[16]

Brantley next produced affidavits. They did not validate his racist excuses. Instead they were accounts that Turner was lynched in a comparatively traditional way. He produced statements by leading Black figures in the region: Rev. Thomas A. Lomax, pastor of Macedonia First Baptist Church in Valdosta; Elder Walter T. Strickland, pastor of the city's Colored Christian Church; William Lissimore, district Sunday school superintendent for Georgia and member of a prominent family in the region; Garrett Taylor, a local upholsterer who had a furniture repair business on Patterson Street, Valdosta's principal thoroughfare; and Benjamin Solomon, an undertaker with his own shop on Oak Street, all claiming that the pregnancy and knifing were "fabrication pure and simple, as no such act of brutality could have occurred without its being brought to their notice." He also had affidavits from "every citizen in the neighborhood where this alleged brutality occurred," stating that the lynching happened but "in the usual way." All "deny that she was hanged by the heels, or that her body was mutilated in any way."[17]

This reliance on the leading Black citizens of Valdosta is an argumentative tactic used in other lynching cases. Jean describes a 1901 lynching in Bartow, Florida, after which a group of Black residents wrote a public letter printed in the local newspaper condemning the actions of a Black teenager accused of raping a white woman and assuring the white population that Black Bartow did not support him and had, in fact, turned him over to authorities. "The letter suggests that there was a limited space for blacks to participate in the discussion *if* they appealed to white sensibilities," Jean argues. The letter couched itself in the language of white southern defenses of lynching but subverted such defenses by arguing that the behavior of the teenager was fundamentally unique within the community. And the white newspaper responded as the letter writers hoped it would. "It is extremely gratifying that ALL OF THE VERY BEST of our negro population stand heartily with us in this matter," the local editor proclaimed.[18]

It was language similar to that of Brantley in his *Oregonian* debate, but it differs in important contextual ways. Jean argues that the public display of solidarity in the Black citizens of Bartow was a protective measure, a way of demonstrating to white people that there was no need for further reprisal. Thus it was not only the message that made a difference but also its presentation to the local white audience. The leading Black citizens of Valdosta, meanwhile, were not providing affidavits for public consumption. The documents were never shared locally in any public forum. They were not legally binding. There might very well have been a sense of protectionism in the affidavits—we cannot know what they actually said—but it was a limited effort, to be sure. Not only were they not presented to the local white public, but also they were presented five years after the attack, when no threat of continued actions from an angry mob was pressing. Finally, it is important to note that letters like the one from representatives of Black Bartow were not false. They were simply strategic. Many surely did disapprove of rape. The Black population had in fact turned over the teenager to the authorities. Strategic thinking was not a signifier of untruth.

"It is not my purpose to defend a mob for anything it does," Brantley explained, "but it is my purpose to show that the barbarism, which these negro writers said occurred in this part of the state, never has been practiced." Barbarism was obviously a relative term. Brantley continued by quoting Alexander Stevens, Georgia's former Confederate vice president, who claimed that "no gentleman would belong to a mob," but that "mobs sometimes do things that ought to be done." Again Brantley reverted to respectability politics. He argued for Black inferiority based on a warped understanding of biology. "The negro is different from the white man; the sun does not blister his back as it does the white man's; and he can sleep standing up like a cow or a horse, which the white man cannot do."[19]

Again, Brantley was not ashamed of the lynchings or his racist understanding of the world. He justified the events of May 1918 in his own skewed, bigoted way. But when it came to Turner's method of lynching, he was consistent and adamant, even producing several affidavits that so convinced the *Oregonian* that the paper printed his lengthy six-column response. When taken together with Shillady's earlier evidence that stopped the NAACP effort in the region, and White's single, far less influential witness, Brantley's adamance only serves to bolster the historical assumption that the pregnancy and mutilation of Turner were fictive. Of course, Brantley's arguments do not constitute proof, and they do not diminish the actual brutality of lynching. There are plenty of reasons to doubt Brantley. But there are also reasons to believe him, and when taken in conjunction with other evidence, they do support the necessarily circumstantial case for Brantley's version of events.

In early March 1925, Cannady wrote to White, including a copy of Brantley's December response. A frustrated White again called the Valdosta editor a liar and assured Cannady that those producing affidavits "were intimidated into doing so or else they are the type of sycophantic creatures who are willing to sell out the race for cheap favor from white people." He would write to find out who they were.[20]

White wrote to Bishop John Hurst in Baltimore explaining the situation. "When I was in Valdosta," he told Hurst, "I talked with all of the leading colored people and I remember none of these individuals as being there at that time." That being the case, he wanted to find out "just what sort of individuals these Negroes are" and "whether they were terrorized into making such affidavits or if they are just the sort of sycophantic creatures with which we are cursed." It was a strange strategy. White was not interested in what the witnesses knew, despite the fact that among them were some of the leading citizens of the region, and instead only looked for ways to discredit them, even though his only on-the-record witness when in Valdosta was a reluctant employee of a white undertaker participating in the lynching. It was also a strange response considering that none of the witnesses denied that any of the lynchings took place; they really were only denying White's particularly wrenching account of one of them. It was, however, an account in which White had much invested. "Can you get me any information on these people through any reliable parties in Valdosta?" he asked Hurst.[21]

Hurst made the effort but had little luck. AME bishop John E. Hurst was born in Port Au Prince, Haiti, before moving to the United States, where he married an American, Katherine Bertha Thompson of South Carolina. He had been the chancellor of Edward Waters College in Jacksonville for part of his career, but that was as close as his work or family life had taken him to Valdosta or Quitman, Georgia. "I approached a number of persons in Jacksonville," he told White, "trying to interest them in that situation that obtained at Valdosta." No one was interested, however, in making the trip to south Georgia. "Some of them know the Rev. T. A. Lomax well and didn't seem to have anything especially good to say about him and his manliness in his dealings with white people," he claimed, but they refused to investigate the others. "Finally, I had to give it up. It is such a pity that in the South, you cannot get colored men to stand up straight when it comes to matters affecting the well being of their people where white people are involved." Hurst's reaction to White's request was equally strange, blaming Black southerners for not investigating the legitimacy of other Black southerners.[22]

To be sure, there are historical instances where Black citizens attempted to curry favor with or pander to powerful whites by writing letters in support of locals with potential criminal exposure, but such attempts were almost always countered by other local Black citizens who stood against them and provided a counternarrative.[23] No such local counternarrative appeared in Valdosta, and it could not be generated by those working from outside the area. In January 1919, for example, Thomas Lomax was part of a large program at St. Paul AME, then hosted Richard R. Wright, president of Georgia State Industrial College for Colored Youth and one of the nation's leading figures in Black higher education, at his own Macedonia First Baptist Church. His son fostered Valdosta's Black public schools through the era of Jim Crow segregation, and his grandson, Louis Lomax, became a central figure in the civil rights movement.[24] Thomas A. Lomax was undeniably a giant in Valdosta's Black community. Hurst was mistaken.

White's response, however, was typical, insulting the affidavit writers and using them as an excuse for his inability to counter Brantley's narrative. "It is pretty hard," he wrote to Cannady, to "not be able to refute him because of the cowardice of the very people for whom you are working. I suppose Lomax is afraid of the white people there and they have forced him to swear to a lie. While one can understand it, nevertheless, it is rather galling to have a minister of the gospel be a party to such a scheme."[25] It was a bitter and unsubstantiated claim from someone with far more at stake in the debate than credit on the editorial page of a local newspaper in the Pacific Northwest.

Again White's account of his experience in the 1906 Atlanta race riot is instructive. White's family knew that his account of facing down the white mob at the family home in Atlanta was not true. After White published a version in the *Nation*, his sister Alice wrote to him: "Read the one in Nation with much amusement. Where did the shot-gun come from?"[26] When White asked his sister Madeline to consult with their mother about her memories of the event, she responded for both herself and their mother that there were no guns in the house and that the women of the house were not hidden away in the back. They watched the mob from an upstairs bedroom window. White, however, denied their versions of events, claiming that "Mother's memory is not correct" and that the version he was now telling was.[27] Once the embellishment became calcified in his mind, even those who had been present could not dissuade him from his account of events.

Even more important, the *Oregonian* debate served another dubious function, as well, one that White's focus on Turner and the pregnancy narrative had served for years. It neglected both the true horror of a comparatively normal lynching and obscured the full scope of the larger race riot that occurred in Brooks and Lowndes Counties in May 1918. It was a trend that would continue.

TALL TALES

In June 1918 reports emerged that Shorty Ford's Jacksonville confession had implicated another man, Simon Shuman, as being part of the plot. The accusation against Shuman was that he used his car to drive the killers to the Smith house. Ford described the automobile, claiming that Shuman did not take part in the actual crime but knew what he was taking his coconspirators to do. Investigators found that Shuman had owned such a vehicle but had sold it after the crime. Local authorities arrested Shuman at his home near Morven and held him in the Brooks County jail in Quitman. Officials still refused to send Ford to Brooks or Lowndes County, and an effort was made to remove Shuman to a new location as well. Days after his arrest, Shuman was taken "to parts unknown, for safe keeping," according to the Associated Press.[28]

Simon Shuman Jr. was born in the late 1870s in Bryan County, Georgia, the son of a farmer and his wife, a housekeeper named Cylar Shuman. He moved, however, to Brooks County upon coming of age, where he married Mollie, only fourteen at the time of their marriage. Shuman found himself in a tenant farming situation in the county, struggling to survive with no education and six children in the first ten years of his and Mollie's marriage.[29]

Shuman was another problematic hole in White's coverage. The newly minted NAACP investigator claimed in his report that he had verified Shuman's lynching. A white mob had called Shuman from his Colquitt County house and destroyed everything inside. Shuman, he claimed, had not been seen since. His disappearance, however, was related to his arrest and removal. He was in a tenuous sharecropping situation only made worse by the charges, and after his release he left the area, settling for the rest of his life in Brunswick, Georgia.[30]

The problems in White's report, however, while too substantial to present under oath in the Senate, were not a problem for the NAACP's more public efforts to fight against the scourge of lynching. In April 1919, after Shillady and the NAACP knew that White's original account was mistaken, the group included White's version of the Mary Turner story in a pamphlet titled "Twelve Months of Lynching in America: Is This Democracy?" It created another pamphlet specifically devoted to the events in south Georgia: "Lynchings of May, 1918, in Brooks and Lowndes Counties, Georgia, an Investigation by the NAACP."[31]

It was clear that White either kept believing in his version or maintained it for consistency's sake. In September 1924 he related the story of the Turner lynching to the director of Philadelphia's Federation of Jewish Charities. He was trying to explain the harsh reality of life in the South in response to the director's query about White's depiction of the racism in the region in his 1924 novel *The Fire in the Flint.* Turner was pregnant and disemboweled, her only crime seeking justice for her husband, he told the director. The other victims and the white mobs roaming the area were all subsumed into the story of Mary Turner, which accurately represented the racial vindictiveness of the white South but distorted the nature of the actual mob violence of 1918.[32]

In 1929 White's relationship with the Turner lynching became even more problematic. In an autobiographical piece for *American Mercury,* the NAACP leader told the stories of some of his most harrowing investigations, and the lynching of Mary Turner was the first on his list. His account was problematic partly because he used direct quotations that could not have been accurate. White describes entering a general store and, passing as a white man, engaging the shopkeeper in typical conversation. Though the shopkeeper goes unnamed in the piece, White is clearly referring to William A. Whipple, whom he implicated as one of the mob's leaders. Whipple was the only listed member of the mob who owned a store. Eventually the shopkeeper feels comfortable enough with White to talk of the lynching:

> "You'll pardon me, Mister," he began, "for seeming suspicious but we have to be careful. In ordinary times we wouldn't have anything to worry about, but with the war there's been some talk of the Federal government looking into lynchings. It seems there's some sort of law during wartime making it treason to lower the man power of the country."
>
> "In that case I don't blame you for being careful," I assured him. "But couldn't the Federal government do something if it wanted to when a lynching takes place, even if no war is going on at the moment?"
>
> "Naw," he said, confidently, proud of the opportunity of displaying his store of information to one who he assumed knew nothing whatever about the subject. "There's no such law, in spite of all the agitation by a lot of fools who don't know the niggers as we do. States' rights won't permit Congress to meddle in lynching in peace time."
>
> "But what about your State government—your Governor, your sheriff, your police officers?"
>
> "Humph! Them? We elected them to office, didn't we? And the niggers, we've got them disfranchised, ain't we? Sheriffs and police and Governors and prosecuting attorneys have got too much sense to mix in lynching-bees. If they do they know they might as well give up all idea of running for office any more—if something worse don't happen to them—" This last with a tightening of the lips and a hard look in the eyes.
>
> I sought to lead the conversation into less dangerous channels. "Who was the white man who was killed—whose killing caused the lynchings?" I asked.
>
> "Oh, he was a hard one, all right. Never paid his debts to white men or niggers and wasn't liked much around here. He was a mean 'un all right, all right."
>
> "Why, then, did you lynch the niggers for killing such a man?"

> "It's a matter of safety—we gotta show niggers that they mustn't touch a white man, no matter how low-down and ornery he is."
>
> Little by little he revealed the whole story. When he told of the manner in which the pregnant woman had been killed he chuckled and slapped his thigh and declared it to be "the best show, Mister, I ever did see. You ought to have heard the wench howl when we strung her up."[33]

Eventually, on White's third day in town, the store owner discovered that his new acquaintance was a "government agent," he explained in the magazine, and White spent an unrestful night with a loaded gun hoping to make it out alive.[34] Though White certainly was able to pass for white during most of his investigations in the South, and though his attempt was to get an honest account of the south Georgia race killings, his 1929 story is absurd, from a white local thinking poorly of Smith for treating his Black workers poorly but reveling in the gruesome murder of a pregnant woman to that same white local using phraseology like "we've got them disfranchised, ain't we?" The notion that a general store owner would find a local plantation owner "low-down and ornery" was similarly far-fetched. In the *American Mercury* story White's life was in danger, but in his real investigation, he returned to Quitman to plead with George Spratling, his Black witness, to testify in Washington. It was an account that was no doubt truly representative of the kinds of conversations he might have had in south Georgia and truly representative of the kinds of experiences he had while investigating lynchings, but it was not a faithful account of his time in Brooks or Lowndes County.

The *New Yorker* in 1948 called the Mary Turner attack White's "favorite lynching, from a propagandistic point of view." And his use of the story lasted long after his *Crisis* article. "His harrowing recital of this incident became known, after a while, as 'the Mary Turner Speech,' and it rarely failed to elicit shudders from his audiences. Every now and then, White would inadvertently make the Mary Turner speech, with diminishing effect, to an audience containing people who had already heard it a couple of times. Once, as White prepared to lecture a crowd in Harlem, a man stood up and called out, 'Please don't lynch Mary Turner tonight, Walter.'"[35] The story as presented in the *New Yorker* was played for laughs, and the man in the crowd may have meant his request as a joke. But the statement could also be interpreted as a plea for respite against the collective trauma that emanated from such gruesome events. Every recounting became a reliving of the lynching for those hearing it. It was trauma that spread across time and space into the minds of all those still living in a nation defined largely by white supremacy and the dangers it posed—even if those hearing the story were in Harlem, far from the cotton fields of south Georgia.

The story's continued repetition by White was not an effort to exacerbate trauma among his listeners, but it demonstrated that the story was part not only of his argument against lynch law in the South and the horrible things of which some white southerners were capable, but also part of White's self-definition, part of his own story that had come to loom large in the way he presented himself as the leader of the NAACP. The story of Turner became less a story of south Georgia, and vastly less the stories of the other victims, and more a story of White's autobiographical identity, a defining moment of his early career and of the first decade of the fledgling NAACP's existence. They had failed to secure federal intervention in the case, but they had documented it for posterity. Except that the organization's failure to secure federal intervention in that particular effort was a direct result of its failure to document the case accurately.

James Weldon Johnson, White's mentor, also told a story of participating in the investigation, one that has no evidence in the historical record. The NAACP field secretary had traveled to Jacksonville, he claimed, for a mass meeting to prompt the sale of liberty bonds. While there Shillady contacted him, asking Johnson to go to Quitman to try again to convince Spratling to testify publicly about the violence in the area. When he arrived, he went to the house of either Athens Grant or Maurice Cobb, the two physicians who had helped White during his original investigation. The doctor told Johnson "that the town was still alive over the lynching, and much incensed over Mr. White's disclosures." His fear transferred to Johnson, who was unable to sleep. The next day, Johnson found Spratling "in one of those dingy restaurants for Negroes, common in the South." Spratling's mother ran the restaurant and worked as Johnson tried to convince the young man to testify, or, barring that, to "give me the names of such members of the mob as he knew. He refused to do either." He reasoned that his mother would be in peril as a response to any such testimony or information.[36]

While they were talking, a car with six white men pulled up to the restaurant. "There they are now," said Spratling. "What'll I tell 'em if they ask about you?" Johnson claimed to be taking subscriptions for a Black newspaper. Spratling went out, talked to the men, and then returned. "They asked me what you were doing here, and I told them you were taking subscriptions. They told me to keep my damned mouth shut." It was a threat Johnson knew all too well. "I got out of Quitman that afternoon and I did not feel safe or comfortable until the train had crossed the Florida line."[37]

There is no corroborating record of either Johnson's liberty bonds speech in Jacksonville or his trip to Quitman. Johnson was a native of Jacksonville who attended college in Atlanta. He was familiar with the area, would have many reasons to return to his hometown for that speech, and would surely be interested in convincing Spratling to testify in Washington. Still, when the NAACP's knowledge of false information about the Turner case is combined with the association's extensive record-keeping that would, in most circumstances, leave a trace of such activities, there is the possibility that Johnson is conflating his own efforts with the possible experience of White on his second trip to Quitman. If the town had been "incensed over Mr. White's disclosures," his trip would have been late in 1918, after the September edition of the *Crisis* in which White's account appeared. By that point, however, contact with senators had been severed after evidence surfaced that White had made mistakes.

Like a rumor through a crowd, the NAACP story of Turner's lynching continued to change in repetition. In 1935 journalist Tom Poston retold the tale for the *New York Amsterdam News*, using White's account as a starting point, to convince readers to contact their congressmen about the Costigan-Wagner anti-lynching bill then making its way through the legislature. The large feature purported to tell of the "Brooks and Lowndes County terror of May 1918," wherein nineteen victims were killed. Even that high number, however, was subsumed in Poston's story to the lynching of Mary Turner. Her abdomen was not just cut open; it was cut open with a butcher knife. The fetus was not just crushed underfoot; it was crushed underfoot with a "hobnailed boot of a Southern gentleman." He "crushed the skull of this prematurely born infant as it uttered its first and final cry in this last stronghold of White Civilization." Hampton Smith's Old Joyce Place was operated "under conditions more revolting than those exposed in the immortal 'Uncle Tom's Cabin.'" The story continued to metastasize as its temporal distance from the actual event grew, Poston building on White's story instead of seeking out evidence for himself. And he did so for the same reason that White never adjusted his claims after new evidence: because those claims were made in aid of generating legislation against lynching.[38]

Three years prior, in 1932, the *Pittsburgh Courier* grew the tale in yet another direction. In the *Courier* version, Turner was "sought out by a white dentist, a superior nordic, to be his concubine." It was "the Nordic" who impregnated her, then decided she needed to die. After she was hanged upside down and set aflame, the "big Nordic drew near to her with a great knife," then cut out the baby and crushed its skull. It was so far afield from any version that any evidence provided, but the *Courier* story demonstrates again how such tales can grow in the mythmaking of lynching horrors.[39]

Late in his life, White again retold the story of the Turner lynching and his role in the investigation in *Rope and Faggot*, his 1969 study of lynching. He argued that the number of lynchings decreased over the decades but that the diminished numbers were balanced against a "greatly aggravated brutality, often extending to almost unbelievable torture of the victim." Between the beginning of 1918 and 1927, 454 people were lynched, 416 of them Black and 11 of them women, "three of them at that time of lynching with child," surely also referring to the lynchings in Shubuta, Mississippi, of Maggie and Alma House, whose pregnancies were also problematically reported and clearly suspect. He noted that 42 of the victims were burned alive and that "14.9 per cent—a little less than one out of each seven—were done to death with abnormal savagery."[40]

Rope and Faggot is an important work, one that defined the scholarship of lynching in the late 1960s. But whatever its accuracy, whatever White and the NAACP knew about that accuracy in the later reporting on the event, the indisputable fact of their mythmaking about Turner is that the emphasis pulled focus from the other deaths surrounding the rampage and caricatured the mob violence as an exception to the rule rather than part of a pattern sweeping the nation from 1917 to 1921. Turner's death undoubtedly included both a rope and faggot, but it was part of a larger racial sentiment in south Georgia, an all-consuming white supremacy represented by the fuses of debt peonage, economic uncertainty, labor shortages, and the everyday atrocities associated with racial retrenchment, which were then lit by the murder of Hampton Smith.

That mythmaking was fueled most directly by the media, whether in later books such as *Rope and Faggot* or earlier conflicting accounts in contemporary newspapers. There were decided differences in coverage as the story of the race riot moved outward from Brooks and Lowndes Counties, like changing ripples after a stone is dropped in water. There were differences in interpretation between local papers and national papers, between rural papers and urban, between the Black press and white, and between the editors of the *Portland Morning Oregonian* and the *Valdosta Times*. That confusion of multiple clarifications led to a varied history of the events of May 1918, most of them centering on the death of one of the white mob's several victims. Throughout that troubled mediation, however, there were still the victims and the murderers, and the collective trauma of an event that scared thousands, accelerated the Great Migration in the region, and left a contested legacy that remains in Brooks and Lowndes Counties in the twenty-first century.

Conclusion

The Turner Legacy

On January 29, 1919, Nashville, Georgia, deputy sheriff J. M. Studstill killed Black prisoner J. M. McPhatten. He claimed that McPhatten, in jail on a forgery charge, had assaulted him, taken a gun, and escaped from the Berrien County jail. Just north and adjoining Lowndes County, Berrien provided many potential hiding places for McPhatten, but after the sheriff "secured assistance of a number of men" and a bloodhound, the group found the escapee a mile and a half away in a mill pond. The posse claimed that McPhatten shot at them, forcing them to kill him. It was another killing, this time by a mob led by a sheriff's deputy who no one would dare dispute.[1]

Less than a year after the violence in Brooks and Lowndes Counties, another racial rampage occurred 170 miles east in Jenkins County. On April 13, 1919, a conflict between two white police officers and congregants at Carswell Grove Baptist Church led to the deaths of the officers and one of the congregants. Another of the church members, Joe Ruffin, was shot in the head while trying to calm the argument that led to the violence. He survived, but an angry white mob that formed in response to the deaths of two white deputies killed two of his sons. They burned down the church, threw the two bodies into the flames, then killed several unknown others while destroying businesses and other places of worship. Ruffin himself survived in exile, taken to safety in Augusta by a white county commissioner, but Cameron McWhirter credits the riot as the opening event of what would become known as Red Summer.[2] Racial violence was ubiquitous in the age, and East St. Louis in 1917 and Chicago and Washington, DC, in 1919 were decidedly urban, but the Jenkins County violence demonstrated the white rural sensitivity to the deaths of white authority figures and the willingness of those rural residents to take matters into their own hands. And while the Black residents of Jenkins County did not organize a chapter of the NAACP, they did resolutely rebuild the church that the white mob took from them.[3]

Still, while incidents of such violence happened in many places, they did not happen everywhere, and the riot in Jenkins County was a rare conflagration. It was less rare 170 miles southeast in Brooks and Lowndes Counties. The Equal Justice Initiative counts twenty lynchings in Brooks County, the most for any county in south Georgia and north Florida, an area with one of the highest rates of racial violence in the nation.[4]

"See that little nigger?" the *Bainbridge Post-Search Light* asked in the weeks following the May 1918 attacks. "Yes, well that is the little nigger that was asked if he would give a days work to the Red Cross and he volunteered TWO days work. Every time that little nigger passes down the streets he will be looked at in a kind way by all men because he did his best." It was a strange way of encouraging volunteerism in the Black population, one that clearly played on Black fears emerging from the violence in Brooks and Lowndes Counties. Such was the leverage created by the constant threat of death. While most white citizens and newspapers did not parlay the lynchings into efforts at wartime volunteerism, however, their use as racial intimidation was all too common in the weeks and months following the attacks.[5]

South Georgia was not monolithically violent and exclusionary, but it was full of Michael Rothberg's "implicated subjects," those whose "actions and inactions help produce and reproduce the positions of victims and perpetrators."[6] In May 1919, for example, C. M. Killian, chair of the Lowndes County Democratic Executive Committee, took a full-page advertisement in the *Valdosta Times* directed "to the Negro voters of Lowndes County." Killian explained that he was raised in northeast Mississippi with a majority Black population. He was "nursed by a negro boy named George, who later nursed my brother Dan." George wore the same clothes and ate the same food as the Killian family, "and when large enough to make his way in the world left us with the very best training that my father and mother could give him." There was an upcoming election for both a road-building bond issue and a new sheriff. Killian explained that he "refused to call a white primary to elect a sheriff." He was "not afraid to trust the negro. I feel sure that he will not take advantage of the great privilege granted him to vote for a sheriff on the same day he votes for bonds." The vote for sheriff had been called to reelect J. F. Passmore, who later earned local infamy for beating *Times* editor C. C. Brantley on the street. While the leader of the Sidney Johnson assault was Valdosta chief of police Calvin Dampier, Passmore and his deputies had been part of the search party, and he was a powerful representative of law enforcement and the white racial line it upheld in the region. After his role in the violence, and after law enforcement's role in the violence more broadly, the call from the Democratic Party to open the primary, complete with paternalistic paeans to Black nurses of privileged white youth, was present not as a Damascus moment from whites concerning voter equality, but instead as a cudgel to reimpose white racial order. Killian was telling Black readers to publicly support one of their attackers by using a mechanism, the franchise, that the county and state usually denied them. It was a different kind of assault on the victims of the riot, but it was an assault nonetheless. At best the divided mind of the white South could compartmentalize lynchings as frontier justice and paternalistically encourage Black voting while still dominating an apartheid state bounded by Jim Crow. At worst it could marshal its apartheid power to encourage Black voters to support one of their abusers.[7]

There was, however, real organization in response to the attack. On May 23, 1919, one year after the rampage and one week after Killian's advertisement, a group of fifty Black residents created Valdosta's first branch of the NAACP.[8] The group existed in fits and starts over the next two decades. It was reestablished in 1943 after a wartime lag and had fifty members in 1948 before disbanding again after the election of Herman Talmadge as governor, from 1949 until 1951.[9] But another murder, that of Willie Watson by two white police officers in 1951, galvanized many. The Valdosta branch reorganized in October of that year under the leadership of local Leonard D. Davis; director of the Southeast Regional Office Ruby Hurley visited that month to aid in the process.[10] It was a demonstration that racial violence, either in the wake of World War I or World War II, sparked civil rights activism in the city and the region and served as a driver of that activism rather than a deterrent in a region with a schizophrenic relationship with race.

Even prior to the May 1918 riot, the region demonstrated its racial schizophrenia early in the century. Historian Bill Boyd describes a 1905 murder case in Valdosta wherein a longstanding family feud boiled over into a murder for hire that put a father and son on trial for a capital killing. The prosecution in the case hinged on the testimony of Alf Moore, a Black farmworker from Tennessee who was first asked to commit the crime, then after refusing witnessed the machinations that ultimately led to the murder. "They came to me and asked me for the truth," Moore testified, "and I told them." Moore was not the only witness, but he was the one with the eyewitness account, and despite being grilled on cross-examination by defense attorneys who tried to play on his race to invalidate his testimony, he was convincing. The white father and son who were being tried for the crime were convicted and hanged in the prison across the street from the Lowndes County courthouse. "It may have been the first time in Georgia history," Boyd explains, "that the testimony of a black man put a white man on the gallows."[11]

Still, such moments were conspicuous by their rarity, the moral arc of the region bending usually toward racial exclusion. At the beginning of August 1919, the *Valdosta Times*'s lead story was the riot in Chicago. "The main negro quarters of the city were patrolled by six thousand troops Thursday," the paper explained, "after four nights of race rioting that caused thirty deaths and the injury of more than five hundred others." In October the paper gave the same treatment to the violence in Elaine, printing wire stories above the fold to demonstrate the trouble of racial mass action in other parts of the country. In an editorial on the Chicago violence, the *Times* argued that "race riots and race friction generally are directly traceable to the 'black belt' politics of the city hall organization," that Chicago politicians "encouraged gambling and disorderly resorts in an effort to 'corral the negro vote,'" and that they appealed to "the criminal, vicious, idle and ignorant classes of negroes." All race friction, the paper argued, "is mainly due to nature's law that birds of a feather must flock together in order to secure harmony."[12]

In another editorial, the *Times* explained that "when American negroes were drafted in large numbers and sent to the war in Europe it was predicted that on their return they would make trouble." The paper laid much of the blame for Red Summer at the feet of Black radicalism and national disloyalty fed by the Black press, which agitated the population to potential violence. It quoted from a government report on the violence that "permeating even the negro masses, there has been aroused a dangerous sense of radical antagonism which is being thoroughly exploited by their leader of the press." The trend, so it seemed, was toward "organized alignment with the most destructive forces of our political life today."[13] It was yet another example of the bigoted nationalism permeating the mob violence narrative in the era of World War I, assuming that Black voices in defense of the race were dangerous because of their inherent challenge to the government, just as, first, German American voices were dangerous, then communist voices were dangerous. Tying dissident groups together as anti-American would continue through the later civil rights movement and into the twenty-first century.

Two years after the south Georgia rampage, while Governor Dorsey was in the process of refusing Shorty Ford's request for clemency, he published a statement condemning lynching and mob violence. "To me it seems that we stand indicted as a people before the world. If the conditions indicated by these charges should continue, both God and man would justly condemn Georgia more severely than man and God have condemned Belgium and Leopold for the Congo atrocities." He then put forward 135 examples of white cruelty to Black Georgians from between 1919 and 1921, examples of lynchings, peonage abuse, forced evacuation, and acts of nonlethal physical violence, each with locations and identifiers removed. It was an overwhelming litany of grotesque racist behavior.[14]

Dorsey's proposed solutions to such incidents were practical. He wanted compulsory education for both races, segregated state committees on race relations, increased publicity, and "an organized campaign by the Churches." He also sought repeal of state laws that excused debt peonage and the addition of laws that granted the governor power to investigate local lynching cases and to empanel statewide grand juries to prosecute offenders. It was not an overtly radical proposal, but it was radical for its time and place. The same leader who dragged his feet in the face of NAACP pressure during the May 1918 ordeal had, on April 22, 1921, just over a month prior to Ford's scheduled execution, discovered a new vigor for regulating such behavior.[15]

The *Atlanta Independent* wholeheartedly supported Dorsey's effort, realizing the power that such a statement by a sitting southern governor could have on the white population. Groups of white Baptist and Presbyterian ministers, for example, adopted resolutions to support the governor's effort to end lynching and mob violence in Georgia.[16]

There were similar efforts going on throughout the country. World War I intensified race conflict and helped ignite a spasm of racially motivated mob violence across the nation. The mob violence in Brooks and Lowndes Counties was part of that spasm. After the south Georgia violence, in July 1918, the Northeastern Federation of Colored Women passed a resolution in support of federal anti-lynching legislation and wrote their own missive to Woodrow Wilson. The autumn following the Turner lynching and the press surrounding it, Missouri's Leonidas Dyer first introduced his anti-lynching bill. It had prominent, but not overwhelming, support, and thus the real effort to pass the Dyer bill would come after the expanded Red Summer wave had run its course, after the Tulsa race riot of 1921, and after Shorty Ford's execution in Savannah two days later, the last victim of the Turner saga in south Georgia. The Dyer bill saw its full flower in 1922, when it was passed by the House only to fall to a filibuster in the Senate. The first introduction of the bill happened in the wake of the Turner publicity, and its last gasp came in the wake of the Turner conclusion.[17]

Six months after the south Georgia rampage, the Commission on Interracial Cooperation (CIC) was founded in Atlanta with the goal of calming racial tensions and ending white mob violence and debt peonage. While the group was not a direct response to the violence in Brooks and Lowndes Counties, that violence and the peonage that helped breed it were part of the motivating force. The white leaders who created the commission were frustrated by the racial tensions of the war years and wanted to find a viable path to ending the region's more odious practices. That said, the group remained decidedly moderate, never challenging, for example, the broader segregationist practices of Jim Crow, instead only focusing on the more publicly scandalous outgrowths of the southern apartheid state such as overt violence and debt peonage, one a violation of life, the other a violation of liberty. White liberal leaders in Atlanta interpreted the violence in cities like East St. Louis in 1917 and in south Georgia in 1918 as precursors to larger upheavals, an assumption that proved to be prescient. Such is not to say that the violence made infamous by the Turner lynching was the impetus for the creation of CIC, but it was part of the narrative of racial violence and the most public intersection of mob killings and debt peonage in the state in the months before the creation of a Georgia organization designed to prevent them. CIC cofounder Jack Woofter, for example, was publicly frustrated with Governor Dorsey's waffling response to the riot and his patronizing response to the Colored Welfare League of Augusta.[18]

Dorsey's waffling response also solidified as the violence wore on. In April 1921, less than two months before Shorty Ford's execution in Savannah, the governor convened a conference in Atlanta to discuss the continued mob violence against Black lives in the state, including several leading members of the CIC. At its conclusion he issued "A Statement from Governor Hugh M. Dorsey as to the Negro in Georgia," in which he cataloged those 135 cases of "alleged mistreatment of negroes in Georgia in the last two years." He noted that he made no special effort to investigate, instead relying on those instances reported to his office. "If such an effort were made, I believe the number could be multiplied," he explained. He noted that only two of the instances included alleged defenses of white womanhood, demonstrating the shibboleth that the excuse almost always was. The statement was a radical act from a moderately progressive southern governor, one far more in line with his public speechifying than was his behavior during 1918.[19]

A generation later Georgia's contract labor law was declared unconstitutional in 1942. "Peonage is a form of involuntary servitude within the meaning of the Thirteenth Amendment and the Congressional Act of 1867 is an appropriate implementation of that amendment," wrote Justice James F. Byrnes. "The sections of the Georgia Code are repugnant to the Thirteenth Amendment and the Act of 1867."[20]

While the end of debt peonage may have killed the possibility of the kind of race riot sparked in south Georgia in 1918, the story of that riot never died. Both Jennifer Williams and Julie Buckner Armstrong have demonstrated how continued sharing developed not only in media reports about the case and White's own retellings of his investigation, but also in the visual and literary narratives that accompanied such violent displays. In the immediate aftermath of the crisis in 1919, Meta Warrick Fuller sculpted *Mary Turner (A Silent Protest Against Mob Violence)*. The following year Angelina Weld Grimké published her story "Goldie." Two years after that, Carrie Williams Clifford's poem "Little Mother" first appeared. And in 1923, Jean Toomer's *Cane* was published. Along with the media and political fallout, the emotional trauma of White's account also played itself out, fittingly, in artistic production, a series of important responses to an unsettling lynching counternarrative but also agents of reification for the assumed validity of White's account. They were works, like White's, that maintained an intellectual honesty without necessarily being grounded in historical fact.[21]

The problem of reading the south Georgia rampage as a lynching, particularly the lynching of one pregnant woman, has also led to a disjointed historical understanding of the event in the twenty-first century. The National Museum of African American History and Culture includes a panel titled "The Rise of Lynching" and uses Turner's case as one of its examples, reprinting a newspaper article describing the attack and framing the killing as a largely singular incident.[22] The Equal Justice Initiative describes the lynching on its website, mentioning seven other people who were killed but following the traditional narrative and focusing almost exclusively on Turner. At the initiative's National Memorial for Peace and Justice, hanging stones representing American counties list the lynchings that occurred in each one. Brooks County's includes some but not all of the victims of the riot, but along with Mary and Hayes Turner, the stone includes Turner's unborn child, listed without a first name.[23] The Turner lynching, divorced from any other victims, is also featured as part of the Zinn Education Project.[24] Carol Anderson's *White Rage*, an important academic analysis of the development of America's racial divide but also a popular bestselling book, includes the traditional Turner lynching narrative, adding that "at least eleven African Americans, ten of whom had absolutely nothing to do with Smith's death, were hunted down and slaughtered."[25] Mariame Kaba's introduction to Rachel Marie-Crane Williams's 2021 *Elegy for Mary Turner* describes Turner as nineteen years old. While Kaba mentions her husband's death, nothing about the race riot is included. Williams's *Elegy* itself is a breathtaking and moving artistic account of the tragedy, hewing directly to Walter White's report of the event. Like Anderson's work, *Elegy* repeats the mistakes of White but gives space to the broader racial violence of May 1918, representing the deaths of Will Head and Will Thompson, Eugene Rice, Chime Riley, Hayes Turner, Sidney Johnson, the bodies later found in the Little River, and Simon Shuman. Shuman, of course, was not actually killed, but the artistic representations in the book of multiple victims does the work of presenting the broad range of violence in the region.[26]

When rumor moves through a crowd, it can also metastasize in the other direction. In 1975, for example, the *Valdosta Times* interviewed a seventy-four-year-old man who recalled the racial terror in Brooks County in 1918. "If you and your brother get in the buggy and ride on down the road," he remembered his father telling him, "you'll see what meanness can do." They did and saw the hanging body of one of the men lynched in the Smith attack. He remembered Hampton Smith as a kind man who "fed the farm hands in the kitchen of his house while he and his wife ate in the dining room." He was not sure why Smith was killed, but he heard from older relations that it was an attempted robbery. In his version of events, Bertha Smith climbed a tree after being shot to hide from her Black attackers, protecting her purity. An elderly woman who lived near Brooks County's "Hanging Tree" remembered hearing the gunshots that night. "It sounded like a war must sound," she said. The man they caught was "strung up right then and there, no questions asked." Both accounts remembered the event as primarily affecting white victims. "For a long time after that we locked our doors every night," the woman said. "We were really scared back then." The man remembered that the race conflict was "one of the worst happenings I ever remember happening around here." But then he began to smile. "Miz Smith's baby was born not too long after and you know, that was one of the healthiest young 'uns I've ever seen."[27]

It was a self-serving account of a lynching based partially in lived experience and partly in fantasy, an accidentally nefarious version of White's good faith effort more than half a century prior, both of them emphasizing a lynching over and against the broader temporal and regional racial tumult. Historian

David F. Krugler, when describing the violence of the period, has argued that the term *race riot* is useful because of its historical resonance but problematic because of its implications. It implies, for example, that there is equal responsibility for violence on both sides of the racial line. It also implies spontaneity. The Black role in race riots of the period, however, was one of resistance, of defense. It was one of fighting back against white attack. And that attack was not spontaneous, either; it was "deliberate, methodical, purposeful," Krugler explains. He suggests instead referring to riots during the period as "antiblack collective violence."[28]

The events in south Georgia fit Krugler's definition. They were deliberate attacks by the white population against the Black. And while Black residents of Brooks and Lowndes Counties did not resist with guns, they resisted by hiding would-be victims, by escaping the area, by speaking with investigators like White, and by forming their own chapter of the NAACP. They were not passive victims. The entire ordeal was an act of social violence, an assault, again in the words of sociologist Allen Day Grimshaw, "upon individuals, or their property, solely or primarily because of their membership in social categories." The bulk of the violence happened in two counties in south Georgia in the summer of 1918, a year after the violence in East St. Louis and a year before that in Washington, Chicago, and other areas. The last victim of that violence, Shorty Ford, found the end of a rope two days after the violence in Tulsa began to subside. It was multifaceted mob violence that killed at least eight, and possibly many more, in the riotous postwar period around the violent apex that was the Red Summer of 1919. The violence, in fact, would prompt a local outmigration, helping to feed the Red Summer the following year. When interpreted in that light, the Brooks-Lowndes race riot of 1918 can be seen as a vital cog in the wheel that turned so violently after World War I.

It was a wheel that had crushed many underneath and left many attempting to maintain a life in a place that had caused them so much misery. Sidney Johnson's parents, for example, were devastated by the killing of their son, but they eventually had one more child, a girl who they named Mary, in 1920. Staying in the region that had caused them so much pain was too much, however, and the two escaped in the 1920s to St. Petersburg, Florida, where Richard finished his career as a yard worker in the budding city.[29]

George Spratling remained an undertaker with the McGowan Undertaking Company for the rest of his life. He died a decade after his ordeal, on November 27, 1929, from myocarditis. His second son, George Spratling Jr., lived until August 1992, like his father remaining his entire life in Quitman.[30]

Spratling's employer, Samuel McGowan, felt no ill effects from his participation in the murders, keeping Spratling on until his death in 1929 and remaining a prominent undertaker in Quitman into the 1940s, when he himself died. His home on Washington Street continued to rise in value through the decades, as did the revenue from his business. His son, Samuel Jr., lived until April 1995.[31]

For all the problems with the anonymous white commentator in 1975, he was right about Smith's baby. Bertha Smith gave birth on September 13, 1918, and named the boy Claude Hampton Smith Jr., his name a signpost of his inheritance of social dominance defined through acts of racial terror. Dixon Smith, the patriarch of the family, died just before Christmas, on December 24, 1921. Bertha found raising the boy on her own difficult, and so in the 1920s she remarried. Ellis Goston Windham, her new husband, was born in August 1886 in Reynolds, in Taylor County, halfway between Columbus and Macon. He was the middle child of a large family of nine kids born to George and Hattie Windham. In his mid-thirties when he met Bertha, Ellis had never married, beginning his professional life as a carpenter before becoming a grocery store clerk in his hometown. It was there that he met Bertha and her son, Hampton. After marriage the couple stayed just outside of Reynolds in adjacent Macon County. In the early 1940s, a now adult Hamp Smith Jr. married Cherry Wynelle and remained in Reynolds for the rest of his long life. The youngest victim of the 1918 ordeal died August 20, 1984, in Macon County, his only real home.[32]

Willie Loyd Smith, son of Hattie Turner, had been traumatized by the events of May 1918 as no one else could have been. After the death of his mother and stepfather, Smith remained in Brooks County, moving into the home of his grandmother Betty Graham. He was not able to attend school in Brooks, but his grandmother taught him to read and write. When he came of age, Smith understandably wanted to escape south Georgia. He became part of the Great Migration, like so many others before him traveling to Chicago to take a factory job, and put south Georgia far behind him.[33]

Of course, in a story filled with contingency, such an account is one in a group of possibilities. Local genealogist Phillip Williams found Willie in the 1930s still living with Hattie's mother and Perry Graham Jr., in Brooks County. Graham's great-grandson claimed that Smith eventually found his way to Florida. Ossie Ola Smith claimed that a Willie Smith born in June 1909 moved to Cook County, where he died in April 1938. Indeed several of those who trace their family history to Turner today live in Cook County. The family lore from other relatives is that Turner had two children, Ocie Lee and Leaster. They ignore Willie Smith altogether. At least one historical account that draws on such family lore claims that after Hayes Turner had been taken, his wife sent Ocie Lee and Leaster to stay with her parents. They took assumed names, Otha Manning and Conie L. Manning, as a protective measure against possible continued violence from retributive white men. In this version Ocie Lee moved to Florida, while Leaster married a local man and moved to a farm just north of where the violence occurred. That the legacy of Turner's offspring is steeped in the same kind of mythology as the death of his (or their) mother is fitting. It is another story, or set of stories, built on the apocrypha of oral transfer and collective memory.[34]

Many of Turner's family members were there on the cool, sunny morning of Friday, December 10, 2021, in Hahira, Georgia, for the rededication of a historical marker remembering the violence. Originally dedicated in 2010 and placed on the Lowndes County side of the Little River, just across the water from where Mary Turner was killed, the monument had been placed by the Georgia Historical Society after the tireless advocacy of the Mary Turner Project, led by local sociologist and activist Mark Patrick George, and the Turner family. The marker's text was rooted in Walter White's narrative but emphasized the broader scope of violence that took place. It was titled "Mary Turner and the Lynching Rampage of 1918." And like so much historical work, it was a threat to white locals still mired in the lost cause of white supremacy. The marker was repeatedly defaced over the following decade, the bullet holes dotting the text their own monument to the vestiges of racial violence still alive in south Georgia. Eventually the marker was removed and replaced with a steel cross, and the Mary Turner Project and Georgia Historical Society's marker program, led by Elyse Butler, began working to replace it on a new site. They found that site on the grounds of Webb Miller Community Church in Hahira, five miles down the road. The church's pastor, Michael Bryant, knew there was a risk of violence in placing the marker on the property, but he was determined that the marker be revived. He explained his resolve on that December morning. So did the descendants of Turner. Audrey Grant, Turner's great-granddaughter, expressed her gratitude. Randy McClain, the great-grandson of one of Turner's brothers, recalled his family's pain at remembering the events of May 1918. Then the family members gathered and unveiled the new marker to the small crowd that had gathered.

> Five miles from this site on May 19, 1918, thirty-three-year-old Mary Turner, eight months pregnant, was burned, mutilated, and shot to death

by a local mob after publicly denouncing her husband's lynching the previous day. In the days immediately following the murder of a White planter by a Black employee on May 16, 1918, at least eleven local African Americans including the Turners died at the hands of a lynch mob in one of the deadliest waves of vigilantism in Georgia's history. No charges were ever brought against known or suspected participants in these crimes. From 1880–1930, as many as 550 people were killed in Georgia in these illegal acts of mob violence.

Of course, there are other stakeholders and family members of the victims left behind. The brother of Will Head remained in the area after the attack, for example, working as a sharecropper until he was able to purchase a small farm near Pavo, Georgia. His family still owns that land today.[35] But the Head and Turner descendants are not the only ones who have been marked with the brand of the historical trauma of the rampage. The Black population in the region still carries the weight of that burden. When Kendrick Johnson died at Lowndes County High School in 2013, the protests that greeted law enforcement after no charges were filed against his alleged white attacker chanted Turner's name almost as often as Johnson's, Valdosta's Black community clearly seeing similarities in the official indifference to the violent loss of Black life. The collective memory of the story surrounding Turner's death has had a massive impact on local, regional, and national understanding, as did the broader rampage that swept the region, the race riot that is not listed alongside similar rampages in Longview, Elaine, Omaha, and others, but rather hides behind the rosier dispositions of white locals who prefer not to remember that kind of violence.

NOTES

INTRODUCTION: RACE, GENDER, AND VIOLENCE

1. Armstrong, *Mary Turner and the Memory of Lynching*, 76–91, 139–48; Armstrong, "Mary Turner's Blues."

2. J. D. Williams, "'Woman Was Lynched the Other Day,'" 86–87.

3. Litwack, *Trouble in Mind*, 288–89; Bennett, Jr., *Before the Mayflower*, 352; Dray, *At the Hands of Persons Unknown*, 245–46. Such was also the case for the history article that really served as the foundational account of the south Georgia violence and helped build a renewed academic and social interest in the event: Meyers, "'Killing Them by the Wholesale.'"

4. Wood and Donaldson, "Lynching's Legacy in American Culture," 10.

5. Ames, "Editorial Treatment of Lynchings"; Wells, *Southern Horrors*; Waldrep, "War of Words," 76–77. See also Hall, *Revolt against Chivalry*; Jack and Massagee, "Ladies and Lynching."

6. Waldrep, "War of Words," 78. For more on Work, see McMurry, *Recorder of the Black Experience*.

7. Waldrep, "War of Words," 79.

8. Waldrep, "War of Words," 80.

9. *Norfolk (VA) Journal and Guide*, December 31, 1932; Waldrep, "War of Words," 81.

10. Waldrep, "War of Words," 83.

11. White, *Rope and Faggot*, 8–11; Waldrep, "War of Words," 85.

12. For more on historical contingency and a need for that broader view, see, e.g., Novick, *That Noble Dream*.

13. Rushdy, *American Lynching*, 20–21. See also Rushdy, "Many Faces in the New South." Rushdy's definitional efforts are intended, at least in part, to demonstrate that lynchings were relatively commonplace during both the slave and Reconstruction periods, thus pushing back the genesis of the lynching period as commonly understood. Pfeifer's *The Roots of Rough Justice* does much the same work, tracing collective violence from the early colonial period through Reconstruction.

14. Wood and Donaldson, "Lynching's Legacy in American Culture," 6. For a good historiographical overview of the lynching phenomenon in American scholarship, see Pfeifer, "At the Hands of Persons Unknown?"

15. Wood and Donaldson, "Lynching's Legacy in American Culture," 10.

16. Italics original to the source. Felman and Laub, *Testimony*, xv, xvii.

17. Césaire, *Discourse on Colonialism*, 41.

18. Rothberg, *Implicated Subject*, 1.

19. Interview with Lee Henderson, September 21, 2020. Henderson performed the original interview with Morrison in 2002.

20. Caruth, *Unclaimed Experience*, 4.

21. De Longoria, "Stranger Fruit," 1–2.

22. Armstrong, "Mary Turner, Hidden Memory, and Narrative Possibility," 28–29. James Weldon Johnson was White's superior at the NAACP.

23. hooks, *Ain't I a Woman*, 4.

24. Gupta, "Since 2015." See also Ritchie, *Invisible No More*.

25. De Longoria, "Stranger Fruit," 40–41.

26. De Longoria, "Stranger Fruit," 58.

27. De Longoria, "Stranger Fruit," 66–68.

28. Morton, *Disfigured Images*, xi–xv, 1–12, 153–58; De Longoria, "Stranger Fruit," 19.

29. Morton, *Disfigured Images*, 12.

30. Brundage does include Turner in an appendix listing lynching victims; *Lynching in the New South*, 35, 80–81, 231. See also Bailey and Washington, "Lynching in the New South"; Hill, "Lynching and the New South." For more on the broader history of lynching, see Tolnay and Beck, *Festival of Violence*; Waldrep, *Many Faces of Judge Lynch*; Feimster, *Southern Horrors*; Waldrep, *Lynching in America*; Wood, *Lynching and Spectacle*; Waldrep, *African Americans Confront Lynching*; Brundage, *Under Sentence of Death*.

31. Brundage, *Lynching in the New South*, 19. Based on his inaccurate account, Brundage categorizes the south Georgia rampage as a posse. Brundage, *Lynching in the New South*, 19–45.

32. Krugler, *1919*, 10–11. For more on Krugler's reasoning, see the conclusion to the present work.

33. See Campney, *This Is Not Dixie*.

34. Grimshaw, "Study in Social Violence," 32–33, 36–37. Broad, far-reaching studies like those of Brundage and Grimshaw are important, but there is also a historiographical trend toward lynching case studies, under which aegis my own account might fall, despite the argument that what is being described is actually a race riot. See McGovern, *Anatomy of a Lynching*; Smead, *Blood Justice*; Downey and Hyser, *No Crooked Death*; Wexler, *Fire in a Canebrake*.

35. Rice, "Gender, Race, and Public Space"; Lumpkins, *American Pogrom*. Elliott Rudwick's early historical monograph on the East St. Louis race riot explains that racial violence had actually begun the previous year, resulting more broadly from political

shifts from Democrat to Republican and the immigration of a new Black population, two phenomena that were not mutually exclusive. Rudwick, *Race Riot at East St. Louis.* As he had in Brooks County in 1918, Walter White went later to investigate the trouble in East St. Louis. White, *Man Called White*, 47–51.

36. Ellsworth, *Death in a Promised Land*; Brophy, *Reconstructing the Dreamland*; L. E. Williams and L. E. Williams, *Anatomy of Four Race Riots*, 56–73.

37. Tuttle, *Race Riot*, viii.

38. McWhirter, *Red Summer*, 114–26; L. E. Williams and L. E. Williams, *Anatomy of Four Race Riots*, 74–97; Krist, *City of Scoundrels.* See also Kerlin, *Voice of the Negro.*

39. L. E. Williams, "Charleston, South Carolina, Riot of 1919"; Tuttle, "Violence in a 'Heathen' Land"; Lakin, "'Dark Night'"; Lawson, "Omaha"; McWhirter, *Red Summer*, 41–54, 82–113, 170–81, 192–207.

40. Whitaker, *On the Laps of Gods*, 19–38; Wells-Barnett, *Arkansas Race Riot*; Stockley, *Blood in Their Eyes*; L. E. Williams and L. E. Williams, *Anatomy of Four Race Riots*, 38–56.

41. Grimshaw, "Study in Social Violence," 10.

42. Waldrep, *Lynching in America*, 199.

43. Brundage, *Lynching in the New South*, 15.

44. Jean, "'Warranted' Lynchings," 127.

45. Jean, "'Warranted' Lynchings," 141.

46. See Hannah-Jones, *1619 Project*; North and Mackaman, *New York Times' 1619 Project*; Wilkerson, *Caste.*

47. See Jean, "'Warranted' Lynchings."

48. LaCapra, *Representing the Holocaust*, xii.

49. Shah and Kilcline, "Trauma in Pregnancy," 615. See also Mattox and Goetzl, "Trauma in Pregnancy"; H. Brown, "Trauma in Pregnancy."

50. Gavin et al., "Racial Discrimination and Preterm Birth"; Dailey et al., "Exploration of Lifetime Trauma"; Braveman et al., "Role of Socioeconomic Factors"; Roberts et al., "Race/Ethnic Differences in Exposure to Traumatic Events."

51. Wood and Donaldson, "Lynching's Legacy in American Culture," 16.

CHAPTER ONE: THE REVOLT AND THE RAMPAGE

1. Department of Commerce, *Tenth Census of the United States, 1880*, Population Schedule, Quitman District, Brooks County, Georgia, sheet no. 73; Department of Commerce, *Twelfth Census of the United States, 1900*, Population Schedule, Quitman District, Brooks County, Georgia, sheet no. 31B; Department of Commerce, *Thirteenth Census of the United States, 1910*, Population Schedule, 1199 G.M., Brooks County, Georgia, sheet no. 3B; Department of Commerce, *Fourteenth Census of the United States, 1920*, Population Schedule, Quitman District, Brooks County, Georgia, sheet no. 5A; *Georgia Property Tax Digest, 1890*, Quitman, Georgia, 1199, p. 31, Georgia Tax Digests, Georgia State Archives, Morrow, Georgia; *Georgia Property Tax Digest, 1872–1877*, Quitman, Georgia, 1199, p. 31, Georgia Tax Digests, Georgia State Archives, Morrow, Georgia; *Quitman*

(GA) Free Press, May 24, 1918. Emma née Smith lived in Valdosta with her husband, Henry B. Spell. *Quitman (GA) Free Press*, May 24, 1918; *RL Polk & Co.'s Valdosta, Ga. City Directory, 1921*, 203; Department of Commerce, *Fifteenth Census of the United States, 1930*, Population Schedule, Valdosta City, Lowndes County, Georgia, sheet no. 12B.

2. The main provisions of the original statute continued into the Revised Statutes of the United States, Sections 1990, 1991, 5526, 5527. Daniel, *Shadow of Slavery*, 19–20; "Peonage Abolition Act," United States Statutes at Large, 39th Congress, session 2, chapter 187, 546. See also "Peonage in Georgia," *Independent* 55 (December 24, 1903): 3079; Myers and Massey, "Race, Labor, and Punishment in Postbellum Georgia."

3. *Clyatt v. United States*, 197 US 207 (1905); Daniel, *Shadow of Slavery*, 33; Howe, "Peonage Cases"; "Procuring Money on Contract for Service," no. 345, *Acts and Resolutions of the General Assembly of the State of Georgia, 1903*, 90–91. For more on the *Clyatt* case, see Daniel, *Shadow of Slavery*, 3–18. Title 26, section 7408, of the Georgia Code stated, "Any person who shall contract with another to perform for him services of any kind with intent to procure money, or other thing of value thereby, and not to perform the service contracted for, to the loss and damage of the hirer; or after having so contracted, shall procure from the hirer money, or other thing of value, with intent not to perform such service, to the loss and damage of the hirer, he shall be deemed a common cheat and swindler, and, upon conviction, shall be punished as for a misdemeanor"; *Code of Georgia of 1933*, Title 26, §7408. Section 7409 declared: "Satisfactory proof of the contract, the procuring thereon of money or other thing of value, the failure to perform the services so contracted for, or failure to return the money so advanced with interest thereon at the time said labor was to be performed, without good and sufficient cause and loss or damage to the hirer, shall be deemed presumptive evidence of the intent referred to in the preceding section"; *Code of Georgia of 1933*, Title 26, §7409. Section 1065 of the Georgia Penal Code, Title 27, provided: "Except where otherwise provided, every crime declared to be a misdemeanor shall be punishable by a fine not to exceed $1,000, imprisonment not to exceed six months, to work in the chain gang on the public roads, or on such other public works as the county or State authorities may employ the chain gang, not to exceed 12 months, any one or more of these punishments in the discretion of the judge"; *Code of Georgia of 1933*, Title 27, §2506.

4. Quotes from Daniel, *Shadow of Slavery*, 22, 36; Vieth, "Kinderlou." Brooks and Lowndes were rural counties, with the exception of Valdosta, which, despite its status as a small town, served as an urban hub for the region. For more on the historical development of Valdosta and Lowndes County, see Schmier, *Valdosta and Lowndes County*; Shelton, *Pines and Pioneers*. For more on Quitman and Brooks County, see Huxford, *History of Brooks County*.

5. Goldenweiser and Truesdell, *Farm Tenancy in the United States*, 23, 24, 25, 48, 49, 58.

6. Bailey and Tolnay, *Lynched*, 108, 113, 209.

7. Quoted in Cooper, "Damned." See also Daniel, *Peonage Files of the U.S. Department of Justice.*

8. Quoted in Cooper, "Damned." See also Daniel, *Peonage Files of the U.S. Department of Justice.*

9. Daniel, *Shadow of Slavery,* 28; Cooper, "Damned"; Clark-Lewis, *Living In, Living Out,* 20. Much of Daniel's interpretation came from Dan T. Carter's master's thesis at the University of Wisconsin, which makes the case for local corruption and describes the practice in places like Georgia of arresting a poor Black citizen on a minor charge, sentencing him to several months of hard labor, then arresting him immediately after serving his sentence as a vagrant and sentencing him again. Carter also describes the organized practice of companies who watched courts and paid the fines of misdemeanor convicts, thus indebting them to the company. Carter, "Prisons, Politics and Business," 94–95.

10. Daniel, *Shadow of Slavery,* 110–31; Cooper, "Damned." The work of economists like Price V. Fishback has given scholars of early twentieth-century peonage another possible motive for the practice. Fishback's scholarship examines the debt peonage of farmers in the 1880s, what most historians today refer to as crop lien, a system wherein farmers remained in cycles of debt to landlords or furnishing merchants to make crops. It was an economically devastating program that further centralized wealth and metastasized the state's wealth gap. Fishback argues that the system of "postharvest debt peonage," however, actually diminished throughout the decade. But versions of sharecropping, tenant farming, and crop lien did not disappear. There was, therefore, a long tradition of versions of debt peonage in place outside the strictures of misdemeanor fine payments and other forced labor that was, in some regards, race neutral. It is analysis that could theoretically lead scholars of early twentieth-century, non-race-neutral debt peonage to read continuity into the system of locking laborers into a forced labor system, a line drawn from slavery to crop lien to debt peonage. It could also lead to an interpretation of a retributive motive, as the shame of earlier monetary and landed versions of debt peonage for white farmers transitioned to a more systematic, state-sponsored debt peonage program propped up by the criminal justice system and almost universally punishing Black workers. Fishback, "Debt Peonage in Postbellum Georgia."

11. *Moultrie (GA) Observer,* May 3, 1918.

12. Vieth, "Kinderlou"; Returns of White Tax Payers, District 1571, Barney, Georgia, Brooks County Tax Digest, 1917, vol. 2 5622, p. 75; Returns of White Tax Payers, District 1751, Barney, Georgia, Brooks County Tax Digest, 1917, vol. 2 5623, p. 82, Revenue, Property Tax Unit, County Property Tax Digests, Georgia Archives, Morrow, Georgia. See also Lichtenstein, *Twice the Work of Free Labor.*

13. "Claude Hampton Smith," serial no. 1131, order no. 706, US World War II Draft Cards, Young Men, 1940–1947, Records of the Selective Service System, 1926–1975,

R.G. 147; "Leila Bertha Windham," Find A Grave Index, https://www.findagrave.com/memorial/54215061.

14. *Butler (GA) Herald*, May 23, 1918.

15. *Thomasville (GA) Daily Times Enterprise*, May 17, 1918; May 18, 1918; *Butler (GA) Herald*, May 23, 1918. This story was repeated with slight variations in multiple papers in the region. The account here is culled from the most common details of the accounts. See, for example, *Clinch County (GA) News*, May 24, 1918; *Cordele (GA) Dispatch*, May 20, 1918; *Tifton (GA) Gazette*, May 18, 1918; *Macon (GA) News*, May 17, 1918; *Waycross (GA) Journal-Herald*, May 17, 1918; May 18, 1918.

16. W. A. May, "Temporary Letters of Administration, C. Hampton Smith," Brooks County, Georgia, June 3, 1918, p. 50, Brooks County Court of Ordinary, Quitman, Georgia; W. A. May, "Letters of Administration, C. Hampton Smith," Brooks County, Georgia, July 2, 1918, p. 121, Brooks County Court of Ordinary, Quitman, Georgia; *Butler (GA) Herald*, May 23, 1918; *Tifton (GA) Gazette*, May 18, 1918.

17. Department of Commerce, *Fourteenth Census of the United States, 1920,* Population Schedule, Quitman Precinct, Brooks County, Georgia, Sheet no. 10B; Department of Commerce, *Fifteenth Census of the United States, 1930*, Population Schedule, Quitman City, Brooks County, Georgia, Sheet no. 1A; Department of Commerce, *Sixteenth Census of the United States, 1940*, Population Schedule, Quitman City, Brooks County, Georgia, Sheet no. 1A.

18. "George U. Spratling," Certificate of Death, Quitman, Georgia, Georgia State Board of Health, Bureau of Vital Statistics, state file no. 28728, Atlanta, Georgia; "George Spratling," Registration Card, World War I, September 12, 1918, serial no. 547, Local Board for the County of Brooks, Quitman, Georgia; Department of Commerce, *Thirteenth Census of the United States, 1910,* Population Schedule, 1199 G.M., Brooks County, Georgia, Sheet no. 7A; Department of Commerce, *Fourteenth Census of the United States, 1920,* Population Schedule, Quitman, Brooks County, Georgia, Sheet no. 3A.

19. *Quitman (GA) Free Press*, May 24, 1918; *Valdosta (GA) Times*, May 25, 1918.

20. *Butler (GA) Herald*, May 23, 1918; October 31, 1918.

21. For more on this contingency, see Jean, "'Warranted' Lynchings"; Aiello, *Grapevine of the Black South.*

22. "Robbery was a secondary motive," reported the *Butler (GA) Herald.* The "assault upon Mrs. Smith" was not part of the original plan but was "evidently decided upon at the spur of the moment." That attack "is what made the white men 'see red.'" *Butler (GA) Herald*, May 23, 1918; October 31, 1918; Department of Commerce, *Thirteenth Census of the United States, 1910*, Barney District, Brooks County, Georgia, Sheet no. 15B; Department of Commerce, *Fourteenth Census of the United States, 1920*, Barney District, Brooks County Georgia, Sheet no. 8B.

23. *Valdosta (GA) Times*, May 25, 1918.

24. Tomberlin, *Images of America*, 8.

25. Tomberlin, *Images of America*; General James Jackson Chapter, DAR, *History of Lowndes County*, 89.

26. *Atlanta Constitution*, May 28, 1916.

27. *Atlanta Constitution*, August 18, 1917; January 7, 1918; February 28, 1918; *Moultrie (GA) Observer*, March 1, 1918.

28. *Atlanta Constitution*, April 15, 1918. The editorial was also reprinted in Valdosta's local paper, taking a clear stance against this form of vigilante antigovernment protest. *Valdosta (GA) Times*, April 29, 1918.

29. *Atlanta Constitution*, March 23, 1918; March 24, 1918.

30. *Valdosta (GA) Times*, April 27, 1918. There were no further specific incidents of violence in response to dipping, but there were still holdouts. In late July several Colquitt County farmers pled guilty to refusing to dip their cattle and paid a fine for the offense. *Moultrie (GA) Observer*, July 30, 1918.

31. *Moultrie (GA) Observer*, April 9, 1918.

32. *Moultrie (GA) Observer*, April 10, 1918.

33. *Moultrie (GA) Observer*, April 12, 1918. He was not alone. Reports showed that several Black farmers in the region purchased bonds of at least five hundred dollars. *Moultrie (GA) Observer*, April 19, 1918.

34. *Atlanta Constitution*, April 15, 1918.

35. *Atlanta Constitution*, May 8, 1918. The day of Hampton Smith's murder in Barney, Golden Crawford, a Black bootlegger returning from Jacksonville, was arrested at the Valdosta station with thirty bottles of whiskey. *Valdosta (GA) Times*, May 18, 1918.

36. Between 1900 and 1910, Brooks County's population increased from 18,606 to 23,832: 1,561 lived in and around Barney, and 7,634 in Quitman. The rural population in 1910 numbered 19,917. Of the county's Black population, 6,975 were women and 7,111 were men. Between 1900 and 1910, Lowndes County's population increased from 20,036 to 24,436, of which 11,715 lived in and around Valdosta.

Between 1910 and 1920, Brooks County's population increased to 24,538, much slower growth than in the previous decade. Black people made up 58.1 percent of the population, and white people 41.8 percent. There was a decline to 4,393 in Quitman, 2,039 of whom were Black. The county's Black population was made up of 7,329 women and 6,918 men. During the same period, Lowndes County's population increased to 26,521—as in Brooks County, much slower growth than in the previous decade. Black people made up 53 percent of the population, and white people 46.5 percent. Of this population, 10,783 were in and around Valdosta, a drop in the city's numbers that demonstrated a growth in rurality in a largely rural area. Black people made up 54.9 of the city's population. *Thirteenth Census of the United States*, vol. 2, *Population, 1910* (Washington, DC: USGPO, 1913), 340, 343, 352, 372, 373, 389; *Fourteenth Census of the United States*, vol. 3, *Population, 1920* (Washington, DC: USGPO, 1922), 208, 215, 222, 224, 372.

37. Moore, *From Whence We Came*, 17. For more on segregated education in Georgia and the South, see Walker and Archung, "Segregated Schooling of Blacks"; Deutsch, *You*

Need a Schoolhouse; Hoffschwelle, *Rosenwald Schools of the American South*; Faircloth, *Class of Their Own*. For the early development of that education in the generation following the Civil War, see Vaughn, *Schools for All*.

38. Moore, *From Whence We Came*, 18; *Macon (GA) Telegraph*, February 18, 1922. For more on Rosenwald schools in Lowndes County, see Fisk University Rosenwald Fund Card File Database, http://rosenwald.fisk.edu/, accessed May 3, 2019.

39. Shelton, *Pines and Pioneers*, 108, 130.

40. D. Williams and T. C. Williams, *Plain Folk in a Rich Man's War*, 144–50.

41. Brundage, *Lynching in the New South*, 35–36.

42. Brundage, *Lynching in the New South*, 195–96.

43. Wood, *Lynching and Spectacle*, 7.

44. *Butler (GA) Herald*, May 23, 1918.

45. See Robertson, *Denmark Vesey*; Aptheker, *Nat Turner's Slave Rebllion*.

46. Pfeifer, *Rough Justice*, 44.

47. "Guardian's Bond," Butts County, Georgia, May 28, 1920, pp. 287, 339, Butts County Court of Ordinary, Jackson, Georgia.

48. Again, there is the contingency of accounts through time and space. My account has attempted to triangulate facts from a variety of local, state, and regional papers to come to a set of conclusions about agreed-upon facts of the case. The *Tifton (GA) Gazette* listed Rice's alias as "James Dison," though no other account used that name. *Atlanta Journal*, May 18, 1918; *Moultrie (GA) Observer*, May 21, 1918; *Memphis Press*, May 21, 1918, NAACP Administrative File, I-C-355, Papers of the NAACP; *Atlanta Constitution*, May 23, 1918; *Augusta (GA) Chronicle*, May 19, 1918; *Tifton (GA) Gazette*, May 18, 1918; *Griffin (GA) Daily News*, May 18, 1918; *Macon (GA) News*, May 18, 1918; May 19, 1918; *Waycross (GA) Journal-Herald*, May 18, 1918.

49. Local genealogist Phillip Williams has argued that Hattie Graham was likely born in Lowndes County rather than Quitman. Her parents married in Lowndes County in 1880, and Perry Graham was living in the Cat Creek district of the county in the mid-1880s prior to Hattie's birth. Phillip Williams, correspondence with the author.

50. Mary is a Catholic name not common to the region. Department of Commerce, *Twelfth Census of the United States, 1900*, Population Schedule, Quitman District, Brooks County, Georgia, Sheet no. B28; Department of Commerce, *Fourteenth Census of the United States, 1920*, Population Schedule, Briggs District, Brooks County, Georgia, Sheet no. 3B; Marriage License, State of Georgia, Colquitt County, February 10, 1917, and Marriage Certificate, State of Georgia, Colquitt County, February 11, 1917, Colquitt County Courthouse, Moultrie, Georgia; *Butler (GA) Herald*, May 23, 1918; *Atlanta Constitution*, May 23, 1918; Forehand, "Place to Lay Their Heads." Phillip Williams has made several searches to learn about Hattie's first husband, Will Smith, but found that his was too common a name for anything certain. One Will Smith was murdered in the early 1910s; another was sent to state prison on a larceny charge in June 1911. Phillip Williams, correspondence with the author.

51. The *Butler (GA) Herald* reversed the common narrative of other sources, claiming that it was Hayes Turner who confessed and that the meeting of conspirators happened at the home of Will Head. The plan in this version of events was for Turner to get the gun and for Johnson and Head to kill Smith. The arrival of a supposed conspirator known as "Black Trouble" from Macon "caused the plan to be changed," the time postponed, and the new arrival to be made "a party to the crime." While Shorty Ford's arrival may have changed plans (see chapter 5), there is no corroboration that Turner confessed to a meeting in Head's home. Every account that includes a confession narrative reverses those names, with Head confessing to a plot at Turner's house. *Butler (GA) Herald*, May 23, 1918; *Moultrie (GA) Observer*, May 21, 1918.

52. *Tifton (GA) Daily Gazette*, May 20, 1918, NAACP Administrative File, I-C-355, Papers of the NAACP; *Moultrie (GA) Observer*, May 21, 1918; *Butler (GA) Herald*, May 23, 1918; Department of Commerce, *Thirteenth Census of the United States, 1910*, Population Schedule, Militia district 1199, Brooks County, Georgia, Sheet no. 18B; Department of Commerce, *Fourteenth Census of the United States, 1920*, Population Schedule, Quitman Precinct, Brooks County, Georgia, Sheet no. 4A.

53. Department of Commerce, *Fifteenth Census of the United States, 1930*, Population Schedule, Barney District, Brooks County, Georgia, Sheet no. 6B; Department of Commerce, *Sixteenth Census of the United States, 1940*, Population Schedule, Barney, Militia district 1571, Brooks County, Georgia, Sheet no. 8B.

54. *Valdosta (GA) Times*, June 1, 1918.

55. *Moultrie (GA) Observer*, May 21, 1918.

56. Similar accounts appeared in the *Augusta Chronicle*, May 20, 1918; *Fitzgerald (GA) Leader-Enterprise and Press*, May 20, 1918; *Valdosta (GA) Times*, May 20, 1918, June 1, 1918; *Tifton (GA) Gazette*, May 20, 1918. The account in the *Macon (GA) News* argued that Turner "was set on fire first, but when the clothes had burned off her body she was hanged." May 20, 1918. There are also dozens of similar accounts in the NAACP Papers. The above account is synthesized from all of these. See NAACP Administrative File, I-C-355, Papers of the NAACP. Early newspaper reports never mentioned that Turner was pregnant. Several accounts in white newspapers, however, claimed, again with no evidence, that the mob recovered Hampton Smith's gold watch from Turner as they carried her to her death. *Memphis Press*, May 20, 1918; *Atlanta Constitution*, May 20, 1918; *St. Louis Argus*, May 24, 1918; *Memphis Commercial Appeal*, May 20, 1918; *New York World*, May 20, 1918; *New York Tribune*, May 20, 1918; *New York Call*, May 20, 1918, in NAACP Administrative File, I-C-355. The account in the *Moultrie (GA) Observer* argues that members of the lynch mob were from not only Brooks and Lowndes Counties but Berrien and Colquitt Counties as well. *Moultrie (GA) Observer*, May 21, 1918.

57. J. D. Williams, "'Woman was Lynched the Other Day,'" 83–84.

58. For more on the gendered nature of lynching, with a particular emphasis on patriarchal assumptions and the role of the rape myth in defining lynching as a predominantly male phenomenon, see Wiegman, *American Anatomies*, 81–113. She rebuts the

argument above that the rarity of the lynching of women was the source of its power, claiming that "black women were routinely lynched, burned, and summarily mutilated, and their public campaign against such terrorism was itself crucial to the political articulations of African American resistance in the early twentieth century" (84).

59. Feimster, *Southern Horrors*, 74, 174.

60. De Longoria, "Stranger Fruit," 71, 74, 110–41.

61. Four years prior, in 1914, Marie Scott, a pregnant teenager, was lynched in Oklahoma after being accused of murdering her white rapist. On June 1, just days after Turner's lynching, in Huntsville, Texas, Sarah Cabiness, her five sons, and her daughter were lynched in retribution after her husband, George, got into an altercation with a white man. Rape, torture, or mutilation almost invariably accompanied the lynching of Black women. *Atlanta Independent*, June 8, 1918.

62. Pfeifer, *Rough Justice*, 62.

63. Pfeifer, *Rough Justice*. For an important study of the lynching of women in the American West, particularly in the nineteenth century and particularly white, Mexican, Native American, and Chinese women, see McLure, "'Who Dares to Style This Female a Woman?'" McLure also describes attacks on several Black women in Texas and Oklahoma in the 1890s (42–43).

64. *Thomasville (GA) Daily Times Enterprise*, May 20, 1918; *Atlanta Journal*, 18 May 1918, NAACP Administrative File, I-C-355.

65. *Butler (GA) Herald*, May 23, 1918; *Thomasville (GA) Daily Times Enterprise*, May 20, 1918.

66. *Chicago Defender*, May 25, 1918.

67. *Chicago Defender*, May 25, 1918.

68. *Quitman (GA) Free Press*, May 24, 1918. The *Cairo (GA) Messenger*, May 24, 1918, included "a man named Julian" in the list of those lynched, either assuming violence against another who fled or putting a name to one of the unnamed victims. The rest of its story jibed with basic regional accounts.

69. *Chicago Defender*, May 25, 1918. The *Defender*'s account was significantly different than its white counterparts, but its description of the lynchings themselves was basically similar. The *Pittsburgh Courier*'s account was similar, describing members of the mob as "inhuman fiends." *Pittsburgh Courier*, May 23, 1918, NAACP Administrative File, I-C-355.

70. Historical work on the *Defender* is, in the context of Black journalism, vast, but the best and most recent account is Michaeli, *Defender*.

CHAPTER TWO: LYNCHINGS AND RIOTS

1. Department of Commerce, *Tenth Census of the United States, 1880*, Population Schedule, Madison, Madison County, Sheet no. 50; Marriage Record, Lowndes County, September 10, 1899, p. 177, Valdosta, Georgia; Department of Commerce, *Twelfth Census*

of the United States, 1900, Population Schedule, Clyattville District, Lowndes County, Georgia, Sheet no. 7A; Department of Commerce, *Thirteenth Census of the United States, 1910,* Population Schedule, Dasher District, Lowndes County, Georgia, Sheet no. 7A; Department of Commerce, *Fourteenth Census of the United States, 1920,* Population Schedule, 663 Militia District, Lowndes County, Georgia, Sheet 4A.

2. *Atlanta Journal,* May 1918, NAACP Administrative File, I-C-355; *Bainbridge (GA) Post-Search Light,* May 23, 1918; *Waycross (GA) Journal-Herald,* May 20, 1918.

3. *Valdosta (GA) Times,* May 25, 1918; *Tifton (GA) Gazette,* May 22, 1918; *Atlanta Constitution,* May 23, 1918; *Macon (GA) News,* May 22, 1918.

4. *Tifton (GA) Gazette,* May 20, 1918; *Valdosta (GA) Times,* May 25, 1918; *Atlanta Constitution,* May 23, 1918.

5. Members of the Johnson search party included Chief of Police Calvin Dampier, Valdosta marshal Oscar T. Hill, Brooks County sheriff Jesse Wade, Lowndes County sheriff J. F. Passmore, Tift County sheriff J. V. Nix (who arrived "with a posse from Berrien County"), Clinch County sheriff Perry R. Lee, and two sheriffs from nearby counties in north Florida. *Butler (GA) Herald,* May 23, 1918; *Atlanta Journal,* May 1918, NAACP Administrative File, I-C-355; *Tifton (GA) Gazette,* May 18, 1918; May 21, 1918; *Fitzgerald (GA) Leader-Enterprise and Press,* May 20, 1918; *Griffin (GA) Daily News,* May 20, 1918; May 21, 1918; *Macon (GA) News,* May 20, 1918.

6. *Atlanta Journal,* May 24, 1918, NAACP Administrative File, I-C-355; *Valdosta (GA) Times,* May 25, 1918; Valdosta, Lowndes County, Georgia, January 1922: Index Map, Sanborn Map Company, University of Georgia Libraries Map Collection, Athens.

7. *Valdosta (GA) Times,* May 25, 1918; *Moultrie (GA) Observer,* May 24, 1918; *Portland Morning Oregonian,* December 28, 1924.

8. *Butler (GA) Herald,* May 23, 1918.

9. *Thomasville (GA) Daily Times Enterprise,* May 23, 1918; *Valdosta (GA) Times,* May 25, 1918. Accounts of the killing remained remarkably consistent in the regional press: *Augusta Chronicle,* May 20, 1918; *Cordele (GA) Dispatch,* May 23, 1918; *Tifton (GA) Gazette,* May 23, 1918; *Fitzgerald (GA) Leader-Enterprise and Press,* May 24, 1918; *Macon (GA) News,* May 23, 1918; *Griffin (GA) Daily News,* May 23, 1918; *Quitman (GA) Free Press,* May 24, 1918; *Waycross (GA) Journal-Herald,* May 23, 1918.

10. *Valdosta (GA) Times,* May 25, 1918.

11. *Quitman (GA) Free Press,* May 24, 1918. Among the papers making such claims was the *Chicago Defender,* which reported the details about Smith being wounded, supposedly shot in the hand by Johnson. Other accounts claimed that Johnson was "unsexed," that the crowd cut off his genitals before burning his body. *Chicago Defender,* June 1, 1918.

12. *Valdosta (GA) Times,* May 25, 1918.

13. *Valdosta (GA) Times,* May 25, 1918; *Valdosta (GA) Times,* June 1, 1918.

14. *Chicago Defender,* June 1, 1918.

15. *Chicago Defender*, June 1, 1918.; Manly, "[Untitled]." For more on Wilmington, see Kirshenbaum, "Vampire That Hovers Over North Carolina.'" For more on Cincinnati, see Taylor, *Frontiers of Freedom*.

16. Louis R. Lautier, "An Illuminating and Eloquent Oration," *Atlanta Independent*, June 8, 1918. Also known as the Camp Logan riot, the Houston riot of 1917, referred to in the *Independent* as the "Houston horror," was a conflict between Black soldiers and the white Houston Police Department that left twenty dead, another nineteen Black soldiers executed after being court-martialed, and forty-one sentenced to life in prison. Haynes, "Houston Mutiny and Riot of 1917."

17. *Butler (GA) Herald*, May 23, 1918.

18. *Atlanta Independent*, June 1, 1918; *Tifton (GA) Gazette*, May 22, 1918; *Griffin (GA) Daily News*, May 22, 1918.

19. *Atlanta Constitution*, May 24, 1918.

20. Tindall, *Emergence of the New South*, 185–87; Hugh M. Dorsey, "In re: Application of Leo M. Frank for Executive Clemency," box 1, folder 3, Hugh M. Dorsey, Sr. Papers; "Argument of Hugh M. Dorsey, Solicitor-General, Atlanta Judicial Circuit, at the trial of Leo M. Frank," box 1, folder 4, Hugh M. Dorsey, Sr. Papers. See Oney, *And the Dead Shall Rise*; Dinnerstein, *Leo Frank Case*.

21. "State of Insurrection in Lowndes and Brooks," NAACP Administrative File, I-C-355; *Atlanta Constitution*, May 23, 1918; *Tifton (GA) Gazette*, May 23, 1918.

22. *Thomasville (GA) Daily Times Enterprise*, May 23, 1918; May 27, 1918; "State of Insurrection in Lowndes and Brooks"; *Baltimore American*, May 23, 1918; *Atlanta Journal*, May 24, 1918, NAACP Administrative File, I-C-355. Among the officers of the Chatham Home Guard that arrived in Valdosta were battalion commander Maj. Bierne Gordon; from Company A, Capt. A. D. Strobhar, Lt. Gordon Cassels, Lt. E. S. Elliott; Company B, Capt. G. B. Pritchard, Lt. Ernest A. Curts; Company C, Capt. Abram Mimis, Lt. D. S. Atkinson, Lt. J. H. Calais; Company D, Capt. J. P. Doyle, Lt. Albion Gruber, Lt. Fred Moore. *Waycross (GA) Journal-Herald*, May 23, 1918.

23. *Atlanta Independent*, May 25, 1918; *Cordele (GA) Dispatch*, May 22, 1918; *Augusta Chronicle*, May 23, 1918. Dorsey's proclamation was as follows: "Whereas, upon the representation made by the judge of the superior courts of the southern judicial circuits, that in Lowndes and Brooks counties, said counties being in his judicial circuit, he had reasonable cause to apprehend an outbreak of a mob, tumult, insurrection, unlawful assembly or combination to oppose the enforcement of the law by intimidation, force or violence within the jurisdiction of where he is by law conservator of the peace, which cannot be speedily suppressed or effectively prevented by an ordinary posse comitatus, and peace officers, and such apprehension being deemed well founded; therefore, by the authority of Section 1434, Volume 11, Code of Georgia, 1910, as amended by the act of the general assembly, approved August 21, 1916, as required therein, I, Hugh M. Dorsey, governor of the state of Georgia, hereby proclaim a state of insurrection. . . .

"Upon arrival of the military commander he will assume charge of the situation.

"All persons, who may heretofore have given aid or otherwise supported the lawlessness existing in the said locality, who shall return to peaceful occupation, holding no communication of any kind with the lawless persons, will not be disturbed.

"All rights of property of whatever kind will not be disturbed, except as exigencies of the public welfare may necessitate, and by direct command of the commanding officer of the troop.

"All shops and places of business except as otherwise ordered by the military commander, will be kept open as usual in the time of peace, and all persons are enjoined to continue their customary and peaceful occupation, except as herein provided, when the existence of martial law implies to the contrary, the usual laws of the community shall be in force. Crime will be tried by the military commission, or civil court, as may be practicable, as the governor may decide.

"No publication, newspaper, pamphlet, hand-bill or otherwise, reflecting upon the United States, or the state of Georgia, or their officers, and no article commenting in any way on the work and actions of the military authorities, will be permitted.

"All assemblages in the said locality, whether day or night, are prohibited only by permission of the military commander.

"Any persons found in said locality who appears to be habitually idle and without occupation will be placed under arrest.

"While it is the desire of the authorities to exercise the powers of martial law mildly, it must not be supposed that they will not be vigorously enforced as the occasion arises.

"Done under my hand and the Great Seal of the State of Georgia, at the capitol in Atlanta, on the 22d day of May, 1918 . . . .

"H.M. Dorsey, Governor."

(*Atlanta Constitution*, May 23, 1918).

24. *Quitman (GA) Free Press*, May 31, 1918.

25. *Atlanta Journal*, May 24, 1918, NAACP Administrative File, I-C-355.

26. Commons, "Labor Conditions in Meat Packing and the Recent Strike." See also Barrett, *Work and Community in the Jungle*; Brody, *Butcher Workmen*; Halpern, *Down on the Killing Floor.*

27. Wilkerson, *Warmth of Other Suns*, 161.

28. Cohen, "Negro Involuntary Servitude in the South," 39–40; Bernstein, *Only One Place of Redress*, 8–27.

29. *Williams v. Fears*, 179 US 270 (1900).

30. *Allgeyer v. Louisiana*, 165 US 578 (1897).

31. "An Act in Relation to Contracts of Persons of Color," Chapter 1470, no. 7, January 12, 1866, Acts and Resolutions Adopted by the General Assembly of Florida, 1865 (Tallahassee: Office of the Floridian, 1866), 32; "An Act to Punish Vagrants and Vagabonds," 28–29; "An Act to Extend the Provisions of an Act Entitled an Act in Relation to Contracts of Persons of Color to All Persons without Distinction of Color," Chapter 1551, no. 18, December 13, 1866, in *Acts and Resolutions Adopted by the General Assembly of the State of Florida, 1866*, 21–22.

32. Wilkerson, *Warmth of Other Suns*, 533.

33. David Levering Lewis quoted in Stockley, *Blood in Their* Eyes. Dunkley, "Red Summer of 1919". See also Norvell and Tuttle, "Views of a Negro during 'the Red Summer' of 1919"; Ellis, "J. Edgar Hoover and the 'Red Summer' of 1919"; Capeci, "Race Riot Redux."

34. Two years later, in 1829, Russwurm's frustration was such that he migrated to Liberia. There, in 1830, he created the *Liberia Herald.* Painter, "Black Journalism," 30–32.

35. Painter, "Black Journalism," 41. For more on Wells, see McMurry, *To Keep the Waters Troubled*; Bay, *To Tell the Truth Freely*; Schechter, *Ida B. Wells-Barnett and American Reform*; Silkey, *Black Woman Reformer.*

36. Painter, "Black Journalism," 31–32.

37. Fenderson, "Negro Press as a Social Instrument," 182–83.

38. Kellogg, "Northern Liberals and Black America," 109–13; Leonard, "Is That What We Fought For?" 468–69.

39. *Macon (GA) Telegraph*, September 27, 1900; *Atlanta Constitution*, September 27, 1900.

40. *Waycross (GA) Journal*, June 5, 1903; Alexander Ackerman to Attorney General, December 2, 1903, Casefile 909–1898, reel 1, Peonage Files of the Department of Justice, 1901–1945.

41. Terrell, "Misdemeanor Convicts."

42. Catherine McRee Carter, "History of Kinderlou, Georgia, 1860–1940," December 7, 1940, p. 25, box 122, folder 1, Kinderlou Papers, Archive Row 1, Lowndes County Historical Society, Valdosta, Georgia.

43. For more, see Godshalk, *Veiled Visions*; Mixon, *Atlanta Riot.*

44. For more, see Carlson, "'With Malice Towards None'"; Crouthamel, "Springfield Race Riot of 1908"; Senechal, *Sociogenesis of a Race Riot.*

45. The number of lynchings come from the count of the NAACP. Similar counts by the Tuskegee Institute proved even higher for 1919. The different counts stem from different definitions of lynching. Waldrep, *Many Faces of Judge Lynch*, 5–7, 127–45.

46. Bailey and Tolnay, *Lynched*, 123, 131, 134, 141.

47. The *Item* was not the only newspaper to notice. The *Times-Picayune* carried similar commentary, as did the *Southwestern Christian Advocate. New Orleans Item*, May 6, 1919; *New Orleans Times-Picayune*, May 12, 1919; "The Monroe Lynching," *Southwestern Christian Advocate*, June 12, 1919; National Association for the Advancement of Colored

People, *Thirty Years of Lynching in the United States, 1889–1918* (New York: Arno, 1969), 71–73, 104–5; *Papers of the NAACP*, part 7, series A, reel 12, 348–52, 354, 356, 373–80, 383, 393. See also Aiello, "Proximity of Moral Ire."

48. Pfeifer, *Rough Justice*, 68–69, 73.

49. Pfeifer, *Rough Justice*, 74.

50. Interestingly, the address did not specifically demand a federal anti-lynch law, but the association's national conference, held the following month, proclaimed that its goal was "to make America safe for Americans." The NAACP's first Louisiana branch was established in Shreveport in 1914. New Orleans, Alexandria, and Baton Rouge established branches by the end of the decade, with Monroe finally participating in 1925. None, however, wielded any real power. Dr. Claude Hudson, Shreveport branch president, wrote in 1923, "The NAACP is thoroughly hated in this section." "Organizing 100,000 for Negro Rights, 'to Make America Safe for Americans': National Conference in Cleveland, June 21 to 29," *Papers of the NAACP*, part 1, reel 8, *Annual Conference Proceedings, 1910–1950* (Bethesda, MD: University Publications of America, 1982); *New Orleans Item*, May 6, 1919; Grant, *Anti-lynching Movement*, 67; Zangrando, *NAACP Crusade Against Lynching*, 46–50; "For Release, Monday, May 5," *Papers of the NAACP*, part 7: The Anti-lynching Campaign, 1912–1955, Series A, reel 12 of 30, 359–60 [hereinafter cited as *Papers of the NAACP*, part 7, series A, reel 12]; "Minutes of the Meeting of the Board of Directors, March 10, 1919," *Papers of the NAACP*, part 1, reel 1, *Minutes of the Meetings of the Board of Directors, 1909–1950* (Bethesda, MD: University Publications of America, 1982); de Jong, *Different Day*, 67; Fairclough, *Race and Democracy*, 20.

51. McTaggart, "Empty Noose," 794. McTaggart notes that Wells and White were not alone in the practice. Mary Burrill, James Weldon Johnson, and Claude McKay engaged in much the same descriptive literary efforts. As lynching incidents decreased, however, imagery and descriptions of them became more figurative and metaphorical rather than specific and detailed. McTaggart reads the change, moving through the twentieth century, as detrimental to civil rights efforts because the new figurative accounts allowed room for white excuse making and denied the visceral reality of white racial violence.

52. In the early 1930s, Jessie Daniel Ames's Association of Southern Women for the Prevention of Lynching took a similar moral stand against mob violence that argued against federal legislation. If people allowed southern courts to try Black men for crimes considered worthy of lynching, the courts would convict them. She sought to convince white southerners to change by emphasizing successful recourses to law instead of harping on southern male barbarism. Hall, *Revolt against Chivalry*, 62–64, 159–75, 193–97; Waldrep, *Many Faces of Judge Lynch*, 132–34.

53. Moton, "South and the Lynching Evil"; "Lynching Evil from a Southern Standpoint"; Zangrando, *NAACP Crusade against Lynching*, 48; "Lynching Evil"; "Fight in Texas against Lynching"; "New Phases of the Fight against Lynching." For more on the debates on lynching in the first decades of the twentieth century, including the

definitions used to categorize the practice, see Waldrep, *Many Faces of Judge Lynch*; Brundage, *Lynching in the New South*; Tolnay and Beck, *Festival of Violence.*

54. Though African American newspapers such as the *New York Age* and *New Orleans Vindicator* echoed Seligmann's sentiments, they remained far more hopeful that justice would be served. Seligmann, "Protecting Southern Womanhood"; "How Shall the Black Man's Burden Be Lifted?"; "*New York Age*—May 24, 1919," *Papers of the NAACP*, part 7, series A, reel 12, 403–4; "*New Orleans Vindicator*—May 17, 1919," *Papers of the NAACP*, part 7, series A, reel 12, 401.

55. A. V. Collins, *All Hell Broke Loose*, 3–11. Paul Gilje develops a similar model of race riots in the period, in the broader context of riots of all kinds in American history. See Gilje, *Rioting in America*, 87–115.

56. Ifill, *On the Courthouse Lawn*, 57–68.

CHAPTER THREE: MEMORY AND MYTHMAKING

1. *Butler (GA) Herald*, October 31, 1918. The actual taxable value in Brooks County rose from $7,147,548 in 1917 to $7,987,925 in 1918. *Valdosta (GA) Times*, August 3, 1918.

2. *Atlanta Independent*, May 25, 1918; Pratt, "Unicoi County Court: 1876–1918," 27–29; *Johnson City (TN) Daily*, May 23, 1918.

3. *Atlanta Independent*, May 25, 1918.

4. *Atlanta Independent*, May 25, 1918.

5. For coverage of the national run-up to war and Wilson's role, see: Link, *Campaigns for Progressivism and Peace*; Link, *Woodrow Wilson and a Revolutionary World*; Peterson, *Propaganda for War.*

6. Kirschbaum, *Burning Beethoven*; Kennedy, *Over Here*; Murray, *Red Scare*; Shepley, *Palmer Raids and the Red Scare.*

7. *Augusta (GA) Chronicle*, May 24, 1918.

8. Campney, "'State of Violent Contrasts'" 259.

9. *Atlanta Constitution*, May 24, 1918, NAACP Administrative File, I-C-355.

10. *Atlanta Independent*, June 1, 1918.

11. *Augusta (GA) Chronicle*, May 22, 1918; May 25, 1918.

12. *Augusta Chronicle*, May 22, 1918; May 25, 1918. *Augusta (GA) Chronicle* quoted in *New York Times*, May 25, 1918, NAACP Administrative File, I-C-355.

13. *Augusta (GA) Chronicle* quoted in *New York Times*, May 25, 1918; *Augusta (GA) Chronicle* editorial reprinted in *New York Age*, June 1, 1918, NAACP Administrative File, I-C-355.

14. Jean, "'Warranted' Lynchings," 132, 135; Wood, *Lynching and Spectacle*, 7.

15. *Valdosta (GA) Times*, June 1, 1918.

16. *Augusta (GA) Chronicle*, May 27, 1918. The *Chronicle*'s stance generated a variety of reactions, all of which the paper printed. Augusta's Evangelical Ministers Union, a group of Black ministers, wrote supporting the stance. A letter writer from Union Point

called lynching "a crime against civilization," arguing that "just such crimes as those are what caused God to overthrow the world, with a flood, in Noah's day." The *Chronicle* printed such attacks on lynching without comment, but when an anonymous supporter wrote a long screed extolling the virtues of mob rule and defending Dorsey and white Brooks County, the paper included an addendum: "The writer of the above insists that we publish his communication in full," the editor explained, "which we take pleasure in doing—as a better argument against lynching than any we could hope to write. He also demands that we reply to it. Very well, if we must, we must; and our reply is—compulsory education." *Augusta (GA) Chronicle*, May 25, 1918; May 26, 1918. The *Chronicle* also reprinted an editorial from the *Albany (GA) Herald* decrying mob violence. The *Herald* supposed that most who took part in the Brooks County lynchings would have "shuddered" at the prospect of such violence before being swept up in racial fury. "And therein is the hideousness of mob law." The editorial described Sidney Johnson's body being dragged behind a car after his death. But that was a distraction from what really mattered, the paper explained. "The thing that was dragged in the dust was Justice." *Augusta Chronicle*, May 27, 1918.

17. *Atlanta Independent*, June 1, 1918. The paper continued the following week, attacking Dorsey for his response and arguing that the reason for lynching and mob violence was not the rape of white women but instead "race prejudice and race hate." *Atlanta Independent*, June 8, 1918.

18. *Savannah Press*, May 22, 1918. For Cumming see Joseph B. Cumming Recollections, 1920, Collection no. 2560-z, Southern Historical Collection, Louis Round Wilson Special Collections Library, University of North Carolina, Chapel Hill; Joseph B. Cumming Papers, 1889–2009, Collection no. 942, Stuart A. Rose Manuscript Archives, Rare Book Library, Emory University, Atlanta.

19. *Cordele (GA) Dispatch*, May 22, 1918; May 23, 1918.

20. *Tifton (GA) Gazette*, May 24, 1918.

21. *Atlanta Constitution*, May 24, 1918, NAACP Administrative File, I-C-355.

22. *Atlanta Constitution*, May 21, 1918, NAACP Administrative File, I-C-355. "Every recurrence of crime that is taken as provocation of lynching," the paper explained, "supports additional proof of the ineffectiveness of lynch law to stamp out crime."

23. *Atlanta Constitution*, May 24, 1918, NAACP Administrative File, I-C-355.

24. The *Butler (GA) Herald* justified the lynchings prior to Johnson's by describing the attack on Smith's wife, who "soon to give birth to her first child": "One negro held her to prevent her screaming while another attacked her and . . . this was repeated until the woman was almost unconscious"; *Butler (GA) Herald*, May 23, 1918. The mob formed to seek justice for her, the paper explained in traditional self-justifying fashion. Johnson was to be lynched for killing Smith, and white readers understood that behavior as an eye-for-an-eye form of justice, but even though any marginally reasonable excuse would suffice, the murder of the others required a form of explanation unrelated to a killing the victims clearly did not commit. The *Coffee County (GA) Progress* (June 6, 1918)

in Douglas did not mention the violence but did produce editorials condemning "loafers and pacifists" and argued in the wake of the violence that "the only way to build up a town is for everyone to go hand in hand," "banish all feelings of discord," and "let harmony prevail."

25. Jean, "'Warranted' Lynchings," 129.

26. *Camilla (GA) Enterprise*, May 31, 1918. For more on the Camilla race riot, see Butler, "'Almost Too Terrible to Believe.'" The *Waycross (GA) Journal-Herald* (May 24, 1918) wholly endorsed Dorsey's "homeopathic treatment to cure the lynching fever that seems to be prevalent in Georgia just now." Homeopathic doctors, the paper explained, asked "about one hundred and fifty questions, trying to find out the real cause of the trouble." Dorsey's diagnosis blaming Black criminals for the problem met with the *Journal-Herald*'s approval. "There is no use talking about it," the *Cairo (GA) Messenger* (June 7, 1918) claimed after Dorsey's statement. "Hugh M. Dorsey has made Georgia the best Governor she has had in many a day and if he runs, which no doubt he will, he will not have any opposition at all." The *Messenger* (May 31, 1918) endorsed the *Valdosta (GA) Times* in its approval of Dorsey's statement and in its feud with Tom Loyless of the *Augusta Chronicle*.

27. "White women must be inviolate before the hands of force," the *Telegraph* claimed, "and race sanctity, which with white people is vested peculiarly and jealously with their women, calls primitively and savagely when the hand of the black man is laid on the white woman, or the eye of the black man even rests on the white woman." The paper's best suggestion for Black Georgia was to lynch its own Black criminals so that white people did not have to. It speculated that after the rampage in Brooks and Lowndes Counties and a lynching in Crisp County, there would probably be another soon: "Things seem to happen in threes." *Macon (GA) Telegraph*, May 25, 1918, NAACP Administrative File, I-C-355.

28. Graham, *Children of the Slaves*, 203–8.

29. *Valdosta (GA) Times*, May 25, 1918.

30. *Thomasville (GA) Daily Times Enterprise*, May 27, 1918.

31. *Thomasville (GA) Daily Times Enterprise*, May 27, 1918.

32. Whitaker, *On the Laps of Gods*, 37–38; Colored Welfare League of Augusta to Woodrow Wilson, May 21, 1918, Woodrow Wilson Papers: Series 4: Executive Office File, 1912–1921; 543, 1913–1918, July 25, Library of Congress, Washington, DC.

33. Robert Russa Moton to Woodrow Wilson, June 15, 1918, Woodrow Wilson Papers: Series 4: Executive Office File, 1912–1921; 543, 1913–1918, July 25, Library of Congress, Washington, DC.

34. Woodrow Wilson to Robert Russa Moton, June 18, 1918, Woodrow Wilson Papers: Series 4: Executive Office File, 1912–1921; 543, 1913–1918, July 25, Library of Congress, Washington, DC. For examples of other protests sent to the president urging some kind of action, see telegrams and letters from R. L. Bailey to Woodrow Wilson, June 28, 1918; G. A. Gregg and C. F. Matthews to Woodrow Wilson, June 28, 1918; Theodore C. Carter

to Woodrow Wilson, June 29, 1918; Robert McMurdy, June 29, 1918; George W. Gross to Woodrow Wilson, June 29, 1918; J. D. Nesome to Woodrow Wilson, June 29, 1918, Woodrow Wilson Papers: Series 4: Executive Office File, 1912–1921; 543, 1913–1918, July 25, Library of Congress, Washington, DC. The messages listed in this note are just a small fraction of the dozens in file 543 requesting that Wilson make a statement against lynching.

35. Wilson, "Proclamation." Wilson was also responding to the NAACP's investigation into the mobs of south Georgia and the sensational accounts provided by the group's investigator, Walter White (see chapter 4). The *Crisis*, meanwhile, speculated that the motive for the proclamation "was a desire to protect possible victims of Prussian propaganda." Janken, *Walter White*, 33; "We Save Others," *Crisis* 17 (March 1919): 240.

36. *Atlanta Independent*, June 1, 1918. Davidson continued: "Might is still in the saddle. If there were any who indulged the fond delusion that right was on the throne, and that men were governed by it rather than force, that delusion was dispelled in the great orgies that took place in Brooks and Lowndes counties where six human beings were put to death by mobs, without rhyme or reason."

37. *Atlanta Independent*, June 1, 1918.

38. *Bainbridge (GA) Post-Search Light*, May 23, 1918.

39. *Atlanta Journal*, May 1918, NAACP Administrative File, I-C-355.

40. *Memphis News Scimitar*, May 21, 1918, NAACP Administrative File, I-C-355.

41. *Butler (GA) Herald*, May 23, 1918, 7; *Augusta Chronicle*, May 21, 1918, 1; *Bainbridge (GA) Post-Search Light*, May 23, 1918; *Macon (GA) News*, May 20, 1918; *Nashville (GA) Herald*, May 24, 1918, 1; *Shreveport Times*, May 21, 1918, NAACP Administrative File, I-C-355.

42. *Quitman (GA) Free Press*, May 24, 1918.

43. *Butler (GA) Herald*, May 23, 1918.

44. *Memphis Commercial Appeal*, May 21, 1918, NAACP Administrative File, I-C-355.

45. *Baltimore Daily Herald*, May 20, 1918, NAACP Administrative File, I-C-355.

46. *Baltimore Daily Herald*, May 22, 1918, NAACP Administrative File, I-C-355.

47. *New York Post*, May 20, 1918, NAACP Administrative File, I-C-355.

48. *Pittsburgh Courier*, June 1, 1918, NAACP Administrative File, I-C-355.

49. *New York Post*, May 20, 1918.

50. The *New York Tribune* expressed its "horror at the lynching of a colored woman in Georgia," whose only crime was denouncing the lynching of her husband. *New York Tribune*, May 22, 1918, NAACP Administrative File, I-C-355.

51. "One hanging of a white man for participation in negro lynching would mean more for Georgia than almost anything that could happen." *Brooklyn Eagle*, May 20, 1918, NAACP Administrative File, I-C-355.

52. The *New York Age* lamented the "cowardly lynching of female" suspects and celebrated white publications like the *Augusta Chronicle* for taking a stand against the violence. The *Chronicle* denounced the "detestable and cowardly attack" against a woman.

"All civilized people must stand aghast at such a crime, and who does not is at heart a criminal and a coward." *New York Age*, June 1, 1918, NAACP Administrative File, I-C-355.

53. The *New York World* lamented that on the same page that the paper covered the valor of Black soldiers in France, it was also compelled to report on the south Georgia lynchings, emphasizing in particular, as did most sources, the lynching of Mary Turner. In the *World*'s account, as in all of them prior to White's, Turner was not pregnant, but she did not need to be: she was a woman, and of "legal evidence against her there was none"; *New York World* editorial reprinted in *New York Age*, May 25, 1918. The juxtaposition of the account with that of Black service in defense of the country was understandably jarring to the editors, highlighting the problems of racism and of extralegal violence in a country trying to make the world safe for democracy. There was similar commentary in *Commerce and Finance*, an early Wall Street publication. *Commerce and Finance*, May 29, 1918, NAACP Administrative File, I-C-355.

54. The *Baltimore Herald*, in response to the south Georgia riots and Dorsey's impotent response, asked, "How many convictions are recorded in Georgia of white men who in the past fifty years have been convicted and punished for the murder of or the commission of violence upon the body of Negroes?" It was a powerful question, given that each of its readers knew that the answer was zero. *Baltimore Herald*, May 25, 1918, NAACP Administrative File, I-C-355.

55. *Bridgeport (CT) Telegram*, May 25, 1918, NAACP Administrative File, I-C-355.

56. *Griffin (GA) Daily News*, June 5, 1918, 1; *Moultrie (GA) Observer*, June 7, 1918, 14; *Camilla (GA) Enterprise*, June 7, 1918, 5.

57. *Quitman (GA) Free Press*, May 24, 1918.

58. *Quitman (GA) Free Press*, May 24, 1918.

59. *Moultrie (GA) Observer*, May 24, 1918.

60. *Moultrie (GA) Observer*, May 28, 1918.

61. *Moultrie (GA) Observer*, May 21, 1918.

62. *Moultrie (GA) Observer*, May 21, 1918.

63. Ohl and Potter, "United We Lynch," 196.

64. Vivian, *Public Forgetting*, 10.

65. Ohl and Potter, "United We Lynch," 188.

66. Ohl and Potter, "United We Lynch," 196.

67. Williamson, "Wounds Not Scars," 1229, 1252. There is a similar case made in other accounts specifically related to the relationship between photography, lynching, and memory. The emphasis on the visual in such accounts makes them less vital here, but their insights into memory development is still valuable. See, for example, Raiford, "Photography and the Practices of Critical Black Memory."

68. See, for example, the reports of Robin D. G. Kelley and David Levering Lewis in "Referees' Reports," 1258–61, 1261–64; Hall, "Later Comment"; Thelen, "What We See and Can't See in the Past."

69. See, for example, Emma Coleman Jordan's critique of Jacqueline Dowd Hall's *Revolt against Chivalry*, which describes the participation of white women like Jessie Daniel Ames in the anti-lynching crusade of the 1930s. "Although Hall reports the racism of white women leaders of various anti-lynching initiatives toward black women collaborators, she does not provide a sustained examination of the contradictory, often mutually antagonistic impulses these leaders displayed." Jordan, "Crossing the River of Blood between Us," 553–56. See also Metress, "Culture, Memory, and the Legacies of Lynching."

70. Hill, *Beyond the Rope*, 5.

71. For more on this phenomenon, see Ore, *Lynching*; Madison, *Lynching in the Heartland.*

72. Markovitz, *Legacies of Lynching*, xv, xviii, xx.

73. Jordan, "Crossing the River of Blood between Us," 547, 562–63.

74. Halbwachs, *On Collective Memory*, 38; Barthes, *Mythologies*, 13.

75. Assman and Czaplicka, "Collective Memory and Cultural Identity," 129–30.

76. Zelizer, "Reading the Past against the Grain," 226.

77. J. D. Williams, "'Woman Was Lynched the Other Day,'" 86; Alexander, "'Can You Be BLACK and Look at This?'" 83.

78. E. B. Brown, "Imaging Lynching," 114.

79. Crabtree, "Devil Is Watching You," 43–44.

CHAPTER FOUR: LOST IN TRANSLATION

1. *Atlanta Independent*, June 1, 1918; John R. Shillady to Hugh M. Dorsey, May 20, 1918; John R. Shillady to Chamber of Commerce, Atlanta, May 20, 1918, NAACP Administrative File, I-C-353.

2. Shillady, *Planning Public Expenditures*; NAACP, *Mobbing of John R. Shillady*; Harrison, "Shillady Resigns."

3. Walter White to John R. Shillady, telegram, June 3, 1918, NAACP Administrative File, I-C-353.

4. Janken, *Walter White*, 14–15.

5. Among those concerned about White's youth and inexperience in such a vital role was W. E. B. Du Bois, who had left Atlanta University prior to White's attendance but knew the family and had taught White's older siblings. Janken, *Walter White*, 20–57; Dyja, *Walter White*, 12–18.

6. Janken, *Walter White*, 28–31; White, "Burning of Jim McIlherron." It might seem a curious choice to use White's account of the McIlherron case as part of a study that casts doubt on parts of another White investigation, but it was the major national point of entry for the Tennessee incident, and at the very least it reflects White's own interpretation of events as he was preparing to launch a similar investigation in south Georgia.

7. White, *Man Called White*, 40–43.

8. Janken, *Walter White*, 33.

9. Spratling told his tale to White in Grant's office in Quitman. Walter White, "Memo Re Brooks-Lowndes Counties Lynchings of May, 1918," NAACP Administrative File, I-C-353; Walter White, Memorandum for Mr. Dam Re: Georgia Lynchings, November 19, 1918, NAACP Administrative File, I-C-355, Quitman, GA.

10. His youngest son followed in his father's footsteps, traveling to New York to become a dentist. Department of Commerce, *Fourteenth Census of the United States, 1920*, Population Schedule, Quitman, Brooks County, Georgia, 10A; *Nashville City Directory, 1915*, 316; "Athens Nathaniel Grant," Registration Card, World War I, September 12, 1918, Serial no. 807, Local Board for the County of Brooks, Quitman, Georgia; "Athens Nathaniel Grant," US World War II Draft Cards, Young Men, 1940–1947, Records of the Selective Service System, 147, box 165; "Athens N. Grant," December 10, 1943, New York Guard Service Cards and Enlistment Records.

11. Cobb died on August 28, 1938. Department of Commerce, *Twelfth Census of the United States, 1900*, Population Schedule, Valdosta, District M663, Lowndes, Georgia, Sheet no. B27; *RL Polk & Co.'s Valdosta City Directory, 1904*, 85; *RL Polk & Co.'s Valdosta, Ga. City Directory, 1908–9*, 195; Department of Commerce, *Fourteenth Census of the United States, 1920*, Population Schedule, Quitman, Brooks County, Georgia, Sheet no. 9B; "Maurice H. Cobb," Certificate of Death, Georgia State Board of Health, Bureau of Vital Statistics, state file no. 19557, Atlanta.

12. *Banks County (GA) Journal*, December 2, 1903; *Atlanta Constitution*, November 25, 1903; Dittmer, *Black Georgia in the Progressive Era*, 73; Alexander Ackerman to Attorney General, December 2, 1903, Casefile 909–1898, reel 1, Peonage Files of the Department of Justice, 1901–1945.

13. Daniel, *Shadow of Slavery*, 36; "Lowndes County Negroes Entered Pleas of Guilty," unidentified newspaper clipping enclosed in Alexander Ackerman to Attorney General, March 27, 1905, Casefile 909-1898, reel 1, Peonage Files of the Department of Justice, 1901–1945.

14. Athens N. Grant to Walter White, November 20, 1918, NAACP Administrative File, I-C-355, Quitman, GA.

15. Whipple died on March 13, 1934. Department of Commerce, *Tenth Census of the United States, 1880*, Population Schedule, Quitman District, Brooks County, Georgia, Sheet no. 77; Department of Commerce, *Thirteenth Census of the United States, 1910*, Population Schedule, 1199 G.M., Brooks County, Georgia, Sheet no. 16B; Department of Commerce, *Fourteenth Census of the United States, 1920*, Population Schedule, Quitman, Brooks County, Georgia, Sheet no. 4B; "William A. Whipple," 17484, Death Index, 1919–1998, Georgia Health Department, Office of Vital Records, Atlanta.

16. White suggested to Dorsey that each of the men be required to supply alibis to prove their innocence. Walter White, "Memorandum for Governor Dorsey from Walter F. White," July 10, 1918, NAACP Administrative File, I-C-353.

17. Department of Commerce, *Fourteenth Census of the United States, 1920*, Population

Schedule, Quitman District, Brooks County, Georgia, Sheet no. 13B; Department of Commerce, *Thirteenth Census of the United States, 1910*, Population Schedule, 1199 G.M., Brooks County, Georgia, Sheet no.4B; Marriage License, Brooks County, Georgia, November 14, 1914, Brooks County Marriage Records, 1828–1978, p. 102, Georgia State Archives, Morrow.

18. Department of Commerce, *Thirteenth Census of the United States, 1910*, Population Schedule, 1199 .M., Brooks County, Georgia, Sheet no. 1B, 18B; Department of Commerce, *Fourteenth Census of the United States, 1920*, Population Schedule, Quitman Precinct, Brooks County, Georgia, Sheet no. 9B, 18B; Department of Commerce, *Fifteenth Census of the United States, 1930*, Population Schedule, Quitman, Brooks County, Georgia, Sheet no. 11A, 4B; Marriage License, Brooks County, Georgia, November 14, 1914, Brooks County Marriage Records, 1828–1978, p. 288, Georgia State Archives, Morrow; Department of Commerce, *Twelfth Census of the United States, 1900*, Quitman District, Brooks County, Georgia, Sheet no. 2A.

19. John R. Shillady, Press Release, Press Service of the NAACP, August 1, 1918, NAACP Administrative File, I-C-355; White, "Memorandum for Governor Dorsey"; John R. Shillady to Woodrow Wilson, July 24, 1918, NAACP Administrative File, I-C-353.

20. Shillady, Press Release, August 1, 1918; White, "Memorandum for Governor Dorsey."

21. Shillady, Press Release, August 1, 1918; White, "Memorandum for Governor Dorsey."

22. White, "Memorandum for Governor Dorsey."

23. Shillady, Press Release, August 1, 1918; White, "Memorandum for Governor Dorsey."

24. There is a growing body of literature on trauma theory. For more on the relationship between representation and trauma, see, for example, Caruth, *Unclaimed Experience*; Hartman, "On Traumatic Knowledge and Literary Studies"; McNally, *Remembering Trauma*; and Culbertson, "Embodied Memory, Transcendence, and Telling," among many others.

25. See, for example, "Tree on Which Hayes Turner Was Lynched," NAACP Administrative File, I-C-355, Quitman, GA.

26. Untitled memorandum draft, NAACP Administrative File, I-C-353.

27. John R. Shillady to Editor of the *Tribune*, New York City, August 8, 1918, NAACP Administrative File, I-C-353; Press Release, August 5, 1918, NAACP Administrative File, I-C-355, Quitman, GA.

28. Wood, *Lynching and Spectacle*, 14; Bolton Smith to John R. Shillady, November 29, 1918; Office Secretary to Bolton Smith, December 8, 1918, NAACP Administrative File, I-C-337.

29. John R. Shillady to Woodrow Wilson, July 25, 1918, Memorandum for Governor Dorsey from Walter F. White, July 10, 1918, Woodrow Wilson Papers: Series 4: Executive Office File, 1912–1921; 543, 1913–1918, July 25, Library of Congress, Washington, DC.

30. John R. Shillady to Hugh M. Dorsey, telegram, August 21, 1918, Hugh M. Dorsey to John R. Shillady, August 27, 1918, NAACP Administrative File, I-C-353.

31. C. P. Dam to John R. Shillady, September 13, 1918, NAACP Administrative File, I-C-355, Quitman, GA. Dam's lobbying was part of a long-standing effort that never prompted the federal government to take reasonable action on lynching. For an account of the full role of the federal government in lynching and its failure, judicially and executively, to stop the practice, along with such efforts in Congress, see Kato, *Liberalizing Lynching*, which describes the circumstance as "constitutional anarchy."

32. Walter White to C. P. Dam, September 16, 1918, NAACP Administrative File, I-C-353.

33. Walter White to C. P. Dam, September 18, 1918; Dam to White, September 17, 1918, NAACP Administrative File, I-C-353.

34. The House opened its session in late June by declaring its support for the war effort. The Senate denounced alcohol and called for its banning. Neither body commented on the violence in south Georgia. C. P. Dam to Walter White, September 21, 1918, NAACP Administrative File, I-C-353; *Atlanta Constitution*, September 14, 1916; *Journal of the House of Representatives of the State of Georgia*, 12–13, 400–401, 443; *Journal of the Senate of Representatives of the State of Georgia*, 7–10.

35. "Democracy versus Demo-n-cracy," *Survey*, August 3, 1918, NAACP Administrative File, I-C-343; Hixson, "Moorfield Storey and the Defense of the Dyer Anti-lynching Bill"; Harvey, "Constitutional Law." See also Grant, *Anti-lynching Movement.*

36. The lack of federal initiative in prosecuting lynchings and the argument of no jurisdiction changed, at least modestly, in the 1940s, pushed in part by the Justice Department's initial law enforcement incursion into the states during the era of Prohibition from 1920 until 1933. See Waldrep, "National Policing, Lynching, and Constitutional Change."

37. Walter White to C. P. Dam, September 24, 1918, NAACP Administrative File, I-C-353.

38. William Kenyon to John R. Shillady, November 9, 1918, NAACP Administrative File, I-C-353.

39. Walter White to John R. Shillady, Telegram, November 11, 1918, NAACP Administrative File, I-C-353; Memo from Walter White, Assistant Secretary, to John R. Shillady, Re: Interview with George U. Spratling at Quitman, Ga., November 12, 1918; Walter White, Memorandum for Mr. Dam Re: Georgia Lynchings, November 19, 1918, NAACP Administrative File, I-C-355, Quitman, GA.

40. John R. Shillady to William S. Kenyon, November 13, 1918; Walter White to John R. Shillady, telegram, November 13, 1918, NAACP Administrative File, I-C-355, Quitman, GA; White, Memorandum for Mr. Dam Re: Georgia Lynchings.

41. C. P. Dam to John R. Shillady, November 16, 1918; Dam to Shillady, November 19, 1918, NAACP Administrative File, I-C-355, Quitman, GA.

42. Athens N. Grant to Walter White, November 20, 1918, NAACP Administrative File, I-C-355, Quitman, GA.

43. Walter White to Athens N. Grant, December 9, 1918, NAACP Administrative File, I-C-355, Quitman, GA.

44. John R. Shillady to C. P. Dam, November 20, 1918, NAACP Administrative File, I-C-355, Quitman, GA.

45. Hugh M. Dorsey to John R. Shillady, November 30, 1918, NAACP Administrative File, I-C-355, Quitman, GA.

46. Walter White to Samuel Scott Broadnax, December 10, 1918, NAACP Administrative File, I-C-355, Quitman, GA.

47. C. P. Dam to John R. Shillady, December 14, 1918; Shillady to Dam, December 19, 1918; Dam to Shillady, December 24, 1918, NAACP Administrative File, I-C-355, Quitman, GA.

48. [Unnamed] to Archibald Grimké, December 19, 1918, NAACP Administrative File, I-C-355, Quitman, GA. DePriest became a congressman a decade later, serving from 1929 to 1935.

49. John R. Shillady to C. P. Dam, February 13, 1919, NAACP Administrative File, I-C-355, Quitman, GA.

50. White, *Man Called White*, 10–12.

51. Janken, *Walter White*, 17–18.

52. *Palm Beach Post*, August 20, 1916; *Vardaman's Weekly* (Jackson, MS), August 24, 1916; Segrave, *Lynchings of Women in the United States*, 114–15; Bailey and Tolnay, *Lynched*, 181–83.

53. *Ocala (FL) Evening Star*, August 19, 1916.

54. For examples, see the *Lakeland (FL) Evening Telegram*, August 19, 2016; *Palatka (FL) News and Advertiser*, August 24, 1916; *Ocala (FL) Evening Star*, August 21, 1916; *Atlanta Constitution*, August 20, 1916; August 21, 1916; *Washington Post*, August 20, 1916; August 21, 1916.

55. MAH, "Another Lynching." In 1919, the year after the Turner lynching, an NAACP report claimed that Mary Dennis was pregnant. *Thirty Years of Lynching in the United States*, 24. The narrative became influential historically. While it did not inspire a federal anti-lynch law, it became the approved narrative of the event. See, for example, Jones, "Rosewood Massacre and the Women Who Survived It," 193.

56. *Memphis News Scimitar*, December 10, 1918; December 11, 1918; December 21, 1918; *Greenville (TN) Daily Sun*, December 21, 1918; *Stone County Enterprise* (Wiggins, MS), December 14, 1918; *Port Gibson (MS) Reveille*, December 12, 1918; *Jones County News* (Ellisville, MS), December 19, 1918; *Liberty (MS) Southern Herald*, December 20, 1918; *Poplarville (MS) Free Press*, December 19, 1918; *Atlanta Constitution*, December 21, 1918; *New York Times*, December 21, 1918; Segrave, *Lynchings of Women in the United States*, 122–23; Ward, *Hanging Bridge*, 21–51.

57. NAACP, *Thirty Years of Lynching in the United States*, 27. As part of the NAACP's effort to fight for justice in Shubuta, the NAACP also sent a letter of protest to Theodore Bilbo, governor of Mississippi. Bilbo responded that the group could "go to hell." NAACP Papers, Part 7, The Anti-lynching Campaign, 1912–1955, Series A, Anti-lynching Investigative Files, 1912–1953, reels 1 and 2; "The Shubuta Lynchings," *Crisis* 18 (May 1919): 24–25; *Atlanta Constitution*, December 22, 1918; *Washington Bee*, January 4, 1919.

58. *Baltimore Afro-American*, December 27, 1918.

59. The principal secondary source for the Shubuta lynching is Jason Morgan Ward's 2016 *Hanging Bridge: Racial Violence and America's Civil Rights Century*, which is a masterful analysis of the events in Mississippi. Again, however, the only source for Ward's discussions of pregnancy is the NAACP report. Ward, *Hanging Bridge*, 26, 29, 40, 47, 59; Walter White, "An Example of Democracy in Mississippi," unedited typescript, 2–3, Shubuta folders, box I:C360, NAACP Papers, microfilm. See also Feimster, *Southern Horrors*, 172–73.

60. NAACP, *Thirty Years of Lynching in the United States*, 27.

61. P. H. Collins, *Black Feminist Thought*, 22. For more on this phenomenon, see Silkey, "Women's Participation in the Power Struggle over Racial and Sexual Violence."

62. hooks, *Ain't I a Woman*, 7.

63. hooks, *Talking Back*, 14.

64. hooks, *Talking Back*, 5.

65. Lorde, "Transformation of Silence into Language and Action," 30.

66. Beale, "Double Jeopardy," 90.

67. King, "Multiple Jeopardy, Multiple Consciousness," 48.

68. Wood, *Lynching and Spectacle*, 204. For more on the application of such rhetoric, see Wood, *Lynching and Spectacle*, 204–5, 216–17.

69. CSDE Lynching Database, lynching.csde.washington.edu/#/home. The datasets used here are from the Tolnay-Bailey-Beck Database of Southern Lynch Victims, particularly its decade-delineated datasets. For more on atypical lynch victims, see the book based on the datasets, Bailey and Tolnay, *Lynched*, 178–202.

70. Cohen, *Folk Devils and Moral Panics*; Thompson, *Moral Panics*, 31–42; Goode and Ben-Yehuda, "Moral Panics," 150, 154–56.

71. Such concern can be expressed through social movements, media stories, voting, and simple attitudes. Sociologists attempt to measure such concern through organized actions, amount of media coverage, and the passage of new laws. Goode and Ben-Yehuda, "Moral Panics," 150–52.

72. Goode and Ben-Yehuda, "Moral Panics," 156–58. Moral panics also tend to include an increased level of hostility to those affected. For an elaboration on Goode and Ben-Yehuda's arguments, see their book-length treatment of the subject: Goode and Ben-Yehuda, *Moral Panics*. Ben-Yehuda also effectively elaborates on some of this ground in his *Politics and Morality of Deviance*; see also Ben-Yehuda, "Sociology of Moral Panics."

73. If the panic is the result of middle-status organizations like the media, it is almost

impossible to make the argument that there is not an interest seeker involved, because organizational entities in the media do not have a moral status. Under the grassroots model of moral panics, interest groups do not necessarily initiate a panic, but they can facilitate it. Media outlets are unlikely to make something up; rather, they respond to the latent concerns of society. Media is the grapevine upon which the grassroots concern develops. Goode and Ben-Yehuda, "Moral Panics," 159–61, 163–64, 166–67. See also Herdt, *Moral Panics, Sex Panics.* For the relationship between deviance and the media, see Reiner, "Media Made Criminality"; Greer, *Crime and Media.*

74. Bailey and Tolnay, *Lynched*, 187.

75. CSDE Lynching Database.

76. LaPierre and Farnsworth, *Social Psychology*, 322.

77. Allport and Postman, *Psychology of Rumor*, ix.

78. Donovan, Mowen, and Chakraborty, "Urban Legends," 524.

79. Guerini and Strapparava, "Credible or Incredible?" 441.

80. Brunvand, *Vanishing Hitchhiker*, 2–4, 10–11.

81. Gates, *Signifying Monkey*, 124.

82. Daniels, *Saving the Soul of Georgia*, 12.

83. Daniels, *Saving the Soul of Georgia*, 12.

84. *Atlanta Constitution*, January 16, 1915; January 20, 1915; January 22, 1915; *Baltimore Afro-American*, January 23, 1915; January 30, 1915.

85. *Chicago Defender*, January 23, 1915; January 30, 1915; February 6, 1915.

86. *Atlanta Independent*, January 23, 1915.

87. *Augusta Chronicle*, January 16, 1915; January 17, 1915; January 19, 1915; January 20, 1915; January 21, 1915; January 22, 1915; January 24, 1915; January 25, 1915; January 26, 1915.

88. *Denver Star*, January 30, 1915; Feimster, *Southern Horrors*, 172; CSDE Lynching Database.

89. *Chicago Defender*, June 29, 1912; March 10, 1917; *Atlanta Constitution*, July 13, 1914; CSDE Lynching Database.

90. Wexler, *Fire in a Canebrake*, 88. See also Pitch, *Last Lynching*, 165–65.

91. Wexler, *Fire in a Canebrake*, 130, 140–43, 174, 227, 230–34, 243. For a similar account that describes the development of conflicting lore in the wake of mob attack, see Akers, *Flames after Midnight.*

92. Jean, "'Warranted' Lynchings," 125–26.

CHAPTER FIVE: INSTITUTIONAL WHITE SUPREMACY

1. As was the violence specifically in response to the killing of Hamp Smith, the lynching of Jim Cobb was covered extensively by regional news outlets. *Cordele (GA) Dispatch*, May 23, 1918; *Valdosta (GA) Times*, May 25, 1918; *Thomasville (GA) Daily Times Enterprise*, May 23, 1918; "Subject: Lynching, Cordele, Ga.," NAACP Administrative File, I-C-355; *Atlanta Constitution*, May 24, 1918, NAACP Administrative File, I-C-355;

Augusta (GA) Chronicle, May 23, 1918; *Cairo (GA) Messenger*, May 24, 1918; *Tifton (GA) Gazette*, May 23, 1918; *Fitzgerald (GA) Leader-Enterprise and Press*, May 24, 1918; *Griffin (GA) Daily News*, May 23, 1918; *Macon (GA) News*, May 23, 1918; May 24, 1918; *Quitman (GA) Free Press*, May 24, 1918; *Waycross (GA) Journal-Herald*, May 23, 1918.

2. *Atlanta Constitution*, May 24, 1918; C. P. Dam to John R. Shillady, November 21, 1918, NAACP Administrative File, I-C-355, Quitman, GA.

3. *Butler (GA) Herald*, May 23, 1918.

4. *Bainbridge (GA) Post-Search Light*, May 16, 1918.

5. *Atlanta Constitution*, May 23, 1918, NAACP Administrative File, I-C-355.

6. *Atlanta Constitution*, May 24, 1918; *Atlanta Journal*, May 25, 1918, NAACP Administrative File, I-C-355; *Moultrie (GA) Observer*, May 28, 1918.

7. *Moultrie (GA) Observer*, May 28, 1918.

8. *Moultrie (GA) Observer*, June 4, 1918.

9. *Valdosta (GA) Times*, June 8, 1918.

10. *Valdosta (GA) Times*, June 22, 1918; *Moultrie (GA) Observer*, June 21, 1918; June 25, 1918; June 28, 1918.

11. *Moultrie (GA) Observer*, June 21, 1918; July 23, 1918.

12. *Valdosta (GA) Times*, June 22, 1918; July 20, 2018. See also Clifford, "Camp Gordon, Georgia."

13. In early July a Mitchell County farmer, Ben F. Pollock, was stabbed by a Black man named Joe Mathis. Pollock had insulted Mathis, and Mathis, enraged, turned on him and stabbed him in the back. Pollock was not killed, but he was seriously injured, the wound paralyzing him from the waist down. Mathis was not the subject of a retributive lynch mob, however, because Mathis was a "half-wit," a man with a known mental illness. *Albany (GA) Supreme Circle News*, August 17, 1918; *Albany (GA) Herald*, August 13, 1918, NAACP Administrative File, I-C-353; *Moultrie (GA) Observer*, July 2, 1918.

14. *Moultrie (GA) Observer*, August 16, 1918.

15. *New York American*, September 5, 1918; *Shreveport Times*, September 25, 1918, NAACP Administrative File, I-C-353.

16. Because Jones's pay was in bills that had been taped back together after being ripped, his killer, Dewey Callahan, was caught after using one of those torn bills to pay someone to help him haul a trunk to Fargo. *Valdosta (GA) Times*, October 5, 1918.

17. *Valdosta (GA) Times*, October 5, 1918.

18. *Moultrie (GA) Observer*, May 28, 1918.

19. *Valdosta (GA) Times*, December 26, 1919.

20. Litwack, "Hellhounds," 15. See also Fouss, "Lynching Performances, Theatres of Violence"; Halttunen, "Humanitarianism and the Pornography of Pain."

21. Milltown, originally on the periphery of Valdosta, was ultimately consumed by it, though still maintaining its independence. Today it is a city within the city known as Remerton. *Tifton (GA) Gazette*, May 22, 1918; Tolnay and Beck, *Festival of Violence*.

22. *Griffin (GA) Daily News*, May 22, 1918; *Valdosta (GA) Times* coverage reprinted in *Nashville (GA) Herald*, May 24, 1918.

23. *Bainbridge (GA) Post-Search Light*, May 23, 1918; *Chicago Defender*, July 13, 1918.

24. John R. Shillady, Press Release, Press Service of the NAACP, August 1, 1918, NAACP Administrative File, I-C-355. Dorsey quotes from *Atlanta Constitution*, July 4, 1918. For all the public worrying Dorsey did, he was completely silent in his written correspondence when it came to the trouble in Brooks and Lowndes Counties. No letters from south Georgia came to Dorsey from the area, demonstrating that white people saw nothing to worry about and Black people were too frightened or frustrated to think writing worthwhile. "May 1918," "June 1918," Governor-Executive Dept.-Governor's Subject Files-1917–1921; Ben W. Fortson, State of Georgia, Executive Minutes; "Correspondence, invitations, and ephemeral material, 1911–1938, undated," box 1, folder 2, Hugh M. Dorsey, Sr. Papers.

25. "Summary of Laws Related to Lynching of the States (Except Texas) Having More Than 25 Lynchings in Past Thirty Years," NAACP Administrative File, I-C-337; "Article 6" and "Article 7," §359–65, *Park's Annotated Code of the State of Georgia, 1914*, vol. 6, *Penal Code*, 240–43; John R. Shillady to Hugh M. Dorsey, September 11, 1918, NAACP Administrative File, I-C-353.

26. *Butler (GA) Herald*, May 23, 1918; *Moultrie (GA) Observer*, May 24, 1918.

27. *Valdosta (GA) Times*, June 1, 1918; *Moultrie (GA) Observer*, May 31, 1918.

28. *Thomasville (GA) Daily Times Enterprise*, May 31, 1918; *Valdosta (GA) Times*, June 15, 1918.

29. This inclusion demonstrated more than any other element of the confession that it was false. Reese was a Black laborer from Macon who was in central Georgia well before the incident at the Smith farm and well after it. *Valdosta (GA) Times*, June 15, 1918; *Moultrie (GA) Observer*, June 14, 1918. *RL Polk & Co.'s Macon City Directory, 1914*, 579; *Polk's Macon City Directory, 1935*, 304.

30. Leamon Wright, file no. 14053, Georgia State Board of Health, Bureau of Vital Statistics, Standard Certificate of Death, Atlanta.

31. *Florida Times-Union*, June 10, 1918; *Moultrie (GA) Observer*, June 28, 1918; *Valdosta (GA) Times*, June 15, 1918. The reporting on Ford's plight in Jacksonville's *Florida Times-Union* was rare for a Florida newspaper. The major paper in the state closest to Brooks and Lowndes Counties was the *Tallahassee Daily Democrat*, for example, which ignored the events.

32. *State v. Shorty Ford, alias Julius Brown, alias Lemon Wright*, Change of Venue from Brooks County, May 15, 1919, p. 330, Clerk of Superior Court, Chatham County, Eastern Judicial Circuit of Georgia. Thomas made the order again on December 2, just before the actual trial got underway. *State v. Shorty Ford*, Order Transferring Case from Brooks to Chatham County, December 2, 1919, p. 331.

33. *Valdosta (GA) Times*, June 15, 1918. On June 25, 1918, the Associated Press

erroneously stated that Shorty Ford's real name was Edmund Pipkins. *Thomasville (GA) Daily Times Enterprise*, June 25, 1918.

34. *Valdosta (GA) Times*, 15 June 1918; December 20, 1919; *RL Polk & Co.'s Valdosta, GA, City Directory, 1908–9*, 128; *RL Polk & Co.'s Valdosta, GA, City Directory, 1913–1914*, 130; Department of Commerce, *Thirteenth Census of the United States, 1910*, Population Schedule, Valdosta City, Lowndes County, Georgia, Sheet no. 14A.

35. John R. Shillady to L. C. Crogman, May 22, 1919, NAACP Administrative File, I-C-355, Quitman, GA; Bayor, *Race and the Shaping of Twentieth-Century Atlanta*, 17.

36. *Valdosta (GA) Times*, March 29, 1919.

37. *Valdosta (GA) Times*, April 12, 1919.

38. *Savannah Tribune*, November 28, 1919.

39. *Savannah Morning News*, December 16, 1919. See A. Pratt Adams, Jr. Papers, MS 2165, Georgia Historical Society, Savannah; Alexander Robert Lawton Papers, 1774–1952, collection no. 415, Southern Historical Collection, Louis Round Wilson Special Collections Library, University of North Carolina, Chapel Hill.

40. Knight, *Standard History of Georgia and Georgians*, 2337–39; *New York Times*, December 14, 1933.

41. Department of Commerce, *Fourteenth Census of the United States, 1920*, Population Schedule, Valdosta, Lowndes County, Georgia, Sheet No. 2B; *RL Polk & Co.'s Valdosta, Ga. City Directory, 1921*, 131.

42. *Valdosta Times*, December 20, 1919; *Atlanta Constitution*, December 16, 1919; December 17, 1919; December 18, 1919.

43. *Savannah Morning News*, December 16, 1919; December 17, 1919; *Quitman (GA) Free Press*, December 19, 1919.

44. "Believed Victim of Hamp Smith Tragedy," NAACP Administrative File, I-C-353.

45. *Valdosta (GA) Times*, December 20, 1919; *Savannah Morning News*, December 16, 1919.

46. *Thomasville (GA) Times-Enterprise*, July 6, 1920; *Savannah Morning News*, June 24, 1920. Whether it was frustration at the certain outcome of the trial, lack of interest because the trial was not about local events, or a politics of respectability that sought to make no new waves with white Savannah, the Black *Savannah Tribune* did not cover Ford's second trial.

47. Harden, *History of Savannah and South Georgia*, 713–14; *Atlanta Constitution*, June 25, 1920; July 5, 1920; *Savannah Morning News*, July 2, 1920; *Thomasville (GA) Times-Enterprise*, July 6, 1920; *Acts and Resolutions of the General Assembly of the State of Georgia, 1912*, 1620.

48. *Chicago Defender*, August 21, 1920.

49. *Ford, alias Brown, alias Wright, v. State*, 332.

50. Despite corroboration that Ford applied for clemency, his request does not appear in the state's records of such requests under any of the names by which the court referred to him. "Applications for Clemency," Convict and Fugitive Records, Georgia

Governor's Office, 1-4-42, Georgia State Archives, Morrow; *Valdosta (GA) Times*, December 7, 1918; *Americus (GA) Times-Recorder*, August 14, 1921; May 12, 1921.

51. *Americus (GA) Times-Recorder*, August 14, 1921; May 12, 1921; *Atlanta Constitution*, May 29, 1921.

52. *Quitman (GA) Free Press*, June 3, 1921.

53. *Savannah Morning News*, June 3, 1921.

54. *Report of the Thirty-Fifth Annual Session of the Georgia Bar Association, June 7, 8, 1918*, 17; *Savannah Morning News*, June 3, 1921.

55. *Savannah Morning News*, June 3, 1921.

56. *Savannah Morning News*, June 3, 1921; *Savannah Morning News*, June 4, 1921.

57. *Savannah Morning News*, June 4, 1921.

58. *Savannah Morning News*, June 4, 1921; *Quitman (GA) Free Press*, June 10, 1921.

59. *Savannah Morning News*, June 4, 1921; *Quitman (GA) Free Press*, June 10, 1921.

60. *Savannah Morning News*, June 4, 1921. Just as the city's Black press had chosen not to report on Ford's trial, it also failed to report his execution, surely for the combination of reasons previously noted. In the pages where the press would be expected to chronicle the Ford execution, instead it published Associated Negro Press coverage of the Tulsa race riot. *Savannah Tribune*, June 4, 1921; June 11, 1921.

61. *Savannah Morning News*, June 4, 1921; *Atlanta Constitution*, June 4, 1921; *Lyons (GA) Progress*, June 9, 1921; *Americus (GA) Times-Recorder*, June 9, 1921. Though Ford was a Greensboro native, his hometown paper had neither commentary nor coverage of his ordeal in Savannah. Even prior to his difficulties, the paper never covered the conflict in Brooks and Lowndes Counties. *Greensboro Herald-Journal*, May 17, 1918; May 24, 1918; May 31, 1918; December 12, 1919; December 19, 1919; December 26, 1919; June 3, 1921; June 10, 1921.

62. *Bainbridge (GA) Post-Search Light*, June 16, 1921. Only one issue of the *Valdosta (GA) Daily Times* exists for the year 1920, and another for the year 1921; the rest were destroyed, as it is always said, in a fire. *Valdosta (GA) Daily Times*, December 3, 1920; October 25, 1921.

CHAPTER SIX: MEMORY AND MEDIA

1. *Portland Morning Oregonian*, September 14, 1924. Along with arguing against the death penalty for Leopold and Loeb, Cannady made a case for racial equality under the law, advocating that Black deaths at the hands of murderers should be avenged in the same way that white deaths were.

2. Mangun, "'As Citizens of Portland We Must Protest'"; Mangun, "Force for Change." See also Mangun, *Force for Change.*

3. *Portland Morning Oregonian*, November 10, 1924.

4. Florence Williams had originally been the editor of the *Times*'s first competitor paper, the *Valdosta Telescope*, before marrying Brantley. Along with her role in the United Daughters of the Confederacy, she was a founder and member of the first

executive committee of Valdosta's American Legion Auxiliary in 1921. She helped found Valdosta's Floral Club and served as president of the Wymodausis Club for women. She, like her husband, was a scion of the white community in the region. Department of Commerce, *Thirteenth Census of the United States, 1910*, Population Schedule, Valdosta District, Lowndes County, Georgia, Sheet. no. 2A; *RL Polk & Co.'s Valdosta, Ga. City Directory, 1913–1914*, 3: 75; *Polk's Valdosta City Directory, 1925*, 49; Department of Commerce, *Fifteenth Census of the United States, 1930*, Population Schedule, Valdosta City, Lowndes County, Georgia, Sheet no. 11A. See also Wymodausis Collection, SB CLB 14, CLB 15, Lowndes County Historical Society, Valdosta, GA. Brantley moved to California at the end of his life and died in Los Angeles on April 16, 1962. "Charles C. Brantley," April 16, 1962, California Death Index, 1940–1997, State of California Department of Health Services, Center for Health Statistics, Sacramento.

5. *Milledgeville (GA) Union Recorder*, July 3, 1917; December 4, 1917.

6. Mrs. E. D. Cannady to W. E. B. Du Bois, November 12, 1924; Walter White to Mrs. E. D. Cannady, November 21, 1924, NAACP Administrative File, I-C-339, Lynching, July–December 1924.

7. *Portland Morning Oregonian*, November 26, 1924; Walter White to Editor, *Portland Morning Oregonian*, November 21, 1924, NAACP Administrative File, I-C-339, Lynching, July–December 1924.

8. *Portland Morning Oregonian*, December 28, 1924. During Brantley's investigation, he did not publish any part of the debate in his own paper. In lieu of such coverage, the paper contained typically contradictory accounts, one making the case that the South was the best place for Black residents, providing them far more prosperity than that of Black northerners, and another describing the fate of Oliver Johnson, a Black Brooks County man who was pulled from his home, mercilessly flogged, and left for dead on the side of the road. While Johnson survived, no one was arrested for the crime, and there was little official effort in investigating. *Valdosta (GA) Times*, December 3, 1924; December 9, 1924.

9. *Portland Morning Oregonian*, December 28, 1924.

10. *Portland Morning Oregonian*, December 28, 1924.

11. See Waldrep, "Substituting Law for the Lash," 1425.

12. Pfeifer, *Rough Justice*, 3.

13. Jean, "'Warranted' Lynchings," 127–28.

14. Jean, "'Warranted' Lynchings," 137.

15. Jean, "'Warranted' Lynchings," 133.

16. Jean, "'Warranted' Lynchings," 138.

17. *Portland Morning Oregonian*, December 28, 1924; *Polk's Valdosta, Ga. City Directory, 1923*, 155, 156, 201, 207, 209. The affidavits have not survived in either the records of the *Oregonian* or the *Valdosta Daily Times*. Correspondence with both publications in possession of the author.

18. Jean, "'Warranted' Lynchings," 142.

19. *Portland Morning Oregonian*, December 28, 1924.

20. Walter White to Mrs. E. D. Cannady, March 6, 1925, NAACP Administrative File, I-C-339, Lynching, March–April 1925.

21. Walter White to Bishop John Hurst, March 6, 1925, NAACP Administrative File, I-C-339, Lynching, March–April 1925.

22. Today there is both a school and a road in Valdosta bearing the Lomax name. Hurst's letter quoted in Walter White to Mrs. E. D. Cannady, April 25, 1925, NAACP Administrative File, I-C-339, Lynching, March–April 1925; "John Hurst," Prabook, https://prabook.com/web/john.hurst/1100311, accessed July 24, 2018; "African Methodist Episcopal Church Historic Timeline 1703–1987," *A.M.E. Church Review*, 1997, available online, http://s3.amazonaws.com/gcah.org/African_Methodist_Episcopal_Church-1.pdf, accessed July 24, 2018; Department of Commerce, *Twelfth Census of the United States, 1900*, Population Schedule, Eleventh Precinct, Baltimore County, Maryland, Sheet no. 4B; Department of Commerce, *Fifteenth Census of the United States, 1930*, Columbia City, Richland County, South Carolina, Sheet no. 8B.

23. For an example of the phenomenon in the aftermath of a 1933 Maryland lynching, see Ifill, *On the Courthouse Lawn*, 71–73.

24. *Valdosta (GA) Times*, January 11, 1919. For more on Richard R. Wright and his working relationships with other leading educational figures such as Mary McLeod Bethune, Booker T. Washington, Mary Church Terrell, and George Washington Carver, see Patton, "And the Truth Shall Make You Free," 17–30. For more on the Lomaxes, see Aiello, *The Life and Times of Louis Lomax*.

25. Walter White to Mrs. E. D. Cannady, April 25, 1925, NAACP Administrative File, I-C-339, Lynching, March–April 1925.

26. Janken, *Walter White*, 17.

27. Janken, *Walter White*, 17–18.

28. *Moultrie (GA) Observer*, June 21, 1918; June 28, 1918; *Thomasville (GA) Daily Times Enterprise*, June 22, 1918; June 25, 1918.

29. Department of Commerce, *Tenth Census of the United States, 1880*, Population Schedule, Twentieth Militia District, Bryan County, Georgia, Sheet no. 41; Department of Commerce, *Thirteenth Census of the United States, 1910*, Population Schedule, Barney District, Brooks County, Georgia, Sheet no. 6B.

30. John R. Shillady, Press Release, Press Service of the NAACP, August 1, 1918, NAACP Administrative File, I-C-355; White, "Memorandum for Governor Dorsey"; Department of Commerce, *Sixteenth Census of the United States, 1940*, Population Schedule, Brunswick City, Glynn County, Georgia, Sheet no. 18B.

31. "Lynching Pamphlets," NAACP Administrative File, II-L-20.

32. Walter White to Jacob Billikopf, September 25, 1924, NAACP Administrative File, I-C-339.

33. White, "I Investigate Lynchings," 78–79.

34. White, "I Investigate Lynchings," 79–80.

35. Kahn "Profiles." It was a story tailored for public consumption, so it appears less in White's private correspondence. See boxes 1–12, Series I. Correspondence, Walter Francis White and Poppy Cannon Papers.

36. Johnson, *Along This Way*, 332–34.

37. Johnson, *Along This Way*, 334–35.

38. *New York Amsterdam News*, February 23, 1935. This kind of story also developed in the historiography. Lerone Bennett Jr., for example, describes Turner as being "doused with gasoline and motor oil and burned." Bennett claims that "a man stepped forward with a pocket knife and ripped open her abdomen in a crude Caesarean operation." The baby gave "two feeble cries" and "received for the answer the heel of a stalwart man, as life was ground out of the tiny form." Bennett, *Before the Mayflower*, 352.

39. *Pittsburgh Courier*, May 21, 1932.

40. By the NAACP's count, there were 1,665 lynchings from 1890 to 1900, for an average of 166.5 per year; 921 from 1900 to 1910, for an average of 92.1 per year; 840 from 1910 to 1920, for an average of 84 per year; and 304 from 1920 to 1927, an average of 38 per year. White, *Rope and Faggot*, 19–22, 27–29.

CONCLUSION: THE TURNER LEGACY

1. *Valdosta (GA) Times*, February 1, 1919. In July 1919 another Black man in Lowndes County, Ott Johnson, was arrested for raping his fourteen-year-old daughter. It was, in the words of the *Valdosta Times*, "one of the most unspeakable crimes in the history of the county." And yet Johnson was held in the county jail awaiting trial. He was in no danger from a mob, because his crime, however unspeakable, was perpetrated against someone who was not white. Johnson's safety, though rightly expected in any democracy, was itself an indictment of the region's mob violence. *Valdosta (GA) Times*, July 20, 1919.

2. McWhirter, *Red Summer*, 1–7.

3. McWhirter, *Red Summer*, 269.

4. Equal Justice Initiative, "Lynching in America."

5. *Bainbridge (GA) Post-Search Light*, May 30, 1918.

6. Rothberg, *Implicated Subject*, 1.

7. *Valdosta (GA) Times*, May 17, 1919.

8. Crabtree, "Devil Is Watching You," 44–45.

9. "Membership & Financial Support Rec'd from Georgia Branches," Papers of the NAACP, Part 26. Selected Branch Files, 1940–1955. Series A: The South, Group II, Series C, Branch Department Files cont., Geographical File cont., Group II, Box C-42, Georgia State Conference, 1950–1955, 0296; White, " Work of a Mob"; *Pittsburgh Courier*, February 6, 1943. The Macon branch was in a similar position to that of Valdosta. In 1947 Macon's NAACP had 350 members; in 1948 the membership was cut by more than half, with 134 members. The branch went dormant later that year, then through 1949 and 1950, reorganizing late in 1950. Lucille Black to Rev. H. T. Pierce, August 11, 1950; Black

to T. B. Hooper, November 29, 1950, Part 26. Selected Branch Files, 1940–1955. Series A: The South, Reel 10, Group II, Series C, Branch Department Files cont., Geographical File cont., Group II, Box C-40, Macon, Georgia, 1941–1955, 0156, 0168.

10. It had been reorganized "under new and younger leadership," Hurley reported, "precipitated" by the Watson murder in May. Leonard Davis was the group's president, and McKinley Riley its secretary. "Membership & Financial Support Rec'd from Georgia Branches."

11. Boyd, *Blind Obedience*, 105.

12. *Valdosta (GA) Times*, August 2, 1919; October 4, 1919; October 18, 1919.

13. *Valdosta (GA) Times*, November 15, 1919.

14. Hugh M. Dorsey, "A Statement from Governor Hugh M. Dorsey as to the Negro in Georgia," April 22, 1921, 1–21.

15. Hugh M. Dorsey, "A Statement from Governor Hugh M. Dorsey as to the Negro in Georgia," April 22, 1921, 22–23.

16. *Atlanta Independent*, June 2, 1921.

17. Feimster, *Southern Horrors*, 220–23; Hixson, "Moorfield Storey and the Defense of the Dyer Anti-Lynching Bill," 65–67; Pinar, "NAACP and the Struggle for Antilynching Federal Legislation," 684–95; Krugler, *1919*, 274–78.

18. George Tindall has noted that though it was a secular organization, "a strong theme of religiosity" was part of it, with, at one point, one fourth of all members being ministers. In 1925 the commission began giving medals to those who showed "particular bravery or intelligence, or both, in outwitting mobs or defending prisons." Tindall, *Emergence of the New South*, 180. In 1930 the CIC commissioned two important lynching studies, continuing its effort to fight the practice. Berg, *Popular Justice*, 149; Ellis, *Race Harmony and Black Progress*, 119; Pilkington, "Trials of Brotherhood"; Cole, "Role of the Commission on Interracial Cooperation in War and Peace"; Tindall, *Emergence of the New South*, 180, 198, 550. For more on the CIC, see Commission on Interracial Cooperation papers, 1919–; Dykeman and Stokely, *Seeds of Southern Change*.

19. George Brown Tindall has argued that the CIC, in fact, "induced" Dorsey's public statement; Tindall, *Emergence of the New South*, 181 Dorsey, "Statement from Governor Hugh M. Dorsey as to the Negro in Georgia"; Pitts, "Hugh M. Dorsey and 'The Negro in Georgia.'"

20. *Taylor v. Georgia*, 315 US 25 (1942); *New York Times*, January 13, 1942.

21. For a full academic evaluation of artistic work perpetuating the Turner narrative, see J. D. Williams, "'Woman Was Lynched the Other Day,'" 92–98; Longoria, "Stranger Fruit," 5–7. Armstrong, *Mary Turner and the Memory of Lynching*, presents an exhaustive and intricate analysis of the literary production related to Turner through the lens of the broader tropes of gender and lynching.

22. The author saw the panel when visiting the museum.

23. "Mary Turner, Pregnant, Lynched in Georgia for Publicly Criticizing Husband's Lynching." The author personally visited the initiative's memorial.

24. "May 19, 1918: Mary Turner Lynching."

25. Anderson, *White Rage*, 40.

26. Kaba, "Say Her Name"; R. M. Wiliams, *Elegy for Mary Turner*.

27. *Valdosta (GA) Daily Times*, June 29, 1975.

28. Krugler, *1919*, 10–11. See also Krugler, "Mob in Uniform."

29. Department of Commerce, *Fifteenth Census of the United States, 1930*, Population Schedule, Saint Petersburg City, Pinellas County, Florida, Sheet no. 14A.

30. "George U. Spratling," Certificate of Death, Quitman, Georgia, Georgia State Board of Health, Bureau of Vital Statistics, state file no. 28728, Atlanta; "George U. Spratling," 257098303, June 3, 1970, US Social Security Applications and Claims Index.

31. Department of Commerce, *Fifteenth Census of the United States, 1930*, Population Schedule, Quitman City, Brooks County, Georgia, Sheet no. 1A; Department of Commerce, *Sixteenth Census of the United States, 1940*, Population Schedule, Quitman City, Brooks County, Georgia, Sheet no. 1A; "Samuel Edward McGowan, Jr.," 254039690, April 3, 1995, US Social Security Applications and Claims Index.

32. "Dixon Smith," Standard Certificate of Death, District 1199, Quitman, Brooks County, Georgia State Board of Health, Bureau of Vital Statistics, state file no. 30072, Atlanta; Department of Commerce, *Twelfth Census of the United States, 1900*, Population Schedule, District 741, Taylor County, Georgia, Sheet no. 5B; Department of Commerce, *Fourteenth Census of the United States, 1920*, Population Schedule, Militia District 741, Taylor County, Georgia, Sheet No. 5B; Department of Commerce, *Fifteenth Census of the United States, 1930*, Militia District 741, Taylor County, Georgia, Sheet No. 10A; Department of Commerce, *Sixteenth Census of the United States, 1940*, N.D. 1002, Macon County, Georgia, Sheet no. 10A; "Claude Hampton Smith," Serial no. 1131, Order no. 706, US World War II Draft Cards, Young Men, 1940–1947, Records of the Selective Service System, 1926–1975, R.G. 147; "Claude Hampton Smith, Jr.," Find a Grave Index, https://www.findagrave.com/memorial/53559850.

33. Department of Commerce, *Fourteenth Census of the United States, 1920*, Population Schedule, Briggs District, Brooks County, Georgia, Sheet no. 3B; Department of Commerce, *Fifteenth Census of the United States, 1930*, Population Schedule, Precinct 15, Cook County, Illinois, Sheet no. 9B.

34. These accounts based on correspondence with Phillip Williams, in possession of the author; Crabtree, "Devil Is Watching You," 43.

35. Crabtree, "Devil Is Watching You," 42–43.

BIBLIOGRAPHY

NEWSPAPERS

Albany (GA) Herald
Albany (GA) Supreme Circle News
Americus (GA) Times-Recorder
Atlanta Constitution
Atlanta Independent
Atlanta Journal
Augusta (GA) Chronicle
Bainbridge (GA) Post-Search Light
Baltimore Afro-American
Baltimore American
Baltimore Daily Herald
Banks County (GA) Journal
Bridgeport (CT) Telegram
Brooklyn Eagle
Butler (GA) Herald
Cairo (GA) Messenger
Camilla (GA) Enterprise
Chicago Defender
Clinch County (GA) News
Coffee County (TN) Progress
Commerce and Finance
Cordele (GA) Dispatch
Denver Star
Fitzgerald (GA) Leader-Enterprise and Press
Florida Times-Union
Greensboro Herald-Journal
Greenville (TN) Daily Sun
Griffin (GA) Daily News
Johnson City (TN) Daily

Jones County News (Ellisville, MS)
Lakeland (FL) Evening Telegram
Liberty (MS) Southern Herald
Lyons (GA) Progress
Macon (GA) News
Macon (GA) Telegraph
Memphis Commercial Appeal
Memphis News Scimitar
Memphis Press
Milledgeville (GA) Union Recorder
Portland Morning Oregonian
Moultrie (GA) Observer
Nashville (GA) Herald
New Orleans Item
New Orleans Times-Picayune
New York Age
New York American
New York Amsterdam News
New York Call
New York Post
New York Times
New York Tribune
New York World
Norfolk (VA) Journal and Guide
Palatka (FL) News and Advertiser
Palm Beach Post
Pittsburgh Courier
Poplarville (MS) Free Press
Port Gibson (MS) Reveille
Ocala (FL) Evening Star
Quitman (GA) Free Press
Savannah Morning News
Savannah Press
Savannah Tribune
Shreveport Times
St. Louis Argus
Stone County Enterprise (Wiggins, MS)
Tallahassee Daily Democrat
Thomasville (GA) Daily Times Enterprise
Tifton (GA) Gazette
Valdosta (GA) Times

Vardaman's Weekly (Jackson, MS)
Washington Bee
Washington Post
Waycross (GA) Journal
Waycross (GA) Journal-Herald

ARCHIVAL SOURCES

A. Pratt Adams, Jr. Papers, MS 2165, Georgia Historical Society, Savannah.

Alexander Robert Lawton Papers, 1774–1952, collection no. 415, Southern Historical Collection, Louis Round Wilson Special Collections Library, University of North Carolina, Chapel Hill.

Ben W. Fortson, State of Georgia, Executive Minutes, June 26, 1915, to June 25, 1921, reel 1217, Georgia Archives, Morrow.

Brooks County Marriage Records, 1828–1978, Georgia State Archives, Morrow.

California Death Index, 1940–1997, State of California Department of Health Services, Center for Health Statistics, Sacramento.

Commission on Interracial Cooperation papers, 1919–1944. Ann Arbor: University Microfilms International, 1984.

Convict and Fugitive Records, Georgia Governor's Office, 1-4-42, Georgia State Archives, Morrow.

County Property Tax Digests, Georgia Archives, Morrow.

Fisk University Rosenwald Fund Card File Database. http://rosenwald.fisk.edu/. Accessed May 3, 2019.

Georgia State Board of Health, Bureau of Vital Statistics, Standard Certificate of Death, Atlanta.

Georgia Tax Digests, Georgia State Archives, Morrow.

Governor-Executive Dept.-Governor's Subject Files-1917–1921-Gov. Hugh Mason Dorsey-April through August 1918, DOC-3117, 001-01-005, Unit 250, Georgia Archives, Morrow.

"Guardian's Bond." Butts County, Georgia, 28 May 1920, p. 287 and p. 339, Butts County Court of Ordinary, Jackson, Georgia.

Hugh M. Dorsey, Sr. Papers, MSS 279, Kenan Research Center at the Atlanta History Center, Atlanta.

Joseph B. Cumming Recollections, 1920, Collection no. 2560-z, Southern Historical Collection, Louis Round Wilson Special Collections Library, University of North Carolina, Chapel Hill.

Joseph B. Cumming Papers, 1889–2009, Collection no. 942, Stuart A. Rose Manuscript, Archives, and Rare Book Library, Emory University, Atlanta.

Marriage License, State of Georgia, Colquitt County, February 10, 1917, and Marriage Certificate, State of Georgia, Colquitt County, February 11, 1917, Colquitt County Courthouse, Moultrie.

New York Guard Service Cards and Enlistment Records, 1906–1918, 1940–1948, Series B2000, New York State Archives, Albany.

Papers of the NAACP.

Peonage Files of the Department of Justice, 1901–1945.

Records of the Selective Service System, 1926–1975, R.G. 147, National Archives, Fort Worth, Texas.

Records of the Selective Service System, 147, box 165, National Archives, St. Louis, Missouri.

Walter Francis White and Poppy Cannon Papers, JWJ MSS 38, Beinecke Rare Book and Manuscript Library, Yale University Library, New Haven, Connecticut.

Wilson, Woodrow. Proclamation." July 26, 1918. Washington: USGPO, 1918. Rare Books and Special Collections Division, Library of Congress, Washington, DC.

Woodrow Wilson Papers, Library of Congress, Washington, DC.

Wymodausis Collection, SB CLB 14, CLB 15, Lowndes County Historical Society, Valdosta, Georgia.

OTHER PRIMARY MATERIAL

Acts and Resolutions Adopted by the General Assembly of Florida, 1865. Tallahassee: Office of the Floridian, 1866.

Acts and Resolutions Adopted by the General Assembly of the State of Florida, 1866. Tallahassee: Office of the Floridian, 1867.

Acts and Resolutions of the General Assembly of the State of Georgia, 1903. Atlanta: Harrison, 1903.

Acts and Resolutions of the General Assembly of the State of Georgia, 1912. Atlanta: Charles P. Byrd, State Printer, 1912.

Allgeyer v. Louisiana, 165 U.S. 578 (1897).

Ames, Jessie Daniel. "Editorial Treatment of Lynchings." *Public Opinion Quarterly* 2 (January 1938): 77–80.

Carter, Catherine McRee. "History of Kinderlou, Georgia, 1860–1940," December 7, 1940, p. 25, box 122, folder 1, Kinderlou Papers, Archive Row 1, Lowndes County Historical Society, Valdosta, Georgia.

Clyatt v. United States, 197 US 207 (1905)

The Code of the State of Georgia of 1910. Vol. 1. Atlanta: Foote and Davies Co., 1911.

The Code of Georgia of 1933. Atlanta: Harrison, 1935.

Commons, John R. "Labor Conditions in Meat Packing and the Recent Strike." *Quarterly Journal of Economics* 19 (November 1904): 1–32.

Daniel, Pete, ed. *The Peonage Files of the U.S. Department of Justice, 1901–1945.* Frederick, MD: University Publications of America, 1987. Microfilm.

Department of Commerce. *Tenth Census of the United States, 1880.*

Department of Commerce. *Twelfth Census of the United States, 1900.*

Department of Commerce. *Thirteenth Census of the United States, 1910.*

Department of Commerce. *Fourteenth Census of the United States, 1920.*

Department of Commerce. *Fifteenth Census of the United States, 1930.*

Department of Commerce. *Sixteenth Census of the United States, 1940.*

"Dixon Smith." Standard Certificate of Death, District 1199, Quitman, Brooks County, Georgia State Board of Health, Bureau of Vital Statistics, state file no. 30072, Atlanta.

Dorsey, Hugh M. "A Statement from Governor Hugh M. Dorsey as to the Negro in Georgia." April 22, 1921. Atlanta: State Government Printing Office, 1921.

"The Fight in Texas Against Lynching." *World's Work* 37 (April 1919): 616.

Ford, alias Brown, alias Wright, v. State, March 16, 1921, no. 2238. In *Reports of Cases Decided in the Supreme Court of Georgia,* vol. 151, *October Term 1920 and March Term 1921.* Columbia, MO: Stephens, 1921.

Fourteenth Census of the United States, vol. 3, *Population, 1920, Occupations.* Washington, DC: USGPO, 1923.

Fourteenth Census of the United States, vol. 3, *Population, 1920.* Washington, DC: USGPO, 1922.

"George Spratling." Registration Card, World War I, September 12, 1918, Serial number 547, Local Board for the County of Brooks, Quitman, Georgia.

"George U. Spratling." Certificate of Death, Quitman, Georgia, Georgia State Board of Health, Bureau of Vital Statistics, state file no. 28728, Atlanta.

"George U. Spratling," 257098303, June 3, 1970, US Social Security Applications and Claims Index.

Goldenweiser, E. A., and Leon E. Truesdell. *Farm Tenancy in the United States,* Census Monographs IV. Washington, DC: USGPO, 1924.

Graham, Stephen. *Children of the Slaves.* London: Macmillan, 1920.

Harrison, Hubert. "Shillady Resigns." *Negro World* 8 (June 19, 1920): 2.

"How Shall the Black Man's Burden Be Lifted?" *Current Opinion* 67 (August 1919): 111–12.

Howe, William Wirt. "The Peonage Cases." *Columbia Law Review* 4 (April 1904): 279–86.

Johnson, James Weldon. *Along This Way: The Autobiography of James Weldon Johnson.* New York: Da Capo, 1973.

Journal of the House of Representatives of the State of Georgia. Atlanta: Byrd, 1918.

Journal of the Senate of Representatives of the State of Georgia. Atlanta: Index, 1918.

Kahn, E. J., Jr. "Profiles: The Frontal Attack." *New Yorker,* September 11, 1948, 40.

Lautier, Louis R. "An Illuminating and Eloquent Oration." *Atlanta Independent,* June 8, 1918, 1.

"The Lynching Evil." *New Republic,* May 3, 1919, 7.

"The Lynching Evil from a Southern Standpoint." *Review of Reviews* 60 (November 1919): 531–32.

MAH. "Another Lynching." *Crisis* 12 (October 1916): 275–76.

Manly, Alex. "[Untitled]." *Wilmington (NC) Record,* August 18, 1898, UNC Libraries, https://exhibits.lib.unc.edu/items/show/2278.

"Maurice H. Cobb." Certificate of Death, Georgia State Board of Health, Bureau of Vital Statistics, state file no. 19557, Atlanta.

May, W. A. "Letters of Administration, C. Hampton Smith." Brooks County, Georgia, July 2, 1918, p. 121, Brooks County Court of Ordinary, Quitman, Georgia.

May, W. A. "Temporary Letters of Administration, C. Hampton Smith." Brooks County, Georgia, June 3, 1918, p. 50, Brooks County Court of Ordinary, Quitman, Georgia.

"The Monroe Lynching." *Southwestern Christian Advocate*, June 12, 1919, 1–2.

Moton, Robert R. "The South and the Lynching Evil." *South Atlantic Quarterly* 18 (July 1919): 191–93.

NAACP. *The Mobbing of John R. Shillady, Secretary for the National Association for the Advancement of Colored People, Austin, Texas, Aug. 22, 1919*. New York: NAACP, 1919.

NAACP. *Thirty Years of Lynching in the United States, 1889–1918*. New York: Arno, 1969.

Nashville City Directory, 1915. Nashville: Marshall-Bruce-Polk, 1915.

"New Phases of the Fight against Lynching." *Current Opinion* 67 (July 1919): 45.

"Peonage Abolition Act." *United States Statutes at Large*, 39th Congress, Session 2, chapter 187, 546.

"Peonage in Georgia." *Atlanta Independent*, December 24, 1903.

Park's Annotated Code of the State of Georgia, 1914, Vol. 6, *Penal Code*. Atlanta: Harrison, 1918.

Polk's Macon City Directory, 1935. Birmingham: Polk, 1935.

Polk's Valdosta, Ga. City Directory, 1923. Detroit: Polk, 1923.

Polk's Valdosta City Directory, 1925. Detroit: Polk, 1925.

Report of the Thirty-Fifth Annual Session of the Georgia Bar Association, June 7, 8, 1918. Macon, GA: Burke, 1918.

Revised Statutes of the United States.

RL Polk & Co.'s Macon City Directory, 1914. Macon, GA: Polk, 1914.

RL Polk & Co.'s Valdosta City Directory, 1904. Valdosta, GA: Wiggins Directories, 1904.

RL Polk & Co.'s Valdosta, Ga. City Directory, 1908–9. Jacksonville, FL: Polk., 1908.

RL Polk & Co.'s Valdosta, GA, City Directory, 1913–1914. Birmingham, AL: Polk, 1913.

RL Polk & Co.'s Valdosta, Ga. City Directory, 1921. Atlanta: Polk, 1921.

"Samuel Edward McGowan, Jr." 254039690, April 3, 1995, US Social Security Applications and Claims Index.

Seligmann, Herbert J. "Protecting Southern Womanhood." *Nation*, June 14, 1919, 938–39.

Shillady, John R. *Planning Public Expenditures to Compensate for Decreased Private Employment During Business Depressions*. New York: Mayor's Committee on Unemployment, November 1916.

"The Shubuta Lynchings." *Crisis* 18 (May 1919): 24–25.

State v. Shorty Ford, alias Julius Brown, alias Lemon Wright, Change of Venue from Brooks County, May 15, 1919, p. 330, Clerk of Superior Court, Chatham County, Eastern Judicial Circuit of Georgia.

State v. Shorty Ford, alias Julius Brown, alias Lemon Wright, Order Transferring Case from Brooks to Chatham County, December 2, 1919, p. 331, Clerk of Superior Court, Chatham County, Eastern Judicial Circuit of Georgia.

Taylor v. Georgia, 315 US 25 (1942).

Terrell, Joseph Merriwell. "Misdemeanor Convicts." *Journal of the House of Representatives of the State of Georgia, 1902*, 48–52. Atlanta: Franklin, 1902.

Thirteenth Census of the United States, Vol. 2, *Population, 1910*. Washington, DC: USGPO, 1913.

Valdosta, Lowndes County, Georgia, January 1922: Index Map, Sanborn Map Company, University of Georgia Libraries Map Collection, Athens, Georgia.

"We Save Others." *Crisis* 17 (March 1919): 240.

Wells, Ida B. *Southern Horrors: Lynch Law in All Its Phases.* New York: New York Age, 1892.

White, Walter F. "The Burning of Jim McIlherron: An NAACP Investigation." *Crisis* 16 (May 1918): 16–20.

White, Walter F. "I Investigate Lynchings." *American Mercury* 16 (January 1929): 78–80.

White, Walter F. *Rope and Faggot*. New York: Arno, 1969 (1929).

White, Walter F. "The Work of a Mob." *Crisis* 16 (September 1918): 221–23.

"William A. Whipple." 17484, Death Index, 1919–1998, Georgia Health Department, Office of Vital Records, Atlanta, Georgia.

Williams v. Fears, 179 U.S. 270 (1900).

SECONDARY SOURCES

Aiello, Thomas. *The Grapevine of the Black South: The Scott Newspaper Syndicate in the Generation before the Civil Rights Movement.* Athens: University of Georgia Press, 2018.

Aiello, Thomas. *The Life and Times of Louis Lomax: The Art of Deliberate Disunity.* Durham: Duke University Press, 2021.

Aiello, Thomas. "The Proximity of Moral Ire: The 1919 Double-Lynching of George Bolden." *Ozark Historical Review* 35 (2006): 20–33.

Akers, Monte. *Flames after Midnight: Murder, Vengeance, and the Desolation of a Texas Community.* Austin: University of Texas Press, 1999.

Alexander, Elizabeth. "'Can You Be BLACK and Look at This?': Reading the Rodney King Video(s)." In *The Black Public Sphere: A Public Culture Book,* edited by Black Public Sphere Collective, 81–98. Chicago: University of Chicago Press, 1995.

Allport, Gordon W., and Leo Postman. *The Psychology of Rumor.* New York: Holt, 1947.

Anderson, Carol. *White Rage: The Unspoken Truth of Our Racial Divide.* New York: Bloomsbury, 2016.

Aptheker, Herbert. *Nat Turner's Slave Rebllion.* New York: Humanities, 1966.

Armstrong, Julie Buckner. *Mary Turner and the Memory of Lynching.* Athens: University of Georgia Press, 2011.

Armstrong, Julie Buckner. "Mary Turner, Hidden Memory, and Narrative Possibility." In *Gender and Lynching: The Politics of Memory,* edited by Evelyn M. Simien, 15–35. New York: Palgrave Macmillan, 2011.

Armstrong, Julie Buckner. "Mary Turner's Blues." *African American Review* 44 (Spring/Summer 2011): 207–20.

Assman, Jan, and John Czaplicka. "Collective Memory and Cultural Identity." *New German Critique* 65 (Spring–Summer 1995): 125–33.

Bailey, Amy Kate, and Stewart E. Tolnay. *Lynched: The Victims of Southern Mob Violence.* Chapel Hill: University of North Carolina Press, 2015.

Bailey, Amy Kate, and Stewart E. Tolnay. Lynching Violence Website, http://lynching.csde.washington.edu. Accessed December 14, 2021.

Bailey, Amy Kate, and Piere E. Washington. "Lynching in the New South, Festival of Violence, and the Synergy of Two Disciplines." *Journal of the Gilded Age and Progressive Era* 20 (January 2021): 74–80.

Barrett, James R. *Work and Community in the Jungle: Chicago's Packing-House Workers, 1894–1922.* Urbana: University of Illinois Press, 1990.

Barthes, Roland. *Mythologies.* New York: Hill & Wang, 1972.

Bay, Mia. *To Tell the Truth Freely: The Life of Ida B. Wells.* New York: Hill & Wang, 2009.

Bayor, Ronald H. *Race and the Shaping of Twentieth-Century Atlanta.* Chapel Hill: University of North Carolina Press, 1996.

Beale, Frances. "Double Jeopardy: To Be Black and Female." In *The Black Woman: An Anthology,* edited by Toni Cade Bambara, 90–100. New York: New American Library, 1970.

Ben-Yehuda, Nachman. *The Politics and Morality of Deviance: Moral Panics, Drug Abuse, Deviant Science, and Reversed Stigmatization.* Albany: SUNY Press, 1990.

Ben-Yehuda, Nachman. "The Sociology of Moral Panics: Toward a New Synthesis." *Sociological Quarterly* 27 (Winter 1986): 495–513.

Bennett, Lerone, Jr. *Before the Mayflower: A History of Black America.* 5th ed. Chicago: Johnson, 1982.

Berg, Manfred. *Popular Justice: A History of Lynching in America.* Chicago: Dee, 2011.

Bernstein, David E. *Only One Place of Redress: African Americans, Labor Regulations, and the Courts from Reconstruction to the New Deal.* Durham, NC: Duke University Press, 2001.

Boyd, Bill. *Blind Obedience: A True Story of Family Loyalty and Murder in South Georgia.* Macon, GA: Mercer University Press, 2000.

Braveman, Paula A., Katherine Heck, Susan Egerter, Kristen S. Marchi, Tyan Parker Dominguez, Catherine Cubbin, Kathryn Fingar, Jay A. Pearson, and Michael Curtis. "The Role of Socioeconomic Factors in Black-White Disparities in Preterm Birth." *American Journal of Public Health* 105 (April 2015): 694–702.

Brody, David. *The Butcher Workmen: A Study of Unionization.* Cambridge, MA: Harvard University Press, 1964.

Brophy, Alfred L. *Reconstructing the Dreamland: The Tulsa Race Riot of 1921, Race Reparations, and Reconciliation.* New York: Oxford University Press, 2002.

Brown, Elsa Barkley. "Imaging Lynching: African American Women, Communities of Struggle, and Collective Memory." In *African American Women Speak out on Anita Hill--Clarence Thomas,* edited by Geneva Smitherman, 100–124. Detroit: Wayne State University Press, 1995.

Brown, Haywood. "Trauma in Pregnancy." *Obstetrics and Gynecology* 114 (July 2009): 147–60.

Brundage, W. Fitzhugh. *Lynching in the New South: Georgia and Virginia, 1880–1930.* Urbana: University of Illinois Press, 1993.

Brundage, W. Fitzhugh, ed. *Under Sentence of Death: Lynching in the South.* Chapel Hill: University of North Carolina Press, 1997.

Brunvand, Jan Harold. *The Vanishing Hitchhiker: American Urban Legends and Their Meanings.* New York: Norton, 1981.

Butler, Joshua. "'Almost Too Terrible to Believe': The Camilla, Georgia Race Riot and Massacre, September 1868." MA thesis, Valdosta State University, 2012.

Campney, Brent M. S. "'A State of Violent Contrasts': Lynching and the Competing Visions of White Supremacy in Georgia, 1949." *Georgia Historical Quarterly* 95 (Summer 2011): 232–62.

Campney, Brent M. S. *This Is Not Dixie: Racist Violence in Kansas, 1861–1927.* Urbana: University of Illinois Press, 2018.

Capeci, Dominic J., Jr. "Race Riot Redux: William M. Tuttle, Jr. and the Study of Racial Violence." *Reviews in American History* 29 (March 2001): 165–66.

Carlson, Andrew. "'With Malice Towards None': The Springfield, Illinois Race Riot of 1908." *Gettysburg Historical Journal* 7 (2020): 16–40.

Carter, Dan T. "Prisons, Politics and Business: The Convict Lease System in the Post-Civil War South." MA thesis, University of Wisconsin, 1964.

Caruth, Cathy. *Unclaimed Experience: Trauma, Narrative, and History.* Baltimore: Johns Hopkins University Press, 1996.

Césaire, Aimé. *Discourse on Colonialism.* New York: Monthly Review Press, 2000 (1955).

Clark-Lewis, Elizabeth. *Living In, Living Out: African American Domestics in Washington, D.C., 1910–1940.* Washington, DC: Smithsonian Books, 2010.

Clifford, James H. "Camp Gordon, Georgia." *On Point: The Journal of Army History* 14 (Winter 2008–9): 43–47.

Cohen, Stanley. *Folk Devils and Moral Panics: The Creation of the Mods and Rockers.* New York: St. Martin's, 1980 (1972).

Cohen, William. "Negro Involuntary Servitude in the South." *Journal of Southern History* 42 (February 1976): 31–60.

Cole, William E. "The Role of the Commission on Interracial Cooperation in War and Peace." *Social Forces* 21 (May 1943): 456–63.

Collins, Ann V. *All Hell Broke Loose: American Race Riots from the Progressive Era through World War II.* Santa Barbara, CA: Praeger, 2012.

Collins, Patricia Hill. *Black Feminist Thought: Knowledge, Consciousness, and the Politics of Empowerment.* New York: Routledge, 1989.

Cooper, Len. "The Damned." *Washington Post,* June 15, 1996.

Crabtree, Mari N. "The Devil Is Watching You: Lynching and Southern Memory, 1940–1970." PhD dissertation, Cornell University, 2014.

Crouthamel, James L. "The Springfield Race Riot of 1908." *Journal of Negro History* 45 (July 1960): 164–81.

Culbertson, Roberta. "Embodied Memory, Transcendence, and Telling: Recounting Trauma, Re-establishing the Self." *New Literary History* 26, no. 1 (1995): 169–95.

Dailey, Dawn E., Janice C. Humphreys, Sally H. Rankin, and Kathryn A. Lee. "An Exploration of Lifetime Trauma Exposure in Pregnant Low-income African American Women." *Maternal and Child Health Journal* 15 (April 2011): 410–18.

Daniel, Pete. *The Shadow of Slavery: Peonage in the South, 1901–1969.* Urbana: University of Illinois Press, 1972.

Daniels, Maurice C. *Saving the Soul of Georgia: Donald L. Hollowell and the Struggle for Civil Rights.* Athens: University of Georgia Press, 2013.

De Jong, Greta. *A Different Day: African American Struggles for Justice in Rural Louisiana, 1900–1970.* Chapel Hill: University of North Carolina Press, 2002.

De Longoria, Maria. "Stranger Fruit: The Lynching of Black Women, the Cases of Rosa Richardson and Marie Scott." PhD dissertation, University of Missouri-Columbia, 2006.

Deutsch, Stephanie. *You Need a Schoolhouse: Booker T. Washington, Julius Rosenwald, and the Building of Schools for the Segregated South.* Evanston, IL: Northwestern University Press, 2011.

Dinnerstein, Leo. *The Leo Frank Case.* Athens: University of Georgia Press, 1987 (1966).

Dittmer, John. *Black Georgia in the Progressive Era, 1900–1920.* Urbana: University of Illinois Press, 1977.

Donovan, D. Todd, John C. Mowen, and Goutam Chakraborty. "Urban Legends: Diffusion Processes and the Exchange of Resources." *Journal of Consumer Marketing* 18, no. 6 (2001): 521–33.

Downey, Dennis, and Ramond M. Hyser. *No Crooked Death: Coatesville, Pennsylvania, and the Lynching of Zachariah Walker.* Urbana: University of Illinois Press, 1991.

Dray, Philip. *At the Hands of Persons Unknown: The Lynching of Black America.* New York: Modern Library, 2002.

Dunkley, Larnell, Jr. "Red Summer of 1919." In *Encyclopedia of the Harlem Renaissance,* edited by Cary D. Wintz and Paul Finkelman, 1052–56. New York: Routledge, 2004.

Dyja, Tom. *Walter White: The Dilemma of Black Identity in America.* Chicago: Dee, 2008.

Dykeman, Wilma, and James Stokely. *Seeds of Southern Change: The Life of Will Alexander.* New York: Norton, 1976.

Ellis, Mark. "J. Edgar Hoover and the 'Red Summer' of 1919." *Journal of American Studies* 28 (April 1994): 40–43.

Ellis, Mark. *Race Harmony and Black Progress: Jack Woofter and the Interracial Cooperation Movement.* Bloomington: Indiana University Press, 2013.

Ellsworth, Scott. *Death in a Promised Land: The Tulsa Race Riot of 1921.* Baton Rouge: Louisiana State University Press, 1992.

Equal Justice Initiative. "Lynching in America." https://lynchinginamerica.eji.org. Accessed December 14, 2021.

Fairclough, Adam. *A Class of Their Own: Black Teachers in the Segregated South.* Cambridge, MA: Harvard University Press, 2007.

Fairclough, Adam. *Race and Democracy: The Civil Rights Struggle in Louisiana, 1915–1972.* Athens: University of Georgia Press, 1995.

Feimster, Crystal N. *Southern Horrors: Women and the Politics of Rape and Lynching.* Cambridge, MA: Harvard University Press, 2009.

Felman, Shoshana, and Dori Laub. *Testimony: Crises of Witnessing in Literature, Psychoanalysis and History.* New York: Routledge, 1992.

Fenderson, Lewis H. "The Negro Press as a Social Instrument." *Journal of Negro Education* 20 (Spring 1951): 181–88.

Fishback, Price V. "Debt Peonage in Postbellum Georgia." *Explorations in Economic History* 26 (April 1989): 219–36.

Forehand, C. Tyrone. "A Place to Lay Their Heads." In Rachel Marie-Crane Williams, *Elegy for Mary Turner: An Illustrated Account of a Lynching*, 55–58. New York: Verso, 2021.

Fouss, Kirk W. "Lynching Performances, Theatres of Violence." *Text and Performance Quarterly* 19 (January 1999): 1–37.

Gates, Henry Louis. *The Signifying Monkey: A Theory of African-American Literary Criticism.* New York: Oxford University Press, 1988.

Gavin, Amelia R., Nancy Grote, Kyaien O. Conner, and Taurmini Fentress. "Racial Discrimination and Preterm Birth among African American Women: The Important Role of Posttraumatic Stress Disorder." *Journal of Health Disparities Research and Practice* 11 (Winter 2008): 91–109.

General James Jackson Chapter, DAR. *History of Lowndes County, Georgia, 1825–1941.* Valdosta, GA: DAR, 1942.

Gilje, Paul A. *Rioting in America.* Bloomington: Indiana University Press, 1996.

Godshalk, David F. *Veiled Visions: The 1906 Atlanta Race Riot and the Reshaping of American Race Relations.* Chapel Hill: University of North Carolina Press, 2005.

Goode, Erich, and Nachman Ben-Yehuda. "Moral Panics: Culture, Politics, and Social Construction." *Annual Review of Sociology* 20 (1994): 149–71.

Goode, Erich, and Nachman Ben-Yehuda. *Moral Panics: The Social Construction of Deviance.* Oxford: Blackwell, 1994.

Grant, Donald Lee. *The Anti-lynching Movement, 1883–1932.* San Francisco: R & E Research Associates, 1975.

Greer, Chris, ed. *Crime and Media: A Reader.* New York: Routledge, 2009.

Grimshaw, Allen Day. "A Study in Social Violence: Urban Race Riots in the United States." PhD dissertation, University of Pennsylvania, 1959.

Guerini, Marco, and Carlo Strapparava. "Credible or Incredible? Dissecting Urban Legends." In *Computational Linguistics and Intelligent Text Processing: 15th International Conference, CICLing 2014, Kathmandu, Nepal, April 6–12, 2014, Proceedings. Part II,* edited by Alexander Gelbukh, 441–53. Heidelberg: Springer, 2014.

Gupta, Alisha Haridasani. "Since 2015: 48 Black Women Killed by the Police. And Only 2 Charges." *New York Times,* September 24, 2020, https://nyti.ms/33XYxRH.

Halbwachs, Maurice. *On Collective Memory.* Chicago: University of Chicago Press, 1992 (1941).

Hall, Jacquelyn Dowd. "A Later Comment." *Journal of American History* 83 (March 1997): 1268–72.

Hall, Jacquelyn Dowd. *Revolt against Chivalry: Jessie Daniel Ames and the Women's Campaign against Lynching.* New York: Columbia University Press, 1993.

Halpern, Rick. *Down on the Killing Floor: Black and White Workers in Chicago's Packinghouses, 1904–54.* Urbana: University of Illinois Press, 1997.

Halttunen, Karen. "Humanitarianism and the Pornography of Pain in Anglo-American Culture." *American Historical Review* 100 (April 1995): 303–34.

Hannah-Jones, Nikole. *The 1619 Project: A New Origin Story.* New York: Random House, 2021.

Harden, William. *A History of Savannah and South Georgia.* Vol. 2. Chicago: Lewis, 1913.

Hartman, Geoffrey. "On Traumatic Knowledge and Literary Studies." *New Literary History* 26, no. 3 (1995): 537–63.

Harvey, William B. "Constitutional Law: Anti-lynching Legislation." *Michigan Law Review* 47 (January 1949): 369–77.

Haynes, Robert V. "The Houston Mutiny and Riot of 1917." *Southwestern Historical Quarterly* 76 (April 1973): 418–39.

Herdt, Gilbert. *Moral Panics, Sex Panics: Fear and the Fight over Sexual Rights.* New York: New York University Press, 2009.

Hill, Karlos K. *Beyond the Rope: The Impact of Lynching on Black Culture and Memory.* New York: Cambridge University Press, 2016.

Hill, Karlos K. "Lynching and the New South and Its Impact on the Historiography of Black Resistance to Lynching." *Journal of the Gilded Age and Progressive Era* 20 (January 2021): 143–47.

Hixson, William B., Jr. "Moorfield Storey and the Defense of the Dyer Anti-lynching Bill." *New England Quarterly* 42 (March 1969): 65–81.

Hoffschwelle, Mary F. *The Rosenwald Schools of the American South.* Gainesville: University Press of Florida, 2014.

hooks, bell. *Ain't I a Woman: Black Women and Feminism.* New York: Taylor & Francis, 2014 (1981).

hooks, bell. *Talking Back: Thinking Feminist, Thinking Black.* Cambridge: South End, 1989.

Huxford, Folks. *The History of Brooks County, Georgia, 1858–1948.* Quitman, GA: Hannah Clark Chapter, DAR, 1949.

Ifill, Sherrilyn A. *On the Courthouse Lawn: Confronting the Legacy of Lynching in the Twenty-First Century.* Boston: Beacon, 2007.

Jack, Jordynn, and Lucy Massagee. "Ladies and Lynching: Southern Women, Civil Rights, and the Rhetoric of Interracial Cooperation." *Rhetoric and Public Affairs* 14 (Fall 2011): 493–510.

Janken, Kenneth Robert. *Walter White: Mr. NAACP.* Chapel Hill: University of North Carolina Press, 2003.

Jean, Susan. "'Warranted' Lynchings: Narratives of Mob Violence in White Southern Newspapers, 1880–1940." In *Lynching Reconsidered: New Perspectives in the Study of Mob Violence*, edited by William D. Carrigan, 125–46. New York: Routledge, 2008.

Jones, Maxine D. "The Rosewood Massacre and the Women Who Survived It." *Florida Historical Quarterly* 76 (Fall 1997): 193–208.

Jordan, Emma Coleman. "Crossing the River of Blood between Us: Lynching, Violence, Beauty, and the Paradox of Feminist History." *Journal of Gender, Race, and Justice* 3 (2000): 545–80.

Kaba, Mariame. "Say Her Name—1918, 1949, 2021—Mary Turner and the 'Wife of the Victim.'" In *Elegy for Mary Turner*, edited by Rachel Marie-Crane Williams, viii–xi. New York: Verso, 2021.

Kato, Daniel. *Liberalizing Lynching: Building a New Racialized State.* New York: Oxford University Press, 2016.

Kellogg, Peter J. "Northern Liberals and Black America: A History of White Attitudes, 1936–1952." PhD dissertation, Northwestern University, 1971.

Kennedy, David M. *Over Here: The First World War and American Society.* New York: Oxford University Press, 2004 (1980).

Kerlin, Robert T. *The Voice of the Negro (1919).* Edited by Thomas Aiello. Lewiston, NY: Mellen, 2013.

King, Deborah K. "Multiple Jeopardy, Multiple Consciousness: The Context of a Black Feminist Ideology." *Signs* 14 (Autumn 1988): 42–72.

Kirschbaum, Erik. *Burning Beethoven: The Eradication of German Culture in the United States during World War I.* New York: Berlinica, 2015.

Kirshenbaum, Andrea Meryl. "'The Vampire That Hovers over North Carolina': Gender, White Supremacy, and the Wilmington Race Riot of 1898." *Southern Cultures* 4, no. 3 (1998): 6–30.

Knight, Lucien Lamar. *A Standard History of Georgia and Georgians.* Vol. 5. Chicago: Lewis, 1917.

Krist, Gary. *City of Scoundrels: The Twelve Days of Disaster That Gave Birth to Modern Chicago.* New York: Crown, 2012.

Krugler, David F. "A Mob in Uniform: Soldiers and Civilians in Washington's Red Summer, 1919." *Washington History* 21 (2009): 48–77.

Krugler, David F. *1919, the Year of Racial Violence: How Americans Fought Back.* New York: Cambridge University Press, 2014.

LaCapra, Dominick. *Representing the Holocaust: History, Theory, Trauma.* Ithaca, NY: Cornell University Press, 1994.

Lakin, Matthew. "'A Dark Night': The Knoxville Riot of 1919." *Journal of East Tennessee History* 72 (2000): 1–29.

LaPierre, Richard T., and Paul Farnsworth. *Social Psychology.* New York: McGraw-Hill, 1936.

Lawson, Michael. "Omaha, a City in Ferment: Summer of 1919." *Nebraska History* 58 (Autumn 1977): 395–417.

Leonard, Kevin Allen. "Is That What We Fought For? Japanese Americans and Racism in California, the Impact of World War II." *Western Historical Quarterly* 21 (November 1990): 463–82.

Lichtenstein, Alex. *Twice the Work of Free Labor: The Political Economy of Convict Labor in the New South.* New York: Verso Books, 1996.

Link, Arthur S. *Campaigns for Progressivism and Peace, 1916–1917.* Vol. 5 of *Wilson.* Princeton, NJ: Princeton University Press, 1965.

Link, Arthur S. *Woodrow Wilson and a Revolutionary World, 1913–1921.* Chapel Hill: University of North Carolina Press, 1982.

Litwack, Leon F. "Hellhounds." In *Without Sanctuary: Lynching Photography in America,* edited by James Allen, Hilton Als, John Lewis, and Leon Litwack, 8–37. Santa Fe, NM: Twin Palms, 2000.

Litwack, Leon F. *Trouble in Mind: Black Southerners in the Age of Jim Crow.* New York: Knopf, 1998.

Lorde, Audre. "The Transformation of Silence into Language and Action." In *Sister Outsider: Essays and Speeches,* 28–32. New York: Penguin, 2021 (1984).

Lumpkins, Charles. *American Pogrom: The East St. Louis Riot and Black Politics.* Athens: Ohio University Press, 2008.

Madison, James H. *A Lynching in the Heartland: Race and Memory in America.* New York: Palgrave Macmillan, 2016.

Mangun, Kimberley. "'As Citizens of Portland We Must Protest': Beatrice Morrow Cannady and the African American Response to D. W. Griffith's Masterpiece." *Oregon Historical Quarterly* 107 (Fall 2006): 382–409.

Mangun, Kimberley. *A Force for Change: Beatrice Morrow Cannady and the Struggle for Civil Rights in Oregon, 1912–1936.* Corvallis: Oregon State University Press, 2010.

Mangun, Kimberley. "A Force for Change: Beatrice Morrow Cannady's Program for Race Relations in Oregon, 1912–1936." *Pacific Northwest Quarterly* 96 (Spring 2005): 69–75.

Markovitz, Jonathan. *Legacies of Lynching: Racial Violence and Memory*. Minneapolis: University of Minnesota Press, 2004.

"Mary Turner, Pregnant, Lynched in Georgia for Publicly Criticizing Husband's Lynching." A History of Racial Justice, Equal Justice Initiative, https://calendar.eji.org. Accessed January 5, 2022.

Mattox, Kenneth L., and Laura Goetzl. "Trauma in Pregnancy." *Critical Care Medicine* 33 (October 2005): S385–89.

"May 19, 1918: Mary Turner Lynching." Zinn Education Project, https://www.zinnedproject.org. Accessed January 5, 2022.

McGovern, James R. *Anatomy of a Lynching: The Killing of Claude Neal*. Baton Rouge: Louisiana State University Press, 1982.

McLure, Helen. "'Who Dares to Style This Female a Woman?' Lynching, Gender, and Culture in the Nineteenth-Century U.S. West." In *Lynching Beyond Dixie: American Mob Violence Outside the South*, edited by Michael J. Pfeifer, 21–53. Urbana: University of Illinois Press, 2013.

McMurry, Linda O. *To Keep the Waters Troubled: The Life of Ida B. Wells*. New York: Oxford University Press, 1998.

McMurry, Linda O. *Recorder of the Black Experience: A Biography of Monroe Nathan Work*. Baton Rouge: Louisiana State University Press, 1985.

McNally, Richard. *Remembering Trauma*. Cambridge, MA: Belknap Press of Harvard University Press, 2003.

McTaggart, Ursula. "The Empty Noose: The Trouble with Removing Spectacle from Lynching Iconography." *Journal of Black Studies* 45 (November 2014): 792–811.

McWhirter, Cameron. *Red Summer: The Summer of 1919 and the Awakening of Black America*. New York: St. Martin's Griffin, 2011.

Metress, Christopher. "Culture, Memory, and the Legacies of Lynching." *Southern Literary Journal* 46 (Fall 2013): 127–31.

Michaeli, Ethan. *The Defender: How the Legendary Black Newspaper Changed America*. Boston: Houghton Mifflin Harcourt, 2016.

Mixon, Gregory. *The Atlanta Riot: Race, Class, and Violence in a New South City*. Gainesville: University Press of Florida, 2005.

Moore, Tomas Franklin. *From Whence We Came: A Historical Overview of the Black Schools of Lowndes County and Valdosta, Georgia from the Period of Reconstruction to the Time of School Desegregation (1867–1969)*. Valdosta, GA, 2006.

Morton, Patricia. *Disfigured Images: The Historical Assault on Afro-American Women*. Westport, CT: Praeger, 1991.

Murray, Robert K. *Red Scare: A Study in National Hysteria, 1919–1920*. Minneapolis: University of Minnesota Press, 1955.

Meyers, Christopher C. "'Killing Them by the Wholesale': A Lynching Rampage in South Georgia." *Georgia Historical Quarterly* 90 (Summer 2006): 214–35.

Myers, Martha A., and James L. Massey. "Race, Labor, and Punishment in Postbellum Georgia." *Social Problems* 38 (May 1991): 267–86.

North, David, and Thomas Mackaman, *The New York Times' 1619 Project and the Racialist Falsification of History.* Oak Park, MI: Mehring Books, 2021.

Norvell, Stanley B., and William M. Tuttle Jr. "Views of a Negro during 'the Red Summer' of 1919." *Journal of Negro History* 51 (July 1966): 209–18.

Novick, Peter. *That Noble Dream: The "Objectivity Question" and the American Historical Profession.* New York: Cambridge University Press, 1988.

Ohl, Jessy J., and Jennifer E. Potter. "United We Lynch: Post-racism and the (Re)Membering of Racial Violence in *Without Sanctuary: Lynching Photography in America.*" *Southern Communication Journal* 78 (July–August 2013): 185–201.

Oney, Steve. *And the Dead Shall Rise: The Murder of Mary Phagan and the Lynching of Leo Frank.* New York: Pantheon, 2003.

Ore, Ersula J. *Lynching: Violence, Rhetoric, and American Identity.* Jackson: University Press of Mississippi, 2019.

Painter, Nell Irvin. "Black Journalism, the First Hundred Years." *Harvard Journal of Afro-American Affairs* 2, no. 2 (1971): 30–32.

Patton, June O. "And the Truth Shall Make You Free: Richard Robert Wright, Sr., Black Intellectual and Iconoclast, 1877–1897." *Journal of Negro History* 81 (Winter–Fall 1996): 17–30.

Peterson, H. C. *Propaganda for War: The Campaign against American Neutrality, 1914–1917.* Norman: University of Oklahoma Press, 1968.

Pfeifer, Michael J. "At the Hands of Persons Unknown? The State of the Field of Lynching Scholarship." *Journal of American History* 101 (December 2014): 832–46.

Pfeifer, Michael J. *The Roots of Rough Justice: Origins of American Lynching.* Urbana: University of Illinois Press, 2011.

Pfeifer, Michael J. *Rough Justice: Lynching and American Society, 1874–1947.* Urbana: University of Illinois Press, 2004.

Pilkington, Charles Kirk. "The Trials of Brotherhood: The Founding of the Commission on Interracial Cooperation." *Georgia Historical Quarterly* 69 (Spring 1985): 55–80.

Pinar, William F. "The NAACP and the Struggle for Antilynching Federal Legislation, 1917–1950." *Counterpoints* 163 (2001): 683–752.

Pitch, Anthony S. *The Last Lynching: How A Gruesome Mass Murder Rocked a Small Georgia Town.* New York: Skyhorse, 2016.

Pitts, Timothy J. "Hugh M. Dorsey and 'The Negro in Georgia.'" *Georgia Historical Quarterly* 89 (Summer 2005): 185–212.

"Racial Terror Lynchings." Lynching in America, Equal Justice Initiative, https://lynchinginamerica.eji.org. Accessed December 14, 2021.

Raiford, Leigh. "Photography and the Practices of Critical Black Memory." *History and Theory* 48 (December 2009): 112–29.

"Referees' Reports." *Journal of American History* 83 (March 1997): 1254–67.

Reiner, Robert. "Media Made Criminality: The Representation of Crime in the Mass Media." In *The Oxford Handbook of Criminology*, edited by Robert Reiner, Mike Maguire, Rod Morgan, 302–40. New York: Oxford University Press, 2002.

Rice, Anne. "Gender, Race, and Public Space: Photography and Memory in the Massacre of East Saint Louis and the Crisis Magazine." In *Gender and Lynching: The Politics of Memory*, edited by Evelyn M. Simien, 131–72. New York: Palgrave Macmillan, 2011.

Ritchie, Andrea J. *Invisible No More: Police Violence against Black Women and Women of Color.* Boston: Beacon, 2017.

Roberts, A. L., S. E. Gilman, J. Breslau, N. Breslau, and K. C. Koenen. "Race/Ethnic Differences in Exposure to Traumatic Events, Development of Post-traumatic Stress Disorder, and Treatment-Seeking for Post-traumatic Stress Disorder in the United States." *Psychological Medicine* 41 (January 2011): 71–83.

Robertson, David M. *Denmark Vesey: The Buried Story of America's Largest Slave Rebellion and the Man Who Led It.* New York: Vintage, 2009.

Rothberg, Michael. *The Implicated Subject: Beyond Victims and Perpetrators.* Stanford, CA: Stanford University Press, 2019.

Rudwick, Elliott M. *Race Riot at East St. Louis.* Carbondale: Southern Illinois University, 1964.

Rushdy, Ashraf H. A. *American Lynching.* New Haven, CT: Yale University Press, 2012.

Rushdy, Ashraf H. A. "Many Faces in the New South: Word and Deed in Lynching Studies." *Journal of the Gilded Age and Progressive Era* 20 (January 2021): 95–103.

Schechter, Patricia. *Ida B. Wells-Barnett and American Reform: 1880–1930.* Chapel Hill: University of North Carolina Press, 2003.

Schmier, Louis. *Valdosta and Lowndes County: A Ray in the Sunbelt.* Northridge, CA: Windsor, 1988.

Segrave, Kerry. *Lynchings of Women in the United States: The Recorded Cases, 1851–1946.* Jefferson, NC: McFarland, 2010.

Senechal, Roberta. *The Sociogenesis of a Race Riot: Springfield, Illinois, in 1908.* Urbana: University of Illinois Press, 1990.

Shah, Amol J., and Bradford A. Kilcline. "Trauma in Pregnancy." *Emergency Medicine Clinics of North America* 21 (2003): 615–29.

Shelton, Jane Twitty. *Pines and Pioneers: A History of Lowndes County, Georgia, 1825–1900.* Atlanta: Cherokee, 1976.

Shepley, Nick. *The Palmer Raids and the Red Scare: 1918–1920, Justice and Liberty for All.* London: Andrews, 2015.

Silkey, Sarah Lynn. *Black Woman Reformer: Ida B. Wells, Lynching, and Transatlantic Activism.* Athens: University of Georgia Press, 2015.

Silkey, Sarah Lynn. "Women's Participation in the Power Struggle over Racial and Sexual Violence." *Journal of the Gilded Age and Progressive Era* 20 (January 2021): 129–35.

Smead, Howard. *Blood Justice: The Lynching of Mack Charles Parker.* New York: Oxford University Press, 1986.

Stockley, Grif. *Blood in Their Eyes: The Elaine Race Massacres of 1919.* Fayetteville: University of Arkansas Press, 2001.

Taylor, Nikki Marie. *Frontiers of Freedom: Cincinnati's Black Community, 1802–1868.* Columbus: Ohio University Press, 2005.

Thelen, David. "What We See and Can't See in the Past: Responses." *Journal of American History* 84 (September 1997): 748–65.

Thompson, Kenneth. *Moral Panics.* New York: Routledge, 1998.

Tindall, George Brown. *The Emergence of the New South, 1913–1945.* Baton Rouge: Louisiana State University Press, 1967.

Tolnay, Stewart E., and E. M. Beck. *A Festival of Violence: An Analysis of Southern Lynchings, 1882–1930.* Urbana: University of Illinois Press, 1995.

Tomberlin, Joseph A. *Images of America: Lowndes County.* Charleston, SC: Arcadia, 2007.

Tuttle, William M. *Race Riot: Chicago in the Red Summer of 1919.* New York: Atheneum, 1970.

Tuttle, William M. "Violence in a 'Heathen' Land: The Longview Race Riot of 1919." *Phylon* 33, no. 4 (1972): 324–33.

Vaughn, William Preston. *Schools for All: The Blacks and Public Education in the South, 1865–1877.* Lexington: University Press of Kentucky, 2014.

Vieth, Benjamin L. "Kinderlou: Paradise for Vagabond Negroes." Unpublished manuscript in possession of the author.

Vivian, Bradford. *Public Forgetting: The Rhetoric and Politics of Beginning Again.* University Park: Pennsylvania State University Press, 2010.

Waldrep, Christopher. *African Americans Confront Lynching: Strategies of Resistance from the Civil War to the Civil Rights Era.* New York: Rowman & Littlefield, 2008.

Waldrep, Christopher, ed. *Lynching in America: A History in Documents.* New York: New York University Press, 2006.

Waldrep, Christopher. *The Many Faces of Judge Lynch: Extralegal Violence and Punishment in America.* New York: Palgrave, 2004.

Waldrep, Christopher. "National Policing, Lynching, and Constitutional Change." *Journal of Southern History* 74 (August 2008): 589–626.

Waldrep, Christopher. "Substituting Law for the Lash: Emancipation and Legal Formalism in a Mississippi County Court." *Journal of American History* 82 (March 1996): 1425–1451.

Waldrep, Christopher. "War of Words: The Controversy over the Definition of Lynching, 1899–1940." *Journal of Southern History* 66 (February 2000): 75–100.

Walker, Vanessa Siddle, and Kim Nesta Archung. "The Segregated Schooling of Blacks in the Southern United States and South Africa." *Comparative Education Review* 47 (February 2003): 21–40.

Ward, Jason Morgan. *Hanging Bridge: Racial Violence and America's Civil Rights Century*. New York: Oxford University Press, 2016.

Wells-Barnett, Ida B. *The Arkansas Race Riot*. Chicago, 1920.

Wexler, Laura. *Fire in a Canebrake: The Last Mass Lynching in America*. New York: Scribner, 2003.

Whitaker, Robert. *On the Laps of Gods: The Red Summer of 1919 and the Struggle for Justice That Remade a Nation*. New York: Three Rivers, 2008.

White, Walter. *A Man Called White: The Autobiography of Walter White*. Athens: University of Georgia Press, 1995 (1948).

Wiegman, Robyn. *American Anatomies: Theorizing Race and Gender*. Durham, NC: Duke University Press, 1995.

Wilkerson, Isabel. *Caste: The Origins of Our Discontents*. New York: Random House, 2020.

Wilkerson, Isabel. *The Warmth of Other Suns: The Epic Story of America's Great Migration*. New York: Random House, 2010.

Williams, David, and Teresa Crisp Williams. *Plain Folk in a Rich Man's War: Class and Dissent in Confederate Georgia*. Gainesville: University of Florida Press, 2002.

Williams, Jennifer D. "'A Woman Was Lynched the Other Day': Memory, Gender, and the Limits of Traumatic Representation." In *Gender and Lynching: The Politics of Memory*, edited by Evelyn M. Simien, 81–102. New York: Palgrave Macmillan, 2011.

Williams, Lee E. "The Charleston, South Carolina, Riot of 1919." In *Southern Miscellany: Essays in History in Honor of Glover Moore*, edited by Frank Allen Dennis, 150–76. Jackson: University of Press of Mississippi, 1981.

Williams, Lee E., and Lee E. Williams Jr. *Anatomy of Four Race Riots: Racial Conflict in Knoxville, Elaine (Arkansas), Tulsa, and Chicago, 1919–1921*. Jackson: University Press of Mississippi, 2008.

Williams, Rachel Marie-Crane. *Elegy for Mary Turner: An Illustrated Account of a Lynching*. New York: Verso, 2021.

Williamson, Joel. "Wounds Not Scars: Lynching, the National Conscience, and the American Historian." *Journal of American History* 83 (March 1997): 1221–53.

Wood, Amy Louise. *Lynching and Spectacle: Witnessing Racial Violence in America, 1890–1940*. Chapel Hill: University of North Carolina Press, 1999.

Wood, Amy Louise, and Susan V. Donaldson. "Lynching's Legacy in American Culture." *Mississippi Quarterly* 61 (Winter–Spring 2008): 5–25.

Zangrando, Robert L. *The NAACP Crusade against Lynching, 1909–1950*. Philadelphia: Temple University Press, 1980.

Zelizer, Barbie. "Reading the Past against the Grain: The Shape of Memory Studies." *Critical Studies in Mass Communication* 12 (June 1995): 214–39.

INDEX